CONFLICT
WITHOUT MALICE

EMANUEL SHINWELL

Conflict Without Malice

BY

EMANUEL SHINWELL

ODHAMS PRESS LIMITED

LONG ACRE, LONDON

First Published 1955

Copyright T.225.P

MADE AND PRINTED IN
GREAT BRITAIN BY THE GARDEN CITY PRESS LIMITED
LETCHWORTH, HERTFORDSHIRE

CONTENTS

PREFACE   *page* 9

Chapter I   FAMILY AND CHILDHOOD   13

II   EFFORTS AT SELF-EDUCATION   21

III   GLASGOW AT THE TURN OF THE CENTURY   29

IV   EARLY UNION AND TRADES COUNCIL WORK   38

V   UNION WORK ON CLYDESIDE   48

VI   "RED FRIDAY" IN GLASGOW   59

VII   EXPERIENCES IN PRISON   67

VIII THE REVOLUTIONARIES GO TO WESTMINSTER   76

IX   PARLIAMENTARY SUCCESS   82

X   I BECOME A MINISTER   87

XI   DEFEAT—AND RETURN TO OFFICE   97

XII   THE 1931 CRISIS   106

XIII RAMSAY MACDONALD   112

XIV   IN THE WILDERNESS   121

XV   PARLIAMENT IN 1935   132

XVI   THE SPANISH CIVIL WAR   140

XVII WAR-TIME ACTIVITIES IN THE HOUSE   145

XVIII CONTEMPLATION OF POST-WAR PROBLEMS   158

XIX   MINISTER OF FUEL AND POWER   168

XX   THE FUEL CRISIS OF 1947   180

XXI   THE WAR OFFICE   190

XXII OVERSEAS VISITS   200

XXIII MINISTER OF DEFENCE   209

XXIV A VISIT TO ISRAEL   226

XXV   SOME THOUGHTS ABOUT THE FUTURE   235

INDEX   247

5

ILLUSTRATIONS

Emanuel Shinwell	*frontispiece*
The author's parents	*facing page* 30
The author, about 1903	,, ,, 31
Mrs. Emanuel Shinwell, about 1903	,, ,, 31
First election campaign, 1918	,, ,, 62
Glasgow disturbances, February, 1919	,, ,, 62
" Red Friday " in Glasgow	,, ,, 63
Glasgow Riot trial	,, ,, 63
Plymouth, 1923	,, ,, 94
A gathering of Socialists	,, ,, 94
The author, about 1925	,, ,, 95
In West Lothian, 1924	,, ,, 126
With British coal owners	,, ,, 126
Election campaign at Seaham, 1935	,, ,, 127
Off to Spain, 1938	,, ,, 158
Labour Government, 1945	,, ,, 158
Nationalization of the coal mines	,, ,, 159
At the War Office	,, ,, 190
With the soldiers	,, ,, 190
Minister of Defence: Washington, 1950	*between pages* 190 *and* 191
At Arlington Cemetery	,, ,, ,, ,, ,,
With a N.A.T.O. delegation	,, ,, ,, ,, ,,
At a N.A.T.O. conference	*facing page* 191
With General Dwight D. Eisenhower	,, ,, 191
Shinwell with his constituents	,, ,, 222
Durham Miners' Gala	,, ,, 222
The author with two of his grandchildren	,, ,, 223

PREFACE

THE events described in this book are intended as a modest contribution to the history of the Labour movement. They may serve to illustrate some of the struggles and the achievements of a political organization whose original purpose was to arouse the social conscience, and to create by democratic means a planned and beneficent social order. In the progress of that movement I may claim to have played an exciting, and on occasion, a prominent part.

Whether this entitles me to write about a period which extends farther back than that of my own experience, and for the rest is an abbreviated record of events in my public life, I must leave to the judgment of others. To write about one's experiences may seem to be an indication of personal vanity. Should such an accusation be brought against me I can only plead extenuating circumstances.

Those friends who urged me to write about the formative years of the Labour movement on the Clydeside and in the West of Scotland; of those days when Conservatives and Liberals regarded Socialists with amused contempt; when support for Labour at elections was negligible; and when Socialist speakers were often threatened with physical chastisement, received little encouragement from me.

I protested that few people would concern themselves with a past that is dead and gone, and that young men and women seem more concerned about the future. But, to my surprise, the pleadings continued. "Do it now," they said; "the time is passing," "the younger generation should know something of past struggles," and so on. When those voices were mingled with those of several publishers I felt that the time had come to relent; to shake off my natural indolence. Nor could I ignore the opinion of Dr. Samuel Johnson "that only a fool would write for nothing."

9

So here it is, accurate in its details, but I regret to say, incomplete. Much material had to be sifted, a careful selection had to be made. What made my task even more difficult was how to leave out any reference to persons and events which might cause offence.

To relate my experiences at the Ministry of Fuel and Power, at the War Office and the Ministry of Defence presented additional difficulties. Cabinet secrets may not be disclosed, at any rate until some years afterwards, nor can official documents be quoted. I had to rely upon notes taken by me and my Parliamentary Private Secretary, Colonel Wigg, at the time, together with my memory, which though not infallible, retains a vivid picture of contemporary events.

In the task of selecting material and in the presentation I had the help of several friends; notably George Kay, for whose services I am grateful; from George Chetwynd, M.P., who kindly searched through the pages of Hansard seeking for speeches which might be worth quoting; and George Wigg to whom I could always look for advice.

I can only hope that those who read the book will feel that the labour was worth while.

E. S.

DEDICATED TO
THOSE MEN AND WOMEN WHO HAVE
SACRIFICED THEMSELVES IN
A WORTHY CAUSE

FAMILY AND CHILDHOOD

I AM a Londoner, born almost within the sound of Bow Bells— and not in Glasgow, Dublin, or Poland as my friends and adversaries have on occasion suggested. My parents lived in two tiny rooms in a house under the shadow of the Spitalfields fruit market in the area once known as the Dutch Tenterground. Political and religious persecution in the Netherlands from the period of sixteenth-century Spanish domination onwards had sent periodical waves of highly skilled artisans to London; this area became the birthplace of a number of industries of enormous value to England, notably diamond cutting, silk weaving, and lace making. My mother was a descendant of these Dutch people.

I was the first of thirteen children, and was born in 1884, the first year of a severe trade depression. It was—as I learned much later—the year the Fabian Society was founded, the year the three-year-old Democratic Federation added the word "social" to its name, and the year that General Gordon was surrounded in Khartoum. Great Britain was realizing that she had an Empire and also that a considerable number of her new subjects disliked the fact. And in the midst of this power she had appalling problems of poverty: the social conscience of the country was stirring a little and more fortunate people had begun to realize that disease, dirt, poverty, and the evils they brought about, could not be isolated.

I am proud of my heritage as a Londoner—and this maybe will excuse my behaviour in boxing the ears of a Tory Member of Parliament when he invited me to go back to Poland. The fact that he had been a boxer in the Navy was unknown to me at the time, though I doubt whether the knowledge would have made any difference. The truth was that the noble and tragic country of Poland was as foreign to me as to him. My grandfather, the last of a family who had been flour millers in the country for centuries, was compelled to leave his native village a few miles from Warsaw, along with hundreds of others, by the occupying Power, Czarist Russia, which regarded Poland and the Poles as a source of amusement for Cossack cavalry and as an inexhaustible recruiting depot for the labour battalions of her armies in Asiatic Russia. "The more it changes, the more it remains the same" is a truism which certainly applies to the Russian mentality from the time of Ivan the Terrible to the Kremlin of modern times.

My grandfather brought his family to Britain in 1868—a symbol of tolerance and freedom for the oppressed people of the world whatever their race, creed, and colour. He and his family were, in modern jargon, refugees, but this did not mean that they arrived helpless and dependent on charity. My grandfather was a skilled miller and master baker. He brought his family—my father was then about seven years old—to Hull. From there he made his way to Leeds where he set up in business. It was a squalid town in those days, and it was said that while its rival Bradford was the filthiest town in the country, Leeds had the doubtful distinction of achieving the maximum of overcrowding. It must have filled my grandfather with some misgivings to see this town, immeasurably larger and wealthier than anything he had known in Poland, provide such appalling miseries of existence for the hordes of workers who were, so far as they could afford it, his customers. He saw the pathetic efforts of the womenfolk to keep their tawdry homes decent and clean so that, as a writer of the time said, on the weekly washing day the streets of Leeds "were so full of lines and linen as to be impassable for horses and carriages, and almost for foot passengers."

He saw also the effect of the effort to widen the mental horizon of the people who had been torn from their roots in the countryside and had lapsed into a sort of urban savagery. It was, I understand, in 1844 that the Leeds Mutual Improvement Society started in a tumbledown house to teach adults the three R's. By mid-century it was teaching chemistry, French and what was described as "Discussion," to people who would never gain any monetary advantage from the knowledge but thereby immeasurably widened their mental and spiritual horizon.

At the age of ten—about three years after his arrival in England—my father (as I write, still alive and in his ninety-second year) went to work as an errand boy with a tailor. By the time he was twelve he was earning a wage of 6s. a week. One Friday evening he was sent on an errand, took longer over it than expected, and found the shop locked on his return. His father chastised him for coming home without his wages, being convinced that he had spent them. The following Friday my father received two weeks' wages, and with this capital of 12s. decided to seek his fortune in London.

The money was just sufficient for a single ticket on the old Midland line, using the cheap night trains. When next morning the twelve-year-old youngster wandered around the forecourt of St. Pancras Station a policeman asked him what he was doing. The officer roared with laughter when my father replied that he had come to London to look for work, amused either because he did not believe him or regarded the idea as fantastic. However, he told him how to get to the East End where jobs of a kind were more plentiful.

The boy walked towards Islington, still at that time with a few tiny farms, relics of the day when the area was the dairy of London. His method of finding work was simply to stop likely looking people in the street and ask for a job. An elderly Jew took pity on him, invited him home for a meal in the Moorgate area and found him a job. He stayed in London for two years and then returned to Leeds, the boy now a man in earning capacity and appearance but not in years. He again quarrelled with his father (who incidentally emigrated to South Africa after my grandmother's death), and again went to London. This was a short stay, and he then went to Glasgow. Here he organized a strike among his fellow-employees which destroyed all chances of getting more work there. By the age of eighteen he was back in London, working and living in the Spitalfields area.

Spitalfields had a reputation as a bastion of workers' freedom. For generations it had been the centre of the silk-weaving industry in England, and as part of the City of London it had fiercely resisted eighteenth-century efforts by the Government to usurp the civil power by military action, particularly during the Wilkes riots of the mid-eighteenth century. When troops arrested two weavers for rioting and hurried them to execution at Bethnal Green, outside the City limits, the whole of London proper rose in wrath, workers and City merchants allied to defend their ancient legal rights and privileges. Whenever the Lord Mayor and Aldermen wanted aid to resist the monarchy and central government—as they often did—they always knew where man-power could be found: Spitalfields. Its people were quarrelsome, hot-tempered, loyal to their ideals and any master they acknow-ledged. This fierce love of freedom existed well into the present century. It was the spirit and atmosphere into which I was born, for my father took a prominent part in the agitation for better wages and conditions. Although without education—he never went to school—he was a good talker and was in demand at all the meetings of his co-workers in the East End.

He met my mother in Spitalfields. She had a number of brothers, all working as diamond-cutters by the old method of holding the diamond in one short stick while another was used as the cutter. The family was by comparison well off. My maternal grandparents, whom I remember quite well, were a striking couple. My grandfather was small but with very broad shoulders and of tough physique. When he died as the result of an accident at the age of ninety-three he was still fit and strong. My grand-mother was a tall and beautiful woman with the character and serenity of her ancestors whom Rembrandt painted so well. She ruled her family with a rod of iron. My parents' marriage was a love match—certainly my father brought little of a tangible nature to the union. Until my birth they lived in my grand-parents' house. Soon after my father had found some rooms he promptly fell out of work—the inevitable reason being his protest about labour conditions.

My father has told me that at one meeting—they were more like social gatherings in those days and wives and sweethearts were allowed to attend—John Burns, perhaps the most popular Labour leader of that period, took me on his knee. I was then the only child. I can therefore claim that in a way I was cradled in the Labour movement, even if I did not feel attracted to Socialism until I was almost nineteen.

Conditions were very tough indeed in those first years for my parents. A general trade recession was aggravated by political instability which shook the smug satisfaction of Victorian England. The Jubilee of Queen Victoria in 1887 did not endow the working people with many tangible reasons for happiness and celebration. The political situation was a contributory reason for my father's interest in trade unionism. It was, in fact, a time of the parting of the ways for the trade unions on the one hand, largely Liberal in thought and unable to grapple with the economic facts of the depression, and the Socialists on the other, among whom the Social Democratic Federation, inspired by Marx and nurtured by Hyndman, sprang into great but temporary prominence. It had as a competitor the Socialist League, with William Morris and his friends its inspiration. Of more lasting significance were the Fabians and Keir Hardie's drive towards an Independent Labour Party.

In this period of depression my father was forced to leave London and to seek work in the provinces. To place after place he went: Nottingham, Leicester, and then to Newcastle where he had some relations. There, as trade was slack, he obtained some funds and started a seamen's outfitters in High Holborn, South Shields.

Only rarely could he send my mother any money, and she was fortunate in getting a job as a cook in a philanthropic institution for poor children. An early memory that I have is of accompanying her to this institution. It was winter and quite dark as she served platters of porridge to hundreds of hungry youngsters in a gas-lit hall. Food distribution of this kind was a sop to the poor. There were many charitable organizations and philanthropic societies which distributed coal, blankets, tea, clothing and food to the "needy poor." It is not intended as any criticism of the good they did to say that the contributions for their work came mostly from people who thus achieved the twofold result of easing their consciences and lessening the risks of social upheaval. There was a strong belief that poverty was a sin, visited by Divine Providence on the sufferers as a penalty for laziness or to instil the virtues of patient acceptance of the lot to which it had pleased God to call them. And the sinners were legion: I have vivid memories— ugly memories—of crowds clamouring and squabbling for bread distributed by these charities.

The children rightly had some priority in the benefits of this welfare work. The food my mother prepared was for those attending two schools—one in Old Castle Street and the other the Free School in Bell Lane.

When summer came the children's canteen was closed. Although my father could not support his family (my sister had by this time been born), he sent for me. I can still recall when my mother took me the few hundred yards to Liverpool Street Station and put me in charge of the guard of a train on the old Great Northern line. I was only seven years of age. The guard was a kindly man, and pointed out interesting sights on the way— the only one I remember being the grey cathedral of Lincoln rising above the flat lands around it. At York the guard told me where to go to catch the train for Sunderland. I was put in an empty compartment and felt frightened and lonely. At Sunderland I couldn't open the door. My frantic knocks on the window attracted some passengers. A group of wondering people put me on the train for High Shields where, to my relief, I saw my father standing on the platform.

I went to school in Shields for a year. By that time the seamen's outfitter's business was nearing disaster. My father decided to try Glasgow, at the time a big centre of the clothing trade. He sent for my mother and sister, and for nearly three years I had regular schooling. The start was not promising. On the first day at the Adelphi Terrace public school I revolted and hung grimly to the railings round the playground. My fingers were forced away and I was practically carried into the classroom.

Lack of earlier schooling resulted in my being placed in a low standard class. One brief remark made by a visiting inspector has remained in my memory and has been a consolation when I have felt a sense of failure. I was loquacious even then, and I used to give the replies to his questions ahead of my classmates. He turned to the teacher and commented: "That boy has his head screwed on the right way." He never knew what that remark meant to me. Equally, I never forgot a caning I had for talking to another boy in class. It was not the physical pain so much as the sense of injustice that turned my admiration of that teacher into hate. Such are the lasting impressions that minor incidents can make on a child's mind.

When I was eleven years old my father moved to another part of Glasgow and I had to leave the Adelphi Terrace school. My father then employed me as an errand boy in his business, and my organized education was over. Many times I have referred to this when I have addressed meetings where the audience was on a somewhat high intellectual level and the subject of a commensurate standard. I have disclaimed any intellectual pretensions, on the grounds of leaving school at so early an age. I have spoken of my melancholy reflections because of this, and how I was only consoled when years afterwards I arrived at the House of Commons and there saw some of the products of the universities and high scholastic institutions.

But how I regret those early years and the loss I sustained! It has been a long and costly struggle ever since: the lack of direction in my studies, the need for intellectual discipline, the agony of composition, the reading of many books on many erudite subjects that I failed to understand. I know all about those famous people in history who, despite the lack of education, rose to great heights in the field of politics, literature, art, and in world affairs, but it is easier to smooth out the problems of living when one is endowed with all that a good education can give.

Fortunately, although my father read very little apart from those subjects which were his immediate interest, my mother was a great lover of books. She read all kinds of novels, probably her escape from too frequent childbearing and the far too frequent bouts of poverty that occurred. So what she read I also read. Perhaps that is why my romantic interest is easily aroused by stories of adventure and heroism. Boys' books I devoured by the score.

Life was not altogether drab in those days of childhood. I can remember that when we were living in London how, in Petticoat Lane, not far away, I could get a dish of hot peas for a farthing, and liver and mashed potatoes for a penny. Eggs were selling at thirty-six for a shilling—when competition was keen even more cheaply. When my father was in work he liked to enjoy himself. I can recall him singing some of the old-time ditties. One in particular remains in my memory:

"As I walk down the street each friend I do meet, says, there goes Muldoon, he's a solid man."

Irish comedians were then the vogue.

My mother also liked to sing. She preferred "I dreamt I dwelt in marble halls, and that you were by my side," or "Kathleen Mavourneen" and other Irish love songs. Those carefree times occurred, of course, when work was available, and food and money to pay the rent were no longer scarce.

CHAPTER TWO

EFFORTS AT SELF-EDUCATION

My father had many customers in the mining districts around Glasgow. Every Friday or Saturday I was sent with a parcel of suits to places like Cambuslang, Bellshill, Falkirk and Stirling to deliver them. I recall how on one occasion I had to take a parcel to the village of California, near Falkirk. This thrilled me because the name conjured up the picture of cowboys, gold prospectors and horses about which I had read in the various boys' magazines which came my way. It was a stiff climb of about two miles from Falkirk to the village. I found the house and delivered my parcel. While waiting for payment (this was most important because unless I got paid there and then there was doubt as to whether the customer would pay at all) I saw the mother of the household making up the "snap" or "piece" for her two sons who were about to go to the pit. It consisted of two thick slices of bread with cheese. On top of the cheese she spread marmalade. I had never seen this done before.

But I soon became tired of running errands for my father. When I was 12½ years old I got a job with the tobacco firm of Smith's, as a message boy, and later as van-boy. The pay was 5s. a week but sometimes I was lucky enough to get a small tip— it might be a penny or twopence. I shall never forget when on one New Year's Eve, on delivering a parcel of tobacco to a shop in Exchange Place, Glasgow, to my great surprise and joy the proprietor gave me a whole shilling. For many years afterwards whenever I passed the shop I recalled with much delight that notable occasion.

My father then conceived the notion that I should be trained as a tailor's cutter, so back to the workshop I went. It was simply of no use. I had no gift for the job. While I was being instructed my mind was on some story, perhaps a serial in one of the "blood-and-thunders" I avidly read.

A variety of jobs followed. One was with a chair manufacturing firm at 6s. a week. Work started at 6 a.m., which meant getting up at 5 a.m. I remained there long enough to learn how to glue legs on a chair. One rosy prospect came at the Singer sewing machine factory at Kilbowie. I saw a foreman who promised me a job at the fabulous wage of 17s. a week. The fifteen-mile walk to and from the factory seemed to me to have been well worth while. To get this job I had simply walked out of my home that morning. Now came the realization that I dared not return. I met some chums and they collected 8d. between them so I could get a bed in a lodging house for the night. Then my mother, who had been searching the streets for me all day, came along—and home I went. The Singer job was off, and I was back in the family tailoring business.

The shop was in the East End of Glasgow. Many of our neighbours were Roman Catholics, but the customers included Irishmen from both the North and South. My father had a workroom at the back of the shop, and customers and friends would cram into it until long after working hours, talking and consuming many a pint of beer and glass of whisky which I had to bring from the pub at the corner.

My father sat on the fence as regards the arguments on Irish topics, with the result that both the Southern Irish and the Ulstermen respected and liked him. I listened with intense interest to arguments on topics which I did not understand and occasionally I intervened with my own views, much to the chagrin of my father who envisaged one customer or the other taking his trade elsewhere. The fact that virtually none of them ordered more than one cheap suit during scores of visits and time-wasting arguments did not affect him. The place was more like a club than a business, with consequent effects on the turnover and profits.

All too often customers would be out of work and then they borrowed money from my father, but they always paid it back. Sometimes I suspected that he borrowed money from them during his own bad patches. The good and the bad times were accepted with patient philosophy. I remember one man saying that "he was never well when he ate too much but he was worse when he ate too little." Another customer sometimes found he could not obtain the money to take his best suit out of pawn on Saturday, so on Sunday he would lean out of the window of his tenement wearing a boiled shirt but with his moleskin working trousers on. He wore the shirt to keep up appearances. There was nothing disgraceful to these folk about pawning their clothes every Monday but it was always expected that they would get them out in order to appear respectable on Sunday.

By the time I was fourteen the Boer question was the chief source of discussion. It even banished Home Rule from the scene, and by the time war broke out, a day or two before my fifteenth birthday, I was a fervid Tory, ready and willing to go to Africa and fight Kruger with my bare hands. Considering that the war was bitterly opposed by most Liberals and all Socialists it was not surprising that my father banished me from the workroom except on business at this period.

I soon found a better source of education: the Glasgow Public Library. As soon as my father's friends had effectively put a stop to further work I would hurry off and remain there until I was turned out at ten o'clock. The daring theories of evolution by Darwin I found absorbing reading, and I expanded my knowledge by reading such works of his as *The Origin of Species* and *Descent of Man*. On the same shelves were books concerned with similar scientific subjects of the day. I read works on zoology, geology, and palæontology, for example, and was thereby encouraged to study the specimens of stuffed animals and birds, skeletons, rocks, and fossils in the Glasgow museums. I used to spend every Saturday afternoon testing myself on the knowledge I had gained from the verbose and serious works which were the forerunners of the popular scientific works of later years.

During the summer of 1899 I went to Ireland for a holiday— the first I had ever had, except for three days at Rothesay on the Clyde where I went camping with some other boys. My principal possession at that time was a pair of boxing gloves. I took them to fight with by day and use as a pillow at night. So far as I recall I took nothing else.

My friends on the Irish trip were all Irish Catholics. We stayed on a farm—it was really a smallholding—near Warren Point. We slept on straw in a barn, and the food was terrible except for plentiful supplies of butter and eggs. The boys were all older than myself and drank heavily of Irish porter at 1½d. per pint. They used to come back intoxicated every evening, but no matter what their condition they never forgot to kneel down and pray before going to sleep. I had little in common with them, for they were uninterested in running and boxing, in both of which I had become proficient in a youthful way.

After the outbreak of the Boer War I made up my mind to join the Navy—tempted by the enticing pictures outside the recruiting depot in the Gallowgate. Without telling my parents I went there to join up. I looked older than I was and they took various details and gave me a physical check-up without comment. When the officer learned my age he told me to go home and bring my parents' written consent. There was nothing for it but to ask my father for this, and the result was the worst row of my life. Not long afterwards he got me a job with a friend who was also in the tailoring business. I still hated the work, but now at least I got paid. My father had queer ideas about the necessity for any wages for one of the family.

In 1902 the family fortunes at last took a turn for the better. My father was offered the management of a clothing factory in South Shields, and he returned to the town where he had made many friends during the existence of the seamen's outfitting business. I remained in Glasgow as I was earning sufficient to pay for board and lodging, at least for a time.

Most of my spare money had for some years been spent on books. Volume by volume, by dint of searching in second-hand book shops and looking over junk barrows, I had amassed about 250 books. The variety of authors and subjects indicate that my constant reading in the public library had broadened my taste. Among authors of fiction I collected the works of Dickens and Thackeray—the popular classics of the day—as well as Meredith and Hardy who were currently most famous. Keats and Rabbie Burns were my favourite poets. There were scores of scientific and philosophical works: Darwin, Huxley, Kant, Herbert Spencer, Spinoza, and so on.

When work became slack my father said that he needed my help in the South Shields factory and I took my precious library with me. The old disputes began and after a year I decided that

I would return to Glasgow. This was a decision made after some reflection. I had been much attracted by a boxing booth, and would have joined it except for the certainty of Glasgow as a home I liked. But I wanted to get away from the clothing trade at all costs. I had no money for the fare, and my food and lodging until I found work. As a result I was compelled to sell my precious library. Although some of the books had cost me only a few pence I had picked up some really excellent bargains at this price; others had cost me several days' wages. But South Shields had few lovers of literature, and still fewer traders to cater for them. After pushing my library round the town on a barrow and not getting even an offer I settled with a bookseller who grumpily agreed to buy them at twopence a volume. The two guineas I received were my sole capital as I made what I thought would be my final departure from home and my father's employ. The reason why Glasgow was such a magnet was the very reasonable one that I had a sweetheart there. That girl became my wife. At the time I returned to Scotland we had no idea of marrying for some time. A year later, fully conscious that my nineteenth birthday was at hand, and having a good job, we decided to marry—against the wishes of both her family and mine.

By this time I had acquired an interest in Socialism—an interest which had its vague origin in the arguments I had listened to in my father's shop, was nourished by my reading in the public library when my father forbade me to upset his customers by taking sides in those arguments, and then by one of those chance meetings which can alter a life. It came about when I was eighteen because of my liking for Glasgow's "speakers' forum" in Gaol Square, where there was some knowledge as well as a lot of amusement to be picked up. On most evenings and on Sunday mornings I loved to listen to the orators haranguing the crowds on politics and theology, which were the usual topics.

The Boer War had been over for some months, but many speakers were still fighting it. The Irishmen always had big crowds, and they had merely to follow the simple recipe for applause of condemning anything the British Government was doing. There were men protesting at the persecution they had personally suffered through quite unbelievable machinations of justice. There were "philosophical anarchists" who pleaded that their simple solution of the world's troubles was to do away with all governments of all kinds. The way to paradise was opened by a score of different sects and creeds, each speaker warning his audience that the others were in fact primrose paths. Incongruously among these rabid religionists were the atheists who denied the whole business and the agnostics who insisted that the more you sought after God the less likely you were to find Him. Most attractive of all were the Orange and Irish Catholic meetings, whose speakers were in fact preaching to the converted, but they usually managed to cause enough argument to cause free fights to break out.

The specious and superficial arguments of some of these speakers tempted me to ask questions and then to share in the discussion myself. Compared with many in the crowds around me I had remarkable knowledge, particularly of biological subjects— and often it was better than that of the speakers—greybeards who had ridden a particular hobby-horse for years, saying the same thing over and over again. It was, of course, callow impertinence on my part to question their statements, and a few of them resented it, often turning the tables by the adroit joking of a skilled speaker so that the crowd roared with laughter at my expense. Others realized that I was a heaven-sent crowd-gatherer, for nothing pleased the people of Gaol Square more than an argument and the hint of a fight at the end of it.

Soon I was quite a well-known interrupter at these meetings. A sort of paradoxically friendly hostility existed between the speakers and myself. One Sunday afternoon, when I was eloquently giving my views on some scientific topic, a stranger edged his way into the crowd and voiced his doubts as to the veracity of my statement. I resented this, for I was by now the clever young man of Gaol Square and quite unused to being questioned by anyone but the speaker. The crowds had always been on my side.

I launched into an attack on the stranger and soon discovered that he was a Socialist. Although I had found the Socialist idea an attractive one, I had little time for those who expected to put the world right by political action. Science, as outlined by the great prophet H. G. Wells, was the only hope for mankind. The pursuit of science was, to my mind, the key to a better civilization; the well-being of everyone in it would automatically follow.

26

The stranger told me quite gently that I had an abysmal ignorance of economics. This was a serious charge in my estimation for it was a word that was quite as "modern" as any of my -ologies. I got talking to him, and discovered he was a sewing-machine mechanic, Neil McLean, later to be M.P. for Govan and a member of the House for thirty years.

He was a member of the Socialist Labour Party, he told me, which had been formed in that year—1903, a strictly Marxist organization with a policy of class war directed by a rigid political hierarchy. It never had more than a few hundred members although it eventually nourished the young life of the Communist Party, particularly on Clydeside.

As a result of that brief conversation I got hold of a pamphlet by Karl Marx entitled *Wages, Labour and Capital.* I was not the first nor the last young man to discover that Marx is hard going, and his arguments on the theory of surplus value, his explanation of labour's part, and his castigation of the exploitation of the working class, were difficult for my mind to grasp. I read and re-read that pamphlet and eventually succeeded in extracting some worth-while material for discussion.

In due course I got my chance to see if I could expound the Marxist views. I chose as my adversary a theological speaker who was a veteran of the "Bird Market," as the hall where he held his meetings was known. He was ostensibly a speaker on theology; no one, I imagine, understood the doctrine he advocated, but he was a born orator and one could be sure of entertainment as he digressed from the main subject. He loved to persuade people in his audience to begin a debate with him, for he could invariably come out best. He was therefore ready and willing to discuss with me the subject "Socialism versus Individualism."

There were, that evening, at least a thousand people listening. Fortunately for me his knowledge of Socialism was nil, and despite his verbosity I was able to corner him on several points. The crowd was delighted that David had managed to get in some telling thrusts at Goliath, and at the end a collection was taken to pay for expenses.

To my amazement my opponent handed over ten shillings to me as my share of the collection. It was the first fee I had ever earned for public speaking, and one of the very few I have ever collected in this regard. I returned to my home in thoughtful mood. It seemed that I was "in politics."

I ventured to think at the time that my wife had good reason to be proud of a husband who was not unknown to the working class of Glasgow as a political speaker, who had a good job, and had been able to furnish a single room in the Govanhill district as the bridal home. The proverbial fall which hurries after pride soon came. Within a month of my marriage the usual slump arrived in the clothing trade. I was a new employee and an agitator for workers' rights. I was dismissed. Our savings were nil. There was, of course, no unemployment relief. For three terrible months I could find no work anywhere. We sold almost everything we possessed except for the clothes we stood up in. Even some of the furniture had to go.

Eventually I had to admit defeat and return to South Shields to work for my father. My wife remained in Glasgow—another spur to me to return as soon as I could. This I achieved after a few months. There have been plenty of bad patches since then, but none so utterly miserable and (at the time) disheartening, as that period after my marriage when my small domestic world came crashing down.

CHAPTER THREE

GLASGOW AT THE TURN
OF THE CENTURY

THE modern generation, reared and living in a society which approaches much closer to real democracy than did the people of the early 1900's, is naturally unable to appreciate the violent contrasts between poverty and wealth which existed fifty years ago and which were the spur to my desire to enter politics.

Through temperament and from experience in my environment I found it impossible to accept the workers' conditions as part of the divine order of things. In periods when trade was good the people worked harder and for longer hours with no commensurate increase in wages. When foreign competition forced prices down or slumps killed trade the workers were the first, and often the sole, sufferers.

Glasgow was not by any means a vast slum, nor all its inhabitants poverty-stricken. Among the million people of the city and its suburbs who greeted the new century were thousands of very wealthy families. There were large mansions in the Maxwell Park and Dowanhill districts just outside the town. These were still run on the same princely standards as those existing when their first owners spent some of the fortunes they amassed out of the Indian and Oriental trade a century earlier. But the majority of the industrialists and business men—the "new rich" who had sprung up after the ruin of some of Glasgow's wealthy families during the Scottish bank failures of the mid-Victorian period—lived in Pollokshields and Kelvinside. The contrast between these districts and the workers' areas was incongruous. It was akin to moving from one film set to another, so startling was the change. Every weekday business men drove in their carriages through this area, and on most afternoons their wives followed for shopping or taking tea in the popular tea-rooms which flourished in the Renfield Street and Sauchiehall Street districts. The smug acceptance of things as they were which was a relic of the Victorian age pervaded not only the wealthy classes; it also still existed among the older workers. The reason, I think, was that, compared with the savage conditions which their parents and grandparents recounted of the hungry forties, things had improved slightly. For the last quarter of the nineteenth century economic conditions were by comparison making gradual progress. It was the turbulent twentieth century which swept away the acceptance of the situation as inevitable.

The working-class people of Glasgow lived in the grimy and ugly tenements of the Gorbals, Townhead, and Gallowgate, and the dockside areas of Anderton and Finnieston. The luckier families had two rooms: with a recessed bed—set in a hole in the wall in the kitchen for the boys and another in the parents' room for the girls. More usually the family had one room. One of Glasgow's medical officers, Dr. J. B. Russell, who attempted the well-nigh hopeless task of arousing landlords' consciences about housing conditions in the last two decades of the century, had declared that a quarter of Glasgow's 760,000 inhabitants lived in one room. One in seven of such one-room tenants took in a lodger in order to pay the rent. Another quarter of the city's population lived in two-room tenements.

Improvements and new buildings since the middle of the nineteenth century had not kept pace with the growth of population, principally due to the heavy immigration into the city. Large numbers of Irish had been coming over for years. Competition between the shipping companies made it possible for a man to cross the Irish Sea for a few shillings (at one period cut-throat rivalry reduced the price of a ticket to 1s.).

The Irish were often disliked by their Scots neighbours. They were usually single men or had left their wives and families in Ireland and would work for as little as 15s. a week. By sleeping three in a bed as lodgers they could manage on 8s. or 10s. a week, leaving a few shillings to send home. More potent motives of dislike came from religion and suspicion. The Lowland Scotsman of the day was a clannish person and would often pick a quarrel to justify his forebodings that Paddy meant trouble. I have seen a

30

The author's parents.

The author,
about 1903.

Mrs. Emanuel
Shinwell,
about 1903.

gawky Scotsman trail his coat along the street on Saturday night, bawling his challenge to anyone who dared to tread on it. An Irishman would accept the invitation with delight. The battle was on.

In drink the Irishman was a formidable and sometimes not very pleasant fellow, but apart from that I liked him. He was naturally friendly, a born wit, and a loyal comrade. The incursion of the Irish added large numbers of supporters to Labour. They were born politicians and could be readily trained as good organizers. Their trouble was their ruthless desire to attain their ends. In municipal elections they just could not see anything wrong in voting for "dead" men or other absentees.

In addition to the Irish, Glasgow had other immigrants. Many Italians came to open small shops; they monopolized the ice-cream trade. Many Norwegians and Swedes came to work on ships and in shipbuilding. Thousands of miners from Poland and Lithuania worked in the Lanarkshire and Fifeshire pits; many of them imported by the coal-owners when the native miners were on strike.

Living was cheap in those days, but wages were cheaper still. Behind the façade of Edwardian peace and prosperity, Britain's appearance, at any rate in those quarters with which I was familiar, was grim and foreboding. In the fourteen years from 1896 the real wage rates had declined by 4 per cent. For the great mass of the people tied to the productive machine of industry conditions were becoming worse than they had been since the beginning of the Industrial Revolution.

Wages for skilled men in the engineering and shipbuilding industries varied from 27s. to 32s. weekly. Labourers earned about 16s. to 18s., and a little less in the building trade. Railwaymen's wages varied from 17s. for an engine cleaner to 21s. for a fireman and signalman, 22s. 6d. for a guard, and 24s. to 30s. for a driver; the latter figure was attainable only by men on the express runs and with upwards of twenty years' service. Miners in the Lanarkshire pits, if they were on a good seam, could attain 6s. to 6s. 6d. a day by piece-work. On day wages the normal rate was 5s. a day of nine hours. A man would be dismissed if he failed to work a full six shifts a week when the owners wanted him to, though more usually, to cut overheads, the largest possible labour force was taken on for three or four days and the mine then closed till the following week. During the summer, miners rarely worked more than three shifts a week. Thus a miner who averaged 25s. a week for a year was considered very fortunate.

Yet these men were the hard core of the labour force—reliable, skilled, known to employers, adroit from years of experience in knowing how to ferret out a job and hang on to it for a time. The heritage of their forefathers gave them the strength for hard physical work despite the conditions in which they lived.

The frail, the old, the injured—and the women—they had to work too, when they could get work. It was among them that the full indignity of what Robert Burns had described as "man's inhumanity to man" was reached. Most tragic of all were the outworkers, mostly women who, through being unmarried or with a husband incapacitated for work, were compelled to earn a pittance at some job where deft fingers made some sort of remuneration possible.

Ordinary, decent folk were quite unaware that conditions worse than those described in the works of Dickens, which graced every middle-class Edwardian parlour, existed in the slums not only of Glasgow, but in every great city in the land.

Few of the upper and middle classes knew, or tried to find out, that in Glasgow and the North women workers in the tailoring and garment trade averaged 13s. for a 58-hour week, while juniors working shorter hours did not reach 10s. These were typical, and by comparison good, wages for women in Edwardian Britain. About half of all women workers over eighteen earned under 10s. a week, while those who were compelled by family ties to work at home rarely reached 5s. a week.

Small wonder is it that the financial troubles of the bulk of the families I knew in my youth were acute and insoluble. None of the workers in industry could budget on a regular wage from week to week, or even day to day. Short time and laying off were daily occurrences. I learned as a child that the normal greeting of one man to another in the street was not to-day's inquiry about health or family but the simple question:

"Are you working?"

Too often there was a slight shake of the head, as if the lack of work was a shameful thing and the subject had better be ignored as embarrassing. Our womenfolk would talk more anxiously and urgently when the negative came to their question "Is your man in work?" They had, of course, the bad end of the stick. The woman usually held the purse-strings whether there was anything inside or not. It was customary for the man to hand over his pay-packet intact and to be given 2s. back by his wife for himself. I did so myself for years. The housewife worked literally in farthings, for in those days a farthing could sometimes buy a piece of bread, a handful of potatoes or a pinch of tea. Her biggest bugbear was the landlord, or the house factor as we used to call him. The rent might be as low as 4s.—a two-room and kitchen flat could be obtained for 6s. to 7s. 6d. a week according to the district and the number of lavatories in the building (sometimes there was one lavatory on each landing, used by three or four families)—but it must be realized that even at this figure rent represented between one-sixth and one-third of the total income of a full-time working week. Further, these rents were usually paid monthly or quarterly. It was humanly impossible for a woman to watch her man and bairns go hungry while the shillings for the collector piled up in the jug on the mantelpiece. True, she could apply to the relieving officer when utterly destitute, but the majority of Scottish people were so proud that they would rather starve than have recourse to the Poor Law.

These people had no reserves of strength to meet the recurrent crises of unemployment. Apart from the infectious and contagious diseases which were rampant in the vermin- and rat-infested buildings (we often had to move because of this; landlords would do nothing about it), deficiency disease took an enormous toll. I can still see the typical Glasgow tenement child, happy and dirty as he played in the gutter or up and down the stairs of his building. His legs would be bandy or knock-kneed: those more fortunate jeered at them with opprobrious words to describe this freakish-ness. But nobody cared, for the physical abnormality was familiar to them all.

Ignorance of diet was not the fault of the housewife, for most of the facts of nutrition, notably the vitamins, were unknown to us, and even to the scientists. Fortunately the Scots had one splendid food in their oatmeal. It was as yet unspoiled by

33

processing, and provided a basis of nutrition without which the workers could not have survived.

A plate of porridge and a mug of tea was the normal working man's breakfast. On Sunday morning a wife would skimp and save to give her husband ham and eggs. Seldom did the rest of the family expect to enjoy this masculine luxury. If the breakfast consisted of kippers there might be a share for all—father, of course, getting the most.

For the midday meal at the shipyards or factory bench the worker of the day would "take a piece" with him—two or three slices of bread and a sausage or bit of cheese. An apprentice was always around to make a bucket of tea for ten or twenty workmen at a cost which provided a pint mug of sweet dark-brown brew for a halfpenny. When he returned home in the evening the meal often consisted of mince, a hot pie costing twopence, or fish and chips. When times were bad he would make do on a dish of "spuds"—potatoes mashed with salt—and possibly a herring.

Butter was a luxury only the countryfolk and the rich towns-people had. Margarine was then unknown. Milk was too expensive to drink by itself or else suspected as the source of many diseases, as indeed it then was.

This was the field in which the seeds of the Labour movement were sown, and it was naturally fertile ground. James Keir Hardie, descendant of a Scottish collier executed for a so-called armed revolt in 1820, had become a hero to his fellow-miners in Ayrshire in the eighties, when he first emerged as their champion. *The Miner*, his earliest publication, had come out in 1887, and his aid to the hardly treated workers by a policy of education with pleas for "the right to work" was a small but steady flame lighting the way ahead. Hardie was at that time, of course, a Liberal and hoped to be elected for Mid-Lanark, but he was beginning to despair of any real progress through his party.

Thus Scotland led the country in Socialist ideas when the Scottish Labour Party came into existence by the autumn of 1888; a Liberal M.P., R. B. Cunninghame Graham, an aristocrat with the blood of Scottish kings in his veins, was its president and Keir Hardie was secretary. When, in 1893, Hardie formed the Independent Labour Party the inspiration was largely Scottish and the greatest enthusiasm for it in the whole country was among the people of the Clyde and Lowlands. In the simple faith of those days the objective was merely to work for collective ownership and control of the means of production, distribution, and exchange, and the immediate objective was the familiar social reform.

The I.L.P. had still more profound influence on the more intellectual people of Glasgow. It gave much food for thought to clergymen, teachers, the better-off craftsmen and artisans, shopkeepers and quite a number of wealthy people who had already become interested in Socialism through the writings of William Morris and the activities of the Fabians.

My experience among the miners in some of the mining villages of Fife and Lanarkshire was that the policy of the Social Democratic Federation made a greater appeal than that of the I.L.P. The miner everywhere is suspicious of novelty until he has studied its advantages and disadvantages. The Social Democratic Federation was so close to the old Radical movement that the miner could accept it without misgivings despite the fact that it was essentially English, inspired by Marx's best-known English disciple, H. M. Hyndman, and with little Scottish blood in its hierarchy at the outset. *England for All*, the title of Hyndman's exposition of the S.D.F. policy, was hardly conducive to the creation of enthusiasm across the Border, though the nationalism we know in Scotland to-day was not at the time so marked. In the event, the S.D.F.'s powers soon declined, for *England for All* was really just an anglicized simplification of Marxian views, written without acknowledgment to the originator. Marx did not forget the slight, and by the time I began to read Marx it was the I.L.P. which had received the seal of approval from his collaborator, the other great European Socialist force, Engels. Two notable S.D.F. members in my day, who played a leading part on the Clydeside, deserve mention; the likeable but formidable Willie Gallagher, and that great exponent of Socialism, John McLean, both of whom served several terms of imprisonment because of their political activities.

A third force emerged later in the period. This was the Socialist Labour Party, formed in 1903 to advocate strict Marxian ideology. It was an imported concept, based on French syndicalism and American militant trade unionism, the latter being largely the policy of the U.S. Socialist leader, Daniel de Leon, who formulated the then sensational aims of the American Industrial Workers of the World. The S.L.P. never meant very much numerically but so far as it had any influence it was in Glasgow. The paucity of members was to some extent made up by fanatical quality. Its Glasgow leaders included Willie Paul, Arthur McManus (whose name later appeared on the notorious and mysterious Zinoviev letter), Tom Bell, and Neil McLean, who resigned from it and joined the I.L.P. before he became M.P. for Govan. These men were skilled in waging direct industrial conflict, and after the Russian Revolution they became (apart from Neil McLean) the nucleus of the Communist Party.

Most important of all as regards the position of the Scottish workers was the fact that they were a patient and tolerant people. They were bitter about their wrongs but had little time for firebrands who advocated bloody revolution. They were fighting for more profound changes than those which could be obtained by stone-throwing, looting, and futile attacks on the police. They were prepared for a patient war of attrition. If perhaps they had known how long that war was to last it is possible that their patience would not have been so gentle.

The people of Glasgow watched the practical efforts on their behalf with greater interest than that bestowed on ideological movements across the Border. The work of the Glasgow Trades Council, with which body I was long and actively associated, was noted by the people with as much excitement as the affairs of the Glasgow Town Council or of Parliament itself. Every Wednesday evening more than four hundred delegates met and discussed topics which went far beyond the immediate factors of the industries concerned. It dealt with both local and national affairs and gave an impetus to the Labour movement not only on Clydeside but throughout the whole of Scotland.

Gossip about the statements and resolutions of the Trades Council gave both Irish and Scottish workers, who vied with one another in their love of debate, chances for discussion in the dinner break and to and from work as well as at week-ends. More ammunition was provided by Robert Blatchford's *Clarion*, which was a regular joy not only because it discoursed on Socialism but recognized that the artisan and miner, though forced by circumstance to wrestle in the mire and murk of a city for their livelihood, were able to lift their eyes in search of the things that embellished a civilization. Without pomposity or criticism the *Clarion* talked about the arts.

There were literally thousands of workers in Glasgow who knew the name of G. B. Shaw before London playgoers had recognized the advent of a new playwright—and there were as many who thought of Oscar Wilde not as a witty writer of epigrams or as an immoral monster but as the brilliant author of *The Soul of Man under Socialism*. Of even greater influence were Blatchford's books, notably *Britain for the British* and *Merrie England*, which sold by the hundreds of thousands, and each copy had a dozen or a score of readers as it was passed from man to man. There was much the same enthusiasm for the other Socialist weeklies—*Justice*, the organ of the S.D.F., and *The Labour Leader*, edited for many years by Hardie.

It was the inspiration of the work of the Trades Council, and later of my own efforts as a member of it, that fashioned my political future. My own life in early manhood was spent in the environment of Glasgow of the new century, the preliminary of more violent times, when strikes and lock-outs became more frequent and the obstinate fatalism of the statement: "Why be afraid of the employers? You starve when you are working and you starve when not" led inexorably to a clash of power.

In the sense of injustice at what I saw around me, and the feeling of intolerance that such things could continue, my life was contemporary with most of the second wave of Socialist adherents who marched behind the banners of Keir Hardie, John Burns, and Tom Mann. In the formative years of my Socialist experience I admired and revered these men. There were many others whose works and words inspired me: George Carson, Martin Haddow, James Welsh of the Clarion Scouts, Bruce Glasier and his wife Katherine, Harry Quelch, Victor Fisher, Joe Duncan. The present Labour movement owes much to them all.

CHAPTER FOUR

EARLY UNION AND TRADES COUNCIL WORK

I WAS a Socialist before I was twenty, not merely by inclination but through active participation in the work of those bodies which furthered the aims of the movement. Such activities, however, as thousands of workers have discovered before and since, do not enhance the husband's contribution to family life.

My wife had experienced the vicissitudes of marriage during the three months of complete poverty which followed soon after our wedding. At first she very reasonably showed little enthusiasm for my trade-union and Socialist activities which took me away from home for so many evenings and week-ends. But quite soon after our marriage she accepted the fact that my political work was not without importance, and she helped me in the best way possible: by the practical aid of comfort and understanding.

Her greatest interest in social matters was always the welfare of children. Cruelty and neglect aroused her anger in a way that nothing else could. She could sympathize in the case of the most hardened criminals who were in the news when on trial, but where children's happiness and well-being were in jeopardy she was a merciless and unrelenting judge.

I shared her views in this regard. If I have little time for sentimentality I hope that I have plenty for sentiment. I have a reputation for ruthless criticism of both opponents and colleagues when I feel such criticism is necessary, but perhaps not quite so obvious to others is my regard for anyone in a minority. Having been so often in a minority myself—on many occasions consisting of one only—I tend to react against the majority. This has brought its troubles. . . .

Some years after our marriage my wife was involved in strike action with me. Glasgow's landlords had decided on a sharp increase in rents. At this time two of our children had arrived; my wages at the clothing factory of the Scottish Co-operative Society at Shieldhall were 35s. a week. I was able to supplement this with a few modest fees from an insurance society, but feeding, housing, and clothing four human beings on little more than 10s. per head per week was not easy. Yet 35s. was top rate in my trade, and my wages were higher than those most of our neighbours, working in the shipyards and engineering works of Clydeside, were getting.

Thus, even though the rent of a two-roomed flat in a Glasgow tenement was only between £15 and £20 a year, it was impossible for the average tenant to meet an increase. Someone discovered that according to Scots Law landlords could not increase rents before giving a notice to quit. Thousands of tenants agreed not to pay any rent until the notices had been served and dealt with by the courts. My own case was heard as the test one for the area. Eventually the compromise arrived at in court meant the increases were lower than the landlords had originally tried to impose.

Soon afterwards came another strike, this time over school-books. The Glasgow Trades Council advised parents to withhold their children from school attendance until the School Board provided all books free of charge. A large number of summonses was issued, and this was sufficient to break the strike with most parents. We continued to keep our own children away, and as I remained adamant at the court hearing I was fined. The Trades Council paid the fine, and the agitation died down when the more expensive books were provided free.

My work at the Co-op. factory had one advantage: it gave me a fair amount of freedom to continue with my propagandist work without fear of victimization or dismissal. I had joined the Amalgamated Society of Clothing Operatives some years before and had taken an active part in the union's Glasgow branch, though I had refused to become assistant secretary because it would have spoiled my opportunities to undertake I.L.P. work, and to devote the time I considered was necessary to my duties on the Glasgow Trades Council, of which I was the youngest member when I was elected at the age of twenty-two in 1906.

The Trades Councils deserve a better place in the Labour

Party's record than in fact they have. Ernest Bevin once said at a meeting of the T.U.C.: ". . . our predecessors formed this party: it was not Keir Hardie. The Labour Party grew out of the bowels of the T.U.C." The Trades Councils were active long before the T.U.C. Indeed the first national trades union conference in 1864 was held thanks to the work of a member of the Glasgow Trades Council, Alexander Campbell.

The Trades Councils began work in various parts of the country more than one hundred years ago, and their exclusion from the T.U.C. in 1895 in no way weakened their influence at that time. By tradition, and experience, the Councils have always been fighting bodies. Only through them could various organizations and groups of workers in a locality provide a united front. The T.U.C. spent years in ousting the Councils from their original great influence, without at first replacing them with any concerted power.

To-day, of course, the Trades Councils have been emasculated in comparison with their powers in the early part of this century. They cannot now interfere in local elections for local government or Parliament, and must not associate with organizations proscribed by the T.U.C. or the Labour Party. To all intents and purposes they are prohibited from intervening in industrial disputes. This is a different position from that which I knew on the Glasgow Trades Council before the First World War.

Although I was the Council's youngest member I had plenty of self-confidence and was regarded as a good debater. In those days the reports of the Council meetings received widespread publicity and were eagerly read by the thousands of workers the organization represented. The high moral tone of the Trades Council ensured its prestige and the unswerving loyalty of the workers. All members were working men. Apart from a remuneration for a full-time secretary, payment for work, or even for routine expenses, was unknown. Some of the members were deeply religious and exerted strong influence for good in the areas where they lived and the factories where they worked. The slightest clouding of a delegate's reputation or character meant that his union was asked to remove him. It was wonderful training for me, and I can ascribe my lifelong code of action almost entirely to its influence.

Many men who were delegates became well known in public life in later years. Robert Smillie, the miners' leader, John Marchbanks, of the railway union, James Walker, of the steelworkers, and a large number of M.P.s, got their baptism of political fire in the Glasgow Trades Council.

For many years the secretary was George Carson, an associate of Keir Hardie when the Scottish Labour Party was formed, and until his retirement and death a man with more influence in Scottish trade-union circles than anyone else I have known. It was unfortunate that in his seventies his mental powers became impaired. I was by then President of the Council (an office which I held for many years in election after election), and on the platform he was difficult to restrain as he made audible asides about the foolishness and stupidity of some delegate who was speaking. He was a great but obstinate old man; eventually we had to fight hard to get him to take a nominal pension and rest on his laurels.

My name became still more widely known when I was sent as the Glasgow Trades Council delegate to the Scottish T.U.C.; there were also my duties with the Scottish I.L.P. and, early in my political career, with the Clarion Scouts.

The Clarion Scouts were a pleasant social-political association of young men, based largely on the tremendous vogue for cycling clubs which grew up at the turn of the century. The mainspring of the organization was, of course, the *Clarion*, and its famous editor, Robert Blatchford.

I remember on one occasion speaking with him, a great honour for a young man. I took the chair for a meeting he was to address on Glasgow Green. His reputation and influence brought great crowds, but they—like myself—were disappointed. As is the case with many writers, Blatchford was a poor speaker. He said only a few words and left the rest of the meeting to me.

In 1908 the Scottish I.L.P. decided to organize a summer campaign on the coast. We lived in tents at Kilwinning. The other members were much older than I, and most of their names are now forgotten. There was O'Connor Kessack, the ablest orator of all; he was killed in France in the First World War. Others included Joe Duncan, later an expert on agriculture and a member of several Government inquiries, George Kerr, secretary of the Scottish I.L.P., Robert Climie, later M.P. for Kilmarnock, Tom McKerrel, later an official with the Ministry of Labour, and George Dallas, who became an M.P. and has held many important posts in the Labour Party.

Kilwinning was no holiday camp. I remember one Saturday afternoon the secretary told me to take some literature and to address a meeting at Largs, the popular Clydeside holiday and fishing town. He told me I would find a man with a red tie who would take the chair. There was no man with a red tie and no sign of a meeting. It was a disgrace to return to the camp without some money from a collection and pamphlet sales, and a report of a meeting. I found a fish-box and started to speak. A considerable crowd gathered. My difficulty was to get a collection without a chairman to go round with the hat. I explained my difficulty and invited my audience to throw their coppers on the ground near my box. They did. It was dark before I got back and I lost my way, stumbling over several ploughed fields and clambering through hedges and over ditches. When I wearily pulled the tent flap aside the sleepy voice of the secretary inquired: "Did you get a collection?" He was not interested in my difficulties. It was a hard school, but a good one.

By no means all the experiences were of pleasant summer camps and enthusiastic but peaceful street-corner meetings. In the Council there were sharp conflicts between the craft unions and the so-called unskilled workers' unions. The members of the former, who had for the most part served long terms of apprenticeship, resented any entrenchment of the position of workers they regarded not necessarily as inferiors, but as rivals. The shipwright queried the duties of the ship's carpenter; the cabinet-maker the definition of skilled and semi-skilled work. Fear of unemployment was the spur to this selfish attitude; to some extent it lingers on to-day, damaging productivity and unity.

Unemployment in these years was severe, as I have stressed elsewhere. Spontaneous demonstrations were almost an everyday occurrence in Glasgow. In 1908 the Trades Council decided to organize a protest meeting in Cathedral Square on a Sunday morning. The procession was led by Tom Kerr (now Lord Provost of Glasgow) and myself. We addressed the crowd. Their exasperation was such that I was interrupted with calls for an entry into

42

the Cathedral, where morning service was being held, to make a protest. The citizens of Glasgow, although they may suffer from sectarian hatred, are fundamentally pious and this idea was, I am convinced, not born of any disrespect. As soon as we moved towards the church doors the waiting police drew their batons and struck down everybody within reach. Many women went sprawling. I got a bruised arm, and we eventually were all chased down the High Street. The Glasgow policeman of the early 1900s was the most brutal I have ever known. Beef rather than brains was the criterion of entry into the force. Most of them came from the Highlands, and they came with a heritage of clan war against the Lowlands, paying off old scores of the eighteenth century and earlier as if they had occurred yesterday. I am glad to say that this sadistic streak has virtually died out.

I often wonder how many of to-day's youthful entrants to the political arena could have stood up to the exactingly high standard of oratory and the long hours of work which we put in after our normal employment. On the Glasgow Trades Council, to quote only one side of my activities, we were expected to have an almost encyclopædic knowledge of the background to current questions. Our debates ranged from free school meals to resolutions on foreign affairs, from old age pensions (before their introduction) to secular education. None of these questions was as simple as they may sound to-day. Agreement was hard to attain. The proposal for feeding the schoolchildren, for example, was the idea of the " extremists" connected with the Social Democratic Federation; I.L.P. and trade-union delegates opposed it because they thought that the idea might be used as an excuse by the employers to refuse to raise wages. The S.D.F. was proud of its advanced opinions. It used to talk about a Citizen Army. This aroused the I.L.P. people, who were wholly pacifist.

One's opponents in debate had no mercy. I recall a trouncing I received from Keir Hardie when attending an I.L.P. conference in Merthyr Tydfil as a Glasgow delegate. There were no half measures about our resolutions in those days, and I had to move one which in effect demanded the abolition of the Navy. I frankly was not convinced of the validity of the proposal, and this did not aid my oratory. Keir Hardie rose. He treated my speech with withering contempt and simply ignored the resolution. I had feared, or rather hoped for, fireworks from him, but all I got was devastating common sense. It was an example of Hardie's attitude. He was not an extremist. If he were alive and active to-day he would undoubtedly be criticized as a right-wing reactionary.

In those days it was simply not done to speak from notes. Any speaker who did so was regarded as a fake. The longer one spoke the higher the regard of an audience. A thirty-minute speech was the effort of a novice at the game; an hour indicated that the speaker was improving. A first-class man would go on for a couple of hours. Time after time I have heard a comrade say: "My, he's a rare speaker! Did you notice how long he spoke?"

But the chairman spoke at length at his peril. There was in those days a burly steelworker named Sandy Haddow who could always command a big audience. At a meeting by Govan Cross a new chairman made a five-minute introduction; then carried away by his own eloquence, he went on for a further twenty minutes. At long last he said: "And now I call upon our good friend Sandy Haddow to address you."

Sandy, who was a crude and forthright man, stood on the box, glared at his audience and exclaimed: "Do any of you want to ask this b—— any questions?"

The lofty idealism of every Socialist in the first decade of the century might seem rather quaint to the no less sincere newcomers to-day. We tempered pugnacity with poetry, tilted at our capitalist windmills with lances of picturesque phrase.

In the early days of the movement it was a common practice of speakers to recite poetry. Some of our well-known propagandists like W. C. Anderson, Dick Wallhead, Russell Williams and even the severely practical Philip Snowden rarely wound up a speech without some snatches of poetry. I remember a number of popular speakers whose orations consisted entirely of poetic excerpts which their audiences loved. One notable exception was Pat (now Sir Patrick) Dollan, perhaps the most conscientious and hard-working propagandist the Scottish Labour movement ever had. His capacity for work was amazing and there was hardly an agitation in which he was not in the front line. I have no recollection of Pat indulging in poetry in order to embroider his theme, except perhaps an occasional line from Burns. But there

44

was never a need; he was seldom at a loss for a word or an idea. The movement in Scotland owes much to him.

I was not an expert in memorizing poetry and thus failed to reach the oratorical peaks in this regard. I have no parrot-like memory, and did not really regret the fact. It seemed to me a little unfair to reel off stanza after stanza to the applause of the audience. The only extracts I could remember were those closely allied to the topic in which I was interested. Even now I can quote from a fifty-year-old memory of a poem by the Italian poet Campanella. It runs:

> "*The people is a beast of muddy brain,*
> *That knows not its own strength*
> *And therefore stands loaded with wood and stone;*
> *The powerless hands of a mere child*
> *Guide it with bit and rein.*
> *One kick would be enough to break the chain,*
> *But the beast fears.*
> *And what the child demands it does,*
> *Nor its own terror understands.*
> *Confused and stupefied by bugbears vain;*
> *With its own hands it ties itself;*
> *Gives itself death and war*
> *From pence doled out by Kings from its own store.*
> *Its own are all things*
> *Between Earth and Heaven.*
> *But this it knows not,*
> *And when one arises to tell this truth*
> *It kills him unforgiven.*"

Poetry has been described as a criticism of life. I regret its (I hope temporary) eclipse. It has to me been both a joy and a means of education. I hope that I can say that my mind is still open and that my education continues even until this day.

In my late twenties and early thirties self-education was a deliberate part of my daily life, just as it had been in youth and early manhood. To this end I enlisted the aid of my two elder children, then just of school age. In my spare time I used to read aloud, then listen to them reading the same passage. We read the whole of the *Golden Treasury* and, of course, as Glaswegians, we dipped into the more suitable works of Rabbie Burns. A good dictionary stood beside us. Every word which we did not understand or were doubtful as regards pronunciation was looked up. For me these mutual lessons were of invaluable aid in improving my diction and eloquence. For the children, I believe, they were of some help in forming character.

Parental responsibility goes farther than giving exhortations to be good and reproofs for being bad. The heritage of literature is not lost even on young minds. Later influences in the forces or at work will not injure the young mind so readily if it is well provided for in childhood.

The mechanical voices of the cinema and radio have to my regret ousted to some extent the power of the printed word. Their influence is more transient than a book or pamphlet and does not create such lasting interest. In the old days we Socialists read more than the young men and women of to-day. Every new work by a Socialist author was pounced on with enthusiasm. Pamphlets were eagerly bought, and fictional works with a new idea or social message—such as the works of H. G. Wells—were readily accepted as indications of the end of an old and outworn system and the dawn of a better and brighter day.

These works kept the fires of our zeal burning. There was also plenty about which to argue. We argued on the slightest excuse and fought over the interpretation of every principle. Karl Marx provided plenty of obscurity for debate. There was the perpetual topic of the possibility of achieving Socialism through parliamentary means as contrasted with what was euphemistically called direct action. On the whole the youthful spirits favoured the latter. A common expression of farewell was "I shall see you at the barricades." The French Revolution seemed much nearer then than it does to-day.

Our knowledge of the history of that revolution and of social development in Britain of the same era was more profound than is the case among young people now. We were all acquainted with the life of Robert Owen (the reputed father of modern Socialism), and the Chartist movement. We studied current events with a zest almost unknown to-day. I remember the joy we felt when the Duma, the first Russian Parliament, was formed in 1905.

It was, I think, Bernard Shaw who commented at this period that "Socialism would be all right if it were not for the Socialists." He was referring to the innumerable brands of Socialism of the time. While the crowds at our meetings would cheer at the very mention of names like Keir Hardie, Robert Blatchford, John Burns, H. M. Hyndman, Cunninghame Graham, or Victor Grayson, their immediate followers waged unceasing war on one another. Usually the charge was one of moderation. Keir Hardie, whose very name to-day makes old ladies shudder in their beds, was to most of us far too mild and patient. Our leaders were getting on; we had the impatience of youth. The Socialist Rome was to be built in a day. It was all very stimulating, and sometimes I think that the flames could with advantage be fanned afresh. . . . We could certainly derive benefit from a revival of this spirit and school of oratory.

The practice of speaking without notes has stood me in good stead since. Usually I neither use notes nor read from a script, except, of course, in occasional broadcasts where timing is so important. Even then, I prefer the unrehearsed broadcast like the Brains Trusts, in which I often spoke during the war. Of course, in a Commons speech for the Government or Opposition notes are necessary. As Minister of Defence, I confined myself to notes because of the statistical material which was necessary. I remember on one occasion Lord Winterton, normally a good friend, rising to ask the Speaker whether it was in order to read a speech. I could have readily knocked him down, for he knew full well that I was one of the men in the House who disliked using notes. Of course, he could not resist the chance of a rather telling thrust, although in private we were on excellent terms, and my momentary resentment soon passed. It is not usually realized by the public that there is a parliamentary tradition that speeches should not be read. Churchill and many others, of course, do so regularly. My colleague, Herbert Morrison, who invariably carefully prepares and reads his speeches, has often remonstrated with me for not speaking without seemingly rehearsing first. In fact, of course, the "spontaneous" speech needs more preliminary work than the scripted one.

There was plenty of action in those days as well as speaking. This applied in particular after my association with the newly formed Seafarers' Union began in 1911, the start of a period which brought me valuable experience, hard times, and some bitter controversy.

CHAPTER FIVE

UNION WORK ON CLYDESIDE

THE year 1911 was a milestone in Britain's modern history: one in which the pressure of events was ignored by the Liberal Government until step by step it had to yield to circumstance. They had to face the annoyances of the militant Suffragettes, the problems of Ireland and the approaching certainty of war in Europe. While political and Press attention was focused on those problems the growing impatience of the workers, now that the depression of the earlier years was passing, brought inevitable upheaval. Liberal England was dying. The struggle was beginning between Socialism and Toryism. Strikes and lock-outs of increasing size and severity began. They were the symptom of workers' unrest, not of unified action. Before the unions organized these local and spontaneous actions of resistance, and the large-scale dock, railways, and mine strikes began, the first storm broke in the National Sailors' and Firemen's Union. It called its members out on strike: the ports were virtually at a standstill for more than a week.

This involved me, for in that blazing summer of 1911 my twenty-year association with seamen began. At the time I was vice-chairman of the Glasgow Trades Council, and I became one of the delegates loaned to the Seamen's Union at the request of Havelock Wilson. The others were James Walker, later M.P. for Motherwell, and Joe Houghton, later secretary of the Scottish Union of Dock Labourers. Our job was to organize the Clydeside seamen.

Conditions at sea at this period were just about as bad as possible. Able seamen on the transatlantic liners were receiving 60s. to 70s. a month, men in the stokeholds 80s. Firemen working tramps or long-distance liners to Australia and South American ports seldom received more than 60s. a month. They were tough men, awkward to deal with, and without much of a social conscience. It was said that the most poverty-stricken home in Glasgow's slums was that of a marine fireman. The home invariably consisted of just one room. The furniture comprised one communal iron bedstead padded with a few rags, a broken-down table and one chair for the master of the house. But one thing was the pride of the establishment; a shining silver cruet-stand marked Anchor or Allan Line.

It has always interested me to read that the oldest police force in the country, the Thames River Police, was formed in the late eighteenth century because thefts in the Pool of London were causing losses of £700,000 a year, and were the principal calling of 115,000 people. In those days the bargees would steal an anchor, thereby allowing a ship to drift in the night to the nearest mud flat where swarms of men, women, and children stripped her bare. I suppose some pilfering continues to-day. When I first went to the Glasgow docks it was not uncommon to see a couple of men carrying a wardrobe or similar large piece of furniture down the gangway as if they were acting on instructions. It was readily disposed of in one of the dark little junk shops of the area. Eventually the shipping firms had to keep guards on the decks and gangways to stop this wholesale pilfering.

Havelock Wilson was not a popular figure in the Labour circles of the day. He was a Liberal and had been M.P. for Middlesbrough. There were, moreover, indications that his enthusiasm for the seamen's cause fluctuated according to the state of the union's contributions account. In this regard admittedly he was deserving of some sympathy, for the financial difficulties of his job were considerable, and in fact he had twice been made bankrupt. In a flush of zeal a seaman would join the union, pay his dues and proceed to sea on a long voyage. On return he would indulge in the traditional spending spree, for his amusement and also to meet the debts which his family had accumulated in his absence. By the time Wilson caught up with him and demanded past and current contributions he had no money left.

The strike began at Southampton on 13 June, 1911. It spread within a day or so to all ports, and although many impoverished men became blacklegs, by 20 June shipping was paralysed. I was in the thick of the fray and took my two weeks' annual holiday without pay from the Co-operative clothing factory so that I could devote all my time to addressing meetings on the dockside and in persuading the men to hold out.

For a day or so I was on my own, for Wilson had returned to his London headquarters. Then he sent up two men who, to say the least, were not the type for the job. One was a man named Albert French who had a bizarre and varied series of adventures around the world to report, and the other a gentleman who announced himself as Captain E. A. Tupper, V.C., " hon. trustee" of the union. Somehow he had impressed Wilson with his story that he was a born aristocrat and Boer War hero anxious to help the poor seamen as a gesture of friendship and admiration— with the aid of expenses for his trouble, of course. In fact he was a native of Worthing who had launched out on an adventurous life as a change from being an errand boy, and had for a short time been a private in the Army. The limp which, he insinuated, was the aftermath of his heroic deeds resulting in the award of the V.C. was, in fact, caused by the kick of a horse.

Despite the hindrances of this help from headquarters, I managed to keep the men together. We had virtually no funds in the union, and in any event I was not an official with the right to handle it, but I could organize collections in the factories and workshops of Glasgow and this enabled us to hand out a few shillings to the strikers' families. Our most vulnerable adversaries were the liner companies. Every Saturday three large vessels sailed for Canada and the United States with a minimum of 1,000 passengers each. Cut-throat competition for the translatlantic passenger trade was at its height, and the expense of feeding and accommodating 3,000 passengers while the vessels lay at anchor in the Clyde represented a formidable loss for the companies. Consequently, we were soon able to complete negotiations to get a minimum of £5 10s. a month from the owners. Unfortunately Wilson had temporarily patched up his bitter quarrel with the Shipping Federation and simultaneously accepted an all-round payment of £5 a month. Clydeside men strongly resented this and continued to strike. Eventually the ship-owners gave way and £5 10s. became the standard rate.

With agreement reached I was begged by the owners' representatives to get some crews to the liners lying at the Tail of the Bank, Greenock. By this time I knew the typical Glasgow seaman, and I knew that to honour the agreement I would have to shepherd the men on board, not leaving them till they were up the gangways. I chartered a tug and crammed a few hundred men, many of them the worse for drink, into her. At the quayside at Greenock some ships' officers told me that in the meantime they had themselves rounded up a crowd of non-union men and did not want my crews. We went into a dock office to talk it over, but they would not go above the £5 rate accepted in London.

There followed one of the most exciting and alarming half-hours of my life. I climbed up a lamp-post and addressed the men. There were some who wanted to throw those ready to accept £5 into the water, and with seamen the wish is the brief preliminary to action. I managed to calm them down and asked them to have patience while I went out to one of the liners where the company officials were awaiting events. Our argument was a long one. They eventually agreed to pay £5 10s. but not to take all the men I had brought to meet their original order for crews. I was under no illusions whatever as to what would happen to me if I compromised. Those left ashore would have settled matters with vigorous and probably fatal results. In any event there was a principle involved. I demanded full settlement and won.

Union work on Clydeside forty years ago was no job for a weakling. As a boy I had learned how to box, but in later years my arm muscles had got soft, so I bought a punch-ball, fixed it up in our flat and had a work-out every morning except Sundays when the "thump-thump" would have disturbed the neighbours. This morning exercise continued for months, and my fists became as tough as leather and my muscles as hard as those of a docker.

There was little real malice about the opponents I met on Clydeside, but they were very dangerous for all that. When I became an official of the union I had always to be ready for a seaman in drink to assault me because at that moment he happened to dislike the union or had been annoyed by a request for his overdue subscription which he could not pay. The docks were the work-haven of both law-abiding and outlaws. Men out of prison and men who by tradition lived by the sea sought for work there. However varied their background or nationality, they had one common characteristic: a belief that toughness and a bellicose attitude were as good a rule for life as any. I suffered many black eyes, but there were several occasions when my adversary staggered back, more in surprise than through fear, when I retaliated to some account. These men had not heard of Queensberry rules. While many seamen were of the most friendly disposition and hated trouble, some would attack from the rear, pounce at night, use a razor or a broken bottle, and on the whole it was better to be a good runner than a clever pugilist. The self-same pugnacious men would, when sober or unworried by lack of money and work, readily contribute to any and every good cause they came across, and I must say that their treatment of their families, even though they kept them in poverty, was on the whole gentle and affectionate.

Immediately the seamen's strike had been settled the dockers started to come out. The result was further unemployment for seamen, and again we had to depend on funds to provide relief. About this time I was offered the post of secretary to the newly formed Dock Labourers' Union, a local organization. I declined, and was almost immediately offered the position of assistant branch secretary of the Seamen's Union, of which French was secretary. I accepted this offer and was soon busy forming an organization among the shore-workers whose job it was to get the ships ready for sea. Their duties were so closely allied to those of the seamen that I felt it would strengthen our case in any future dispute if both groups could co-operate. Havelock Wilson was very annoyed, and in due course the redoubtable Captain Tupper appeared as a headquarters emissary to see what we were doing. He was accompanied by a remarkable individual named the "Rev." Charles P. Hopkins. He was, in his own words as a witness at a later court hearing, a volunteer "sky pilot," who clad himself in a semi-clerical, semi-nautical garb consisting of discreet black habit with a blue seaman's jersey and a gold crucifix. He was a newcomer, having become a trustee of the union that summer, though an old crony of Wilson's. Our inquisitors promptly sacked the committee and the officials, so that there was no alternative but to continue the organization as a local one. Simultaneously a similar crisis had occurred in Southampton. Within a few

months these two local units combined as the British Seafarers'
Union.

Wilson, who was a great believer in lawsuits, started a series
of actions in the courts. His first one was successful in getting us
evicted from his offices. We departed to new premises with our
books and records, which brought another action for their return.
Wilson lost this case as he had omitted to register his union in
Scotland. His unfortunate solicitors were ordered again and again
to prepare fresh cases on one pretext or another, which failed.

For the sake of peace and quiet the committee agreed to hand
the books over, but I was forced to clear up one of his wilder
charges—that I had misappropriated funds. In fact, I had always
taken an uncompromising attitude to financial matters ever since
I first engaged in Trades Council work, and indeed I had always
felt many misgivings about Wilson's lax arrangements on the
financial side of his union organization. At the Court of Session
in Edinburgh I was awarded £50 damages against Wilson and
costs amounting to nearly £600.

Despite further efforts by Wilson to intimidate our members
we were soon achieving considerable success, and on the outbreak
of war in 1914 the union's negotiations with the owners became
official. Years before as a boy I had tried to join the Navy. Now
I tried again, but at the request of the ship-owners I was reserved
and my job listed as one of "national importance." I was not,
and never have been, a conscientious objector, but when Ramsay
MacDonald began his campaign for peace by negotiation in
1916-17 I spoke in favour of it. As a result I was brought before a
Military Tribunal with the object of silencing me in uniform.
There was nothing I could do, or wished to do, about their
decision, beyond my determination to speak at meetings and say
what I pleased, but in the event George Barnes, a Labour member
of the War Cabinet, intervened. It was thought in Whitehall, I
suppose, that the comparatively peaceful atmosphere among the
seamen of Clydeside, despite the frightful toll of the U-boats, was
well worth a little street-corner criticism from one of their
representatives.

If things were comparatively quiet in the docks this was not
true of the rest of the industrial area of Clydeside. It must be
remembered that in 1914-18 there was not the unity of purpose

which pervaded the public mind when Britain fought Hitlerism. Perhaps Government propaganda was wrong. Anyway, the Whitehall policy was soon to annoy rather than inspire the working population. The trade unions, particularly the craft unions, tried to grapple with the sudden problem of dilution of labour, particularly in the case of women who entered industry on a wide front for the first time. Some employers demanded that all trade-union rules in factories concerned with the output of munitions should be abolished. The War Office, as a leading employer, was well to the fore in this type of campaign. Growing unrest on the employees' side and increasingly impatient demands from the employers resulted in the Government forming a Committee on Production. As a result of its report on the munitions industry the trade unions suffered almost complete defeat. When the Defence of the Realm Act was passed in March, 1915, compulsion and punishment were the twin rules of employment in the war industries. The right to strike had gone; trade-union regulations were to be relaxed, and unskilled or semi-skilled labour could be used provided the rate for the job was not thereby deliberately lowered. Later, thanks to the engineers' union, some control of profits was promised. By this time food prices had risen by 25 per cent. as compared with August, 1914, and were still rising steadily. The workers, disillusioned by events, were ready to risk the consequences of strike action. All the South Wales coal mines stopped, with 200,000 men on strike. In the Clydeside engineering works unofficial stoppages had begun sporadically in February, 1915. They were organized by a group called Withdrawal of Labour Committee, which later became the Clyde Workers' Committee, one of the many bodies of its kind set up in industrial areas during the First World War as a form of insurance when it was realized the large unions would or could do little in the way of direct action. The men in the field for these committees were the shop stewards, now to acquire much more responsibility and power.

The restive situation on the Clyde throughout 1915 came to a climax on Christmas Day, 1915, when Lloyd George came to Glasgow to deal with the situation. He arrived two days before, confident that his Welsh wizardry would smooth away all difficulties. His first setback was at Weir's engineering works where the stewards refused to meet him. As a result of this experience he cancelled a visit arranged to the Fairfield shipyard. Arthur Henderson, one of the Labour members of the War Cabinet, accompanied Lloyd George, and he had an embarrassing time at the Parkhead forge factory of Beardmore's. David Kirkwood was chairman at the meeting, and to Henderson's horror he introduced Lloyd George as " the enemy of the workers."

I will pay credit to Lloyd George for continuing with his resolve to hold the big meeting in St. Andrew's Hall just the same. As it was Christmas Day, work was a little relaxed even though the holiday means little to Scotland, and an immense crowd turned up. The authorities miscalculated badly in their arrangements to ensure success. They indulged in such superficial stunts as bringing khaki-dressed girls from somewhere, and having a choir singing patriotic songs. It burst into "See the Conquering Hero Comes" just as the man who had been pompously introduced at Beardmore's as "the Chief Minister of Munitions for the British Empire" strode on to the flower-bedecked platform. It was too much for the crowd of 3,000 in the hall. It drowned the choir with the strains of the "Red Flag." Henderson was given a hearing as soon as he stood up, but he went on much too long. Lloyd George, who was given a chance at the shouted request of the shop stewards, relied on an emotional appeal to gain his point. He evaded the hard practical points about labour dilution, wages, and the cost of living. There was not a man or woman in that hall without relatives or neighbours fighting in Flanders or dying in the holocaust of Gallipoli, at that very moment coming to its disastrous end. If Lloyd George had dealt with the critical situation of a war that was in danger of being lost, with the need for a common effort in which no man and no section were favoured, he would have got a hearing and could have reached agreement. He failed to do so, and the meeting ended in chaos.

Whitehall issued an "official account" of the meeting which duly appeared in the national Press. No Press release was sent to *Forward*, Tom Johnston's paper, which printed its own and true account, was promptly suppressed and its offices occupied by the military. Two months later the workers at Parkhead struck when the employers forbade Kirkwood from moving from department to department. At three o'clock one morning four policemen

arrived at Kirkwood's house and said that he was under arrest.
At the Central Police Station he was told that he had been court-
martialled the previous day and sentenced to deportation under
section 14 of D.O.R.A., the Defence of the Realm Act. Five other
men, Arthur McManus, James Haggerty, James Messer, Sam
Shields, and Robert Wainwright were arrested at the same time.
They were told that they could go where they liked—"San Fran-
cisco, if you prefer it"—so long as they were five miles beyond
the Clyde munition area. The bizarre penalty and the ominous
sentence-in-absence are symptomatic of the ruthless measures
which were available to authority in 1914-18. They all had a
pleasant holiday in Edinburgh for twelve months, after which they
were allowed to return. Their absence, of course, did not eradicate
the "danger"; it merely deprived the country of a group of skilled
engineers and fomented a burning resentment among tens of
thousands of loyal workers on Clydeside.

Meanwhile my union activities kept me very busy, particularly
as the shipping situation deteriorated when the demands for men
increased after the entry of the United States into the war.
Paradoxically, the Armistice brought a renewal of the earlier
hostilities with the owners and with Havelock Wilson. He succeeded in persuading the owners to refuse employment to members of the British Seafarers' Union. Every man signing on for a
voyage had to produce a card signed by port consultants, one of
whom was a representative of the National Sailors' and Firemen's
Union and the other of the Shipping Federation. The T.U.C.
most unfairly regarded us as a breakaway union and we were
therefore unable to obtain affiliation and through it concerted
action to get this obnoxious arrangement withdrawn. When
fourteen major unions combined in the "octopus" Transport and
General Workers Union under the general secretaryship of
Ernest Bevin, there began negotiations to absorb the seamen's
unions as well. This scheme fell through.

Then began a wasteful and sometimes sordid period of internecine strife. At the outset the prospects seemed good. We
amalgamated with another union known as the National Union
of Ships' Stewards, Cooks, Butchers and Bakers, which was strong
in the great passenger-carrying ports of Southampton and
Liverpool. The increased power we thus obtained annoyed the

ship-owners still more. I became National Organizer and addressed meetings in the principal ports of the country. I found that the seamen had little enthusiasm about their membership of Havelock Wilson's union but were compelled to remain members of it because of the employment card. But they listened to me with interest and friendliness despite the activities of the crowd of toughs Wilson had trailing after me wherever I went.

At last the T.U.C. took action. Fred Bramley, the secretary, and A. W. Walkden began negotiations the basis of which was that the three leading spirits of our union, including myself, should gracefully retire from the fray with compensation of £1,000 each. I was not accustomed to accept bribes and objected strongly to this proposal, though I offered to resign without compensation in an amalgamation in which our union's principles were recognized. Our union was still flourishing until after the General Strike in 1926 when I watched seamen's interests in the London docks. But by 1927, through the recurring litigation and wasteful bickering with Havelock Wilson, together with the owners' ban on our members, we found it impossible to carry on. The union was disbanded.

So ended a period full of melodramatic events, much hard work, and not a little personal danger. There were few holds barred on either side in those days, although we certainly refrained from some of the unpleasant tricks indulged in by Wilson's rough-house gangs. We did not go around with loaded guns but during a skirmish on the dockside on Clydeside, when some seamen threatened French of the N.S.F.U., he drew a revolver and mistakenly thinking I was the instigator of the threatened attack, fired at me. He hit a man named James Martin standing by my side, who died in hospital. The ensuing trial degenerated into a political debate, and French got off on the grounds of self-defence.

All the excitement, danger, and toil of those hectic years were not without reward. From a personal viewpoint I gained a first-hand knowledge of the problems of shipping and the men who man ships which stood me in good stead in the Second World War. I think we also improved the seamen's conditions. The work was hard and often, on the short view, unrewarding. It was, of course, only part of my daily round. Apart from being a member of Glasgow Town Council and a speaker for the I.L.P., I had the task of "nursing" my prospective constituency of West Lothian from 1917 onwards, and then, in 1922, there were my duties as an M.P. Indeed, from 1911, my life had all the features of a busy career—except that my income remained much the same as it had been during easier days in the clothing factory. Trade-union officials and politicians of thirty and forty years ago did not ride to work in cars or have to worry about income tax. . . .

Almost twenty years later came a particularly happy and acceptable ending to my story of adventure on behalf of the seamen's interests. Just after VE Day in 1945, I received a letter from the late Charles Jarman, Acting General Secretary of the National Union of Seamen, which stated:

"Our Finance and General Purposes Committee asked me at their meeting yesterday, to convey to you their appreciation of all the work you have done in the House on behalf of the Merchant Service, and to express the hope that you will again be returned for Seaham to continue your good work in the House of Commons. I can personally assure you that your efforts on behalf of the officers and men of the service are appreciated. So much so, that I am instructed to ask you if you would be prepared to accept the Life Honorary Membership of the National Union of Seamen as a token of our regard for your work."

CHAPTER SIX

"RED FRIDAY" IN GLASGOW

THE hysterical joy of the entire nation (though perhaps it was a sadder and more realistic relief in the ranks of the soldiers) on 11 November, 1918, was a reasonably human emotion after four years of the bloodiest war in history. But it was unreasonable to expect that rejoicing should become a normal condition of life. Fomented by the Liberal and Tory Party machines, the most level-headed people in the world accepted unquestioningly the glib political promises of an immediate paradise rising from the hell of war. By the simple process of hanging the Kaiser and squeezing the vanquished enemy " till the pips squeaked" Britain was to become a "land fit for heroes to live in" overnight. The heroes, not so certain that there would be sufficient to go round, were restless and in some places mutinous. Without plan or policy they were demobilized in their thousands a day.

A fortnight after the Armistice, Parliament was dissolved. Lloyd George's extra Christmas gift to the nation as an addition to all the other glittering promises he had made was an election for a new Government to run the new Utopia. Intelligent electioneering was impossible. All that a candidate needed was the " coupon" from Lloyd George. With that stamp of approval of the Welsh Wizard, the architect of victory, 530 candidates were successful. Asquith's independent Liberals were stripped to 29 seats. Labour put up 363 candidates. Only 57 were returned. I was among the legion of the defeated. Other losers included MacDonald, Snowden, and Lansbury. The Socialist leader in the new House was a virtually unknown and inexperienced politician, Willie Adamson, the Fife Miners' leader, who was shortly afterwards succeeded by J. R. Clynes, a war-time Coalition colleague of Lloyd George, and to most

Socialists not a very fervid adversary of the Prime Minister now that the Coalition was broken.

Disillusion soon set in. The thousands of unemployed ex-servicemen became hundreds of thousands. The great war plants dismissed armies of men and women almost as vast. Unlike 1945, there was no plan in 1919 for the switch-over from a war to a peace economy. While the war profiteers became peace profiteers by holding a starved world to ransom by selling products kept artificially scarce and at a price which was as high as the market could bear, the poor became poorer and the workers were in constant danger of joining the workless. Wholesale prices were 135 per cent above the pre-war level; the cost of living was 120 per cent above 1914; both were rising all the time. War-time food controls both as regards prices and rationing were being withdrawn at a reckless speed. The Government did not believe in official austerity. The mass of the population began to learn what it really meant.

In the New Year the West of Scotland was driven to plans for a general strike to begin on 27 January. George Kerr, a trade-union organizer and Glasgow town councillor, presided over a meeting of shop stewards and trade-union delegates which issued a call for action: "Thousands of men are being demobilized from the Army and Navy every day. Over a hundred thousand workers in Scotland have been dismissed from civil employment. They are now looking for jobs. There are no jobs for them. There is only one remedy. Reduce the number of hours. The time for action is now. Delay means failure. No more than 40 hours per week to be worked. No reduction in wages. No overtime to be worked. No work on Monday, 27 January. No resumption of work until demands have been conceded."

In an era when Labour has shown that a planned economy provides more work, not less, the resolution may appear short-sighted. But in 1919, with a Government false to the lavish promises made during the conflict, it was the only method that seemed open to the workers.

The call gained a ready hearing among workers on both sides of the Border. It also caused alarm farther afield. The Russian Revolution was but fifteen months old. The barricades were up in the streets of Europe's cities. Revolt with all its bloody terror was abroad in the world. Lloyd George had lively memories of the fiery spirit of Clydeside and in particular of the shop stewards. His newspaper-owning friends had propagated the fear of "Red Glasgow."

As a result many people believed that this move was the beginning of revolution in Britain. A few days before there had been mutinous outbreaks at Shorncliffe, near Folkestone, at Dover, and at other camps, involving some 70,000 troops. Some had grabbed lorries and driven to the Houses of Parliament and the War Office demanding satisfaction for their grievances. Yet the Glasgow unrest, at any rate among the workers, was not revolutionary in character. At the outset it never occurred to me that I should be drawn into the agitation. It was largely inspired by the shop-steward movement which had grown up during the war, and undoubtedly had a revolutionary spirit which did not always show itself in action, but certainly pervaded its determination to seek redress for the growing numbers of unemployed.

When, however, the Shop Stewards Committee had an appeal addressed to the Glasgow Trades Council it could not be ignored, even if the trade unions were individually and officially unresponsive. The Council appointed several members to attend a conference, and as the chairman I was among them. At the conference it was suggested that I should be appointed to the chair. I declined, but nobody else was willing to accept the position and the meeting expressed its keen desire to have me associated with the movement. I agreed to become chairman—with some misgivings about the future of the agitation.

Still positive that the mass of workers had no aims beyond remedying the labour situation, I took the opportunity of reiterating my views at a meeting of the Trades Council, knowing that with the current anxieties of the country, my words would obtain national Press coverage and might bring a note of sanity into the hysteria being shown in London.

"This movement for a 40-hour week is not revolutionary in character," I said, "nor is it inspired by the legitimate desire for more leisure. It is attributable solely and entirely to the fear of possible unemployment in the near future and the desire of the workers generally to make room for the demobilized servicemen."

These views were ignored in the Press, which continued to

report the alarmist statements of politicians who seemed able to give a graphic account of the revolutionary situation in Glasgow without coming within three hundred miles of the city. Inevitably and inexorably the day for work to cease drew nearer.

Hundreds of the workers attended a mass meeting on the first day of the strike at St. Andrew's Hall, at which I presided. Even the newspapers which had done their best to foment the belief in revolution admitted that the crowds were quiet and orderly. About 40,000 men were out in the Clydeside area, and there were strikes in many other areas both in and outside Scotland, notably Belfast. By Wednesday the Clydeside strike total had increased to 70,000.

No move to settle the strike was made by the Minister of Labour, Sir Robert Horne, and I went to see the Lord Provost of Glasgow asking him to get in touch with Horne with a request that the Government should intervene in order to settle the strike. The only result was a Press statement by the Minister of Food, G. H. Roberts, by description at least a member of the Labour Party, that the strike was revolutionary in character. The Lord Provost promised to forward an inquiry and it was arranged that we should return for a reply at midday on Friday, 31 January. The Lord Provost did, in fact, receive a reply from Bonar Law: "The Government cannot entertain the request for intervention in the strike," and this was generally known.

About 11 a.m. on Friday a huge mass of people began to assemble in George Square. They brought their brass bands with them. All doors of the City Chambers were locked and a strong force of police guarded the building. My deputation, consisting of eleven members, including David Kirkwood and Neil McLean, struggled through the mass of people in order to meet the Lord Provost. We were taken to the library, when we were told that rioting had broken out. I rushed to the Lord Provost's room with the rest, demanding to know how a perfectly orderly crowd had been transformed in a matter of minutes into an angry mob. We were told that we could not enter until the meeting of the Magistrates' Committee was over. I rushed down in the hope of calming the crowd, but when I got to the door of the City Chambers, the people had been driven back by the police. Men and women were scattering in all directions, many falling under the merciless

First Election Campaign, 1918. Emanuel Shinwell addressing an open-air meeting at Bathgate, West Lothian.

Glasgow disturbances, February, 1919. Tanks in the cattle market.

(*Top*) "Red Friday" in Glasgow. Emanuel Shinwell (left) and Harry Hopkins addressing the crowd from a vantage point before the Municipal Buildings in George Square. (*Bottom*) Glasgow Riot trial. The front row of men in the dock are (left to right): Emanuel Shinwell, William Gallacher, George Ebury, David Brennan, David Kirkwood, Harry Hopkins and James Murray.

attack of the frenzied police. I saw Gallagher standing holding his head, which appeared to be bleeding.

At that moment the crowd on the north side of the square came rushing back to the entrance of the building, and I was surrounded by many who asked what they should do. I had no chance to say a word, for more police charged and we were swept up Hanover Street. A lorry packed with empty bottles stood there. Someone threw a single bottle at the oncoming police, and then the whole lorry was besieged and emptied.

On the other side some ill-advised tramcar driver was attempting to drive his vehicle into this maelstrom of people. It blocked the road and the terrified people invaded the General Post Office—the only possible haven from the police behind them. Immediately mounted police, kept in hiding in the courtyard of the municipal buildings, charged out and scattered the crowds hither and thither.

Mass panic is a frightening sight. I tried to shout to the people to walk steadily from the square to avoid further injury and bloodshed, standing on a seat to make my voice heard above the general bedlam. My advice was futile, for the police turned and made for us, the foot police at the double and the mounted men at a gallop. Having drawn blood, they had literally gone berserk.

It was, I realized, hopeless to do anything and with a few words to those around me to get away from the square, I went accompanied by several men, to the offices of the Trades Council where William Shaw, the secretary, had also arrived. With a vivid foreboding of the repercussions of the riot in our minds, we decided to destroy all the Council's documents associated with the strike.

I went next to the offices of the Socialist Labour Party's printing works and drew up a leaflet calling on the workers to stand firm, promising that the whole ghastly affair would be brought before the authorities and a demand made for action to be taken against those responsible for ordering the police to charge a crowd pursuing their legal rights in approaching the Lord Provost to seek his good offices on their behalf.

Pat Dollan suggested that I should go home with him, as he was certain that I should be arrested. I declined his invitation and returned to my own home in Linthouse. The expected knock on the door came at midnight. I opened the door and invited the detective standing there to come inside. He then told me I would be charged with incitement to riot. He followed me into the children's bedroom when I told him I would like to see them before I went. Then he accompanied me downstairs and I saw that no fewer than ten policemen were loitering about the street. I was taken to Govan Police Station and pushed into a cell without undergoing the usual formalities which are the rights of the most vicious criminal. It was a stone cell with no bed. I was completely worn out, lay down on the floor and slept until I was aroused at 5 a.m. to be taken to the Central Police Station. On the way one of the escorting detectives, appointing himself judge and jury, told me: "You'll get five years for this." I laughed at him, which did not improve his subsequent treatment of me.

At the Central Police Station some of my friends were also being charged. Willie Gallagher was there, despite the fact that he had actually been given police protection so that he could bawl out to the crowd: "March off, for God's sake." David Kirkwood had also been arrested. He was excitable but was really a peaceable soul and had, as a matter of fact, been hit on the head by a policeman almost as soon as he ran down the steps of the City Chambers, being attacked from the back as he raised his hand to quieten the crowd. That might not have meant his discharge at the subsequent trial except for the lucky fact that a press photographer took a picture of the policeman's baton raised and Kirkwood collapsing—evidence which, of course, meant his dismissal from the case when the picture was exhibited.

After being charged we were all taken to Duke Street prison where we remained for four weeks until the authorities agreed to grant bail. While I was there I suffered violent toothache. I shall never forget the extraction on a particularly cold day in an icy cell and without an anæsthetic.

While we were in prison awaiting trial, Whitehall, which had been so uninterested in the agitation, now acted in spectacular and melodramatic fashion. Troops deployed on Glasgow.

They came in steel helmets and with full war equipment. Machine-gun nests were built at strategic points. Over the week-end 10,000 soldiers arrived. Tanks, which few civilians in Glasgow had ever seen, were parked in the Cattle Market. The Press, at first rejoicing in the fact that the strike would fade out now that troops could protect those anxious to work from intimidation, changed its tune when it was seen that the strikers were not returning in any numbers in Glasgow and the 40-hour move was spreading quite spontaneously to many parts of the country, including Sheffield and London. People began to wonder why troops remained in the city, and who was responsible for putting the town under military control in the first place.

The trial took place in the High Court of Justiciary at Edinburgh on 7 April—more than two months after our arrest, and during this time we were for over four weeks kept in prison. Mr. Constable, K.C., and Graham Robertson defended me. The trial lasted eleven days. I was found guilty of incitement in George Square and James Watt Lane on days prior to the riot by a majority verdict of the jury. Gallagher was found guilty of earlier incitement but "strongly recommended to mercy" for trying to pacify the crowd during the riot.

The costs of the trial came to nearly £2,000. The workers of Scotland contributed nearly £1,700 towards them; the rest was never paid, though for years the lawyers sent me demands as if I had been sole defendant.

A huge crowd awaited the verdict outside the court, and hundreds of police stood by expecting trouble. There was, of course, none. Seemingly even the evidence at the trial had not proved to the authorities that the workers did not riot for the sake of making trouble: they only rioted when panic-stricken forces of law enforcement drove them to it. *The Glasgow Herald*, like most of the other papers, had not learned anything. In its leader after the trial, in deprecating the lightness of our sentences, it repeated the charge that the strike had been "the first step towards the squalid terror which the world now describes as Bolshevism." Even the prison official who, against the rules, handed me this effusion, laughed at it.

Before the trial the strikes had, of course, petered out. They had the effect of forcing the Government to pay lip service to the welfare of the State. A Wages (Temporary Regulation) Act forbade any reductions. Rent restriction was retained. The miners got a 7-hour day, and when the National Industrial Conference met in February the employers were no longer dictating terms—they were ready to discuss them. It even agreed in principle on a maximum 48-hour week for all industries and all workers. There can be little doubt that these small concessions were given because of "Red Friday" in Glasgow—red only because of the blood which one of the rare instances of police mishandling of a legal and loyal meeting caused to be spilt.

CHAPTER SEVEN

EXPERIENCES IN PRISON

TOM MANN, the pioneer Socialist who, with John Burns, had led the organization of unskilled workers in the eighteen-eighties, once told me: "Unless a Socialist leader has been in prison his education has been neglected."

This grand old man—he was eighty-five when he died—had been sent to prison in 1912 for his share in circulating a "Don't Shoot!" pamphlet among soldiers ordered to put down strikes.

Now I was to be educated in the same manner, and with the longest "course" of all the defendants. Willie Gallagher was given three months and I received five. The other defendants, including David Kirkwood, were found not guilty.

I had the slight comfort of conscience that I was in a cell of the High Court at Edinburgh awaiting the Black Maria for activities on behalf of the workers and not for picking pockets or bogus company promotion. It was, I admit, only a slight comfort, as I realized when my wife was allowed to see me. Her sole misgivings were about my welfare, but I was deeply worried as to what would become of her. She had our children to look after, and from the £2 a week I received from the union we had naturally been able to save nothing. Incidentally, it is worth noting when mentioning this income of mine that the cost of living in 1919 was 125 per cent above the 1914 level and rising rapidly every month. While I was in prison it soared to 170 per cent.

How she managed then, as on many other occasions of hard times, I do not know. The union gave my wife half-pay, and there were gestures of kindness from friends and strangers just as there had been that spontaneous and general contribution of money for our defence from workers all over Scotland—and, incidentally, not only workers. There were men and women who disliked my politics but loved liberty and justice. The very violence and ill-judged ravings of the Press campaign before our trial—to-day no editor would risk the certainty of prosecution for contempt of court as occurred then—not only influenced the fair-minded judge, Lord Scott Dickson, to sentence us lightly, but hundreds of people were alarmed that we had even been prosecuted.

The time came to take leave of my wife. She went back to Glasgow and I climbed in the Black Maria for the short journey to Calton Gaol. This building has the appearance of a castle and fits in quite well with its historic surroundings—so well, indeed, that it is said that Queen Victoria, during a visit to Holyrood, asked whose castle it was. The diplomatic official in attendance replied: "One of your Majesty's many institutions, ma'am." Since my incarceration it has been renovated and modernized and now presumably makes a reasonably comfortable head-quarters for the Scottish Office. In 1919 it justly had the reputation of being the worst prison in Scotland. It had been condemned over and over again, but retained on the grounds of economy and need.

Films and books have made the routine of reception at a prison familiar to many people. But no director or writer—and certainly not myself—can portray the sense of desolation that it brings. I suppose there are old lags who go through the preliminaries of having a bath, donning the prison garb, and entering a cell without misgivings, though frankly I doubt it. For the newcomer it is a nightmare.

When I arrived at Calton I was given a ragged uniform and a pair of boots which were several sizes too large and as stiff as boards. My cell was at the top of the prison and was so small that I could almost touch each wall without moving. The door was immediately slammed and I was left to brood over my fate for the rest of that evening and through the night.

The cell was temporary accommodation because I had arrived late from the court. When the door opened in the early morning and a warder bawled at me to come out I momentarily imagined that my home for the next five months would be better. I was wrong. The new cell was dark, the window a mere slit in the wall, more suitable for a sharpshooter defending the place than as a source of light and air. But there was no time to protest. The door was immediately slammed on me.

After a time it opened again and a warder shouted at me to take my breakfast, brought round by another prisoner. I was handed a large stone jar of the kind that holds jam or marmalade. It was nearly full of a greyish-looking thickened liquid which I presumed was called porridge—a description which should have made any Scots-born official in the place rise in wrath. Along with it came a small canister of milk. As soon as the door closed I tried the milk. It was sour, a type which was quite a familiar food in poor Scottish homes. I could not drink it and though I tried the porridge my stomach would have nothing to do with it.

When the door was again opened the warder seemed quite uninterested when I handed him over my breakfast almost as I had received it. Next, I was handed a machine and a large pile of sections of horses' nosebags which I was abruptly told "to make." Fortunately for me I had my tailoring experience so I could manage to obey. I cannot imagine what other new prisoners did when they were handed a job like that. The work enabled me to fill in the morning, and I was also given some exercise in the yard. Then came the midday meal when the familiar jar was handed in—this time full of a liquid described as soup. It was undrinkable. There was also a lump of bread, which gave me something to eat. At tea-time, before the cell was shut for the fourteen hours of night, the jar of " porridge " was the only food. I left it untouched.

After two days of eating nothing but the midday piece of bread and drinking nothing but water the warder asked me what I was up to; I suppose he thought I was on some sort of hunger strike—memories of Irish political prisoners and Suffragettes were still vivid among prison officials at that time, of course. I told him that I simply could not eat the porridge or drink the soup. The result was an interview with the prison doctor.

He was unsympathetic, indeed he was extremely annoyed at the trouble I was making. He told me the porridge was appetizing and nutritious.

"Then I suggest you eat it yourself," I replied.

The interview ended abruptly.

For ten days I continued to live on dry bread, and strangely enough I never felt really hungry. Then the Head Warder came. He was not a bad chap and asked me without any threatening attitude what was the matter. I told him that I simply could not swallow the porridge or the sour milk, and I took as much of the soup as I could manage. His job had given him a good insight into the tricks of prisoners and I realized he was convinced my excuse was genuine enough. He sent me to the doctor again.

The interview was more stormy than the previous one. This time he tried intimidation, followed by an almost chummy remark: "After all, that porridge is good enough for me, you know."

"You're welcome to my share," I said politely.

Once again the interview ended abruptly.

I suspect that it was the Head Warder's action that produced a huge jar of tea and a lump of bread the following evening. There were quite two pints of warm and sweet liquid and I drank it all. During the period of four months and ten days I was in prison my diet consisted solely of that tea and the two pieces of bread morning and evening. On some Fridays potatoes were served at the midday meal in place of the soup. I was there in the early part of the year and the potatoes were all frost-bitten and uneatable. Other prisoners somehow managed to swallow that awful concoction of soup, but even they could not eat the blackened pulp of the potatoes boiled in their skins to prevent them disintegrating.

During the First World War the campaign against conscientious objectors was far more severe than in 1939-45. There were about 16,000 of them, and 1,543 were absolutists—men who refused to work directly or indirectly for the war effort. These men received prison sentences of two years, with the result that many were still in gaol long after the Armistice. I met one of them at Calton. He was a miner from the Lanarkshire village of Douglas Water and as his sentence was for hard labour he was put on to trimming coal in the prison cellars. I was not punished by hard labour but was nevertheless told to work with this man. He tore into his work and made me keep up with him, with results to my back and arms which may be imagined. He was allowed to receive food from outside (there had been awkward questions in Parliament because of the deaths of conscientious objectors in prison or immediately after release; altogether seventy-one died in various prisons). He gave me a small bar of chocolate, and I made it last a week, nibbling a tiny piece each evening and letting the grains dissolve slowly in my mouth.

Although I had no objection to the coal-trimming job as it got me out of the cell and gave me someone to talk to I doubted whether the authorities were acting legally in putting me on hard labour. I demanded to see the governor, an ex-Army officer with a very limited outlook, but he told me that in Scotland there was no such thing as a political prisoner. While I was fully aware that the Scottish judicial system differed widely from that of England I was equally certain that war-time legislation, which was at least partly responsible for my arrest and sentence, applied both North and South of the Tweed. I asked to see one of the Prison Commissioners.

One of them arrived a fortnight later. He knew me as a Glasgow town councillor and was friendly. As the result of his interview with me I was transferred shortly afterwards from my normal work of sewing mailbags and horses' nosebags.

The new job was in the ashpit at the back of the furnaces. I was given a sieve and a shovel and told to sift the cinders to save the coke. The job was rather like cleaning out the Augean stables, for other prisoners were bringing barrow-loads of ash faster than I could sieve it, and I seldom had any help. Those who were occasionally sent gave me an insight into the criminal mind, and convinced me that punishment of all and sundry who offend against society is rarely a solution unless some psychological examination is made first.

There was a burly coloured man who told me he was serving a month's sentence for assaulting a woman. I told him I thought it was a terrible thing. "What did you do to her?" I asked. "I hit her with a bottle," he replied. I expressed my horror, and he hastily tried to indicate that it was not so bad as I thought. "She was my own woman," he explained.

Another man was serving a sentence for breaking a jeweller's window and stealing a ring. He had been in prison many times. No sooner was he out than he found a jeweller's, threw a brick, and then took one ring. The police in the Edinburgh and Glasgow areas never put detectives on a robbery of this kind. They simply sent a constable to the man's house to arrest him. There was no sense of misguided adventure or of revenge on society as he told me he would do it again. He was of weak intellect and could grasp no other plan for acquiring what he wanted. By contrast there was a youngster who was typical of the juvenile delinquent and young offender of to-day. He was serving a year's sentence and proudly boasted that the moment he was out he would "do a really big job." No effort was made to rehabilitate him.

In the spring I was occasionally put to work in the prison garden. This was a great relief. I could see the clock of the North British Hotel and hear the rumbling of traffic. I had a young warder to guard me who had a streak of the toughness which is an occupational trait of his profession, but he was decent enough to me, gossiping while I worked although this was against the rules.

His character was usually stern and unrelenting, except when he told me of his love of roses, which amounted to a passion. While he talked about the bushes and standards in his garden he became a gentle, sensitive person.

One morning he mentioned excitedly that he had applied for another job. I imagined that it might be as a gardener on some estate, for he undoubtedly had "green fingers" and would have won his employer many cups and prizes if he had been let loose in a rose garden. But I was wrong.

"The hangman's job is vacant," he said. "That's good money —piece-work, you know. There'll be a wave of murders as a reaction to the war, and I reckon I'll make twice as much as I do as a warder."

Whether he ever got the job I cannot say.

Sunday was the blackest day of the week, for there was no work to do, and apart from the church service or Bible class (I always wonder if the visiting clergy really believe that prisoners are such ardent worshippers as the packed chapel suggests) the boredom was interminable. My cell window was high above the floor, but by piling the books I had on my stool I could just see out and listen to somebody playing an instrument in the Canongate on Sunday afternoons. These books, incidentally, were not only precious as a support. Without them those months would have been unbearable, and I would never have read and re-read Shakespeare so that I can now quote, or place a quotation, from most of his plays.

Whatever the regulations about books may have been the special treatment inflicted on me restricted the privilege to one a week. I suspect this was a private rule, for as soon as I told the governor I would mention the matter to my Prison Visitor the number was increased to two a week. These I collected from the "library"—two cells fitted out with shelves. I made friends with the old warder who had been given the job of librarian to see out the last few years of his service. He used to come to my cell with an authorization for me to carry out some odd job for him and then I exchanged my two books as often as I wanted.

He was virtually unaware of the contents of the volumes under his charge in the non-fiction section, while to him all fiction was written by Sir Walter Scott. Whether I took a book by Dickens or Hardy he would look up and say: "Aye, you'll enjoy Watty Scott."

Worthy philanthropic societies and some idealist in the Scottish Office had equipped the library with an amazing range of books. Philosophy, science, and general interest works were there galore, as well as poetical works of Keats, Tennyson, and so on—and lesser-known classics such as Shelley's prose letters. The virgin whiteness of the pages in most of the books was proof enough that I was the first reader, although the fly-leaves gave publication dates many years earlier. I was sometimes asked to accompany the warder distributing reading material around the cells. Very few prisoners wanted anything but magazines or trashy adventure stories popular among boys.

Literature made prison life bearable for me. I used to keep a notebook of comments on the works I read and even tried my hand at writing poetry myself—some of it, I admit, just caustic stuff about prison life, the food and the governor. Naturally I also used the book as a diary, and that is why I was forbidden to take it out with me. Weeks after my release I made formal application for it to be returned. It duly arrived—with almost all the pages torn out. Shakespearean quotations, together with my reflections on man's inhumanity to man, were doubtless regarded as dangerous material by the prison authorities.

One Sunday afternoon I did not get down from my book-and-stool stand quickly enough as footsteps approached, and the result was that I was taken to the main hall and told to enter a very dark cell. I refused. The warder stormed off to get help. He returned with the Head Warder—the man who had been decent about my food, and was always fair with the prisoners. By that time I had wandered down the corridor past the row of empty cells and saw one with a little more light. In I went and stood there. The Head Warder grinned and told me to stay there if I liked it, much to the fury of the other warder. For a time I had no neighbour. Then a middle-aged man serving a sentence for embezzlement was put in the next cell. I was told to show him how to sew mailbags, and I whispered to him to learn this mundane art as slowly as possible so that I would be sent in again. Whenever the warder moved away we talked in whispers. My fellow-prisoner was a family man and had embarked on his crime in the usual way of "borrowing" a little, and then going on and on until the inevitable discovery. Prison life for men of his type, accustomed to the safe routine of office and home, can be very hard and he took things badly. I used to tap out messages of comfort by the usual prison system of one tap for A and so on to twenty-six for Z. It is surprising how proficient one gets at this, and learns to avoid words like "you," "we," and "very" which involve, in the case of "very," for example, seventy taps. But by this method we both learned each other's complete life stories.

At long last I was told that, with remission for good conduct, I was due for release. The authorities knew—though I did not—that many demonstrations had taken place outside the prison gates demanding my release, and they feared trouble as I left. As a result I was suddenly ordered late one afternoon to get ready. My civilian clothes, strange-looking and ill-fitting, were brought to my cell, and in company with a warder I was taken to the station for the Glasgow train. We had a reserved compartment, and he gave me some tobacco for my pipe: the first smoke I had had for more than four months. It made me feel ill. I had to spend the night in Duke Street prison in Glasgow and I think I suffered more during that single night than during the whole time I was at Calton. The next morning, while my friends awaited me at Edinburgh, I walked through the gates of the Glasgow prison on my way home.

My wife, with a woman's instinct for such things, was awaiting me there with the children. She had the kettle boiling and the cups set out.

"A cup's no good to me," I said. "I want a jar."

There was no jar, so I drank that welcoming brew from a bowl.

I noticed that my wife was looking at me anxiously when she thought I was off my guard. Eventually I asked her: "What's wrong?"

"It's your voice," she said. "You haven't the strength to speak above a whisper."

I had not realized it, but it was true enough. It took me a week to overcome the habit of speaking in a low mumble with almost unmoving lips—a habit one instinctively adopts in a place where walls have ears and cell doors have eyes. But there was nothing wrong with my health: I was stronger and heavier than when I went in.

At last I had graduated in Tom Mann's "academy" for real Socialists. Now I had to take up the reins of life in the ordinary world again. In some ways it was much tougher than in prison. But it was freedom.

CHAPTER EIGHT

THE REVOLUTIONARIES GO TO WESTMINSTER

SIXTY thousand people were crammed into St. Enoch's Square and the surrounding streets on a November night in 1922. They were singing, shouting, arguing, merry-making. The "Wild Men of the Clyde" were on the way to the Mother of Parliaments, and Glasgow was giving them a deliriously happy send-off.

Scotland had returned seventeen Labour members in the General Election of 15 November, and thirteen of them, with leanings of varying degrees towards the extreme left, came from Glasgow and the surrounding area. The Press of London shudderingly reported that Clydeside had gone red. Thousands of ordinary folk in England genuinely believed that the seeds of a revolution akin to that which had begun a mere five years earlier in Petrograd had already been sown in the munition works, the shipyards, and the mines of the Glasgow area. The Clydeside brand of Bolshevism, it was whispered, would out-bolshevize the Kerensky and Lenin brands.

It was, of course, quite untrue. Those of us who knew the workers of Clydeside ridiculed any suggestion of bloody revolution. But we did believe that Socialism would remedy the evils which had seeped for generations into their lives, their families, and their homes. We of the Socialist movement on the Clyde knew from the packed meetings, the stream of questions, and the demand for literature and information that a political change was imminent. But we had no conception how profound that change would be.

Those crowds which spontaneously came to see us off on the night train to London were permeated with hope. There were many, it is true, who made it an excuse for a bit of a celebration.

Some had taken a dram or two to keep the cold out. Others enjoyed the contagious excitement of a big crowd. But my most vivid impression, as I struggled with my wife through that orderly mass of men and women with whom I had worked and lived before and during the dark days of war, was of the almost frightening faith in us which touched one's face like a soft breeze. In the gaslight of the street lamps shawled women, white-faced and haggard with the poverty and worry of months of unemployment of their menfolk, stood silent, staring at us. Only their eyes were bright with expectation, even admiration. I nodded to a six-foot-six constable, the ruddy glow of his Highland upbringing still on his face, as he shouted "good luck." He was a policeman whose regular beat was on the Broomielaw where the seamen congregated. He knew me well. On orders, in harsher times, he had used his baton on the people who now stood around him. I was slapped on the back, given advice in pawky Glaswegian humour, had my hand shaken a hundred times. Whatever the method of greeting there were always the eyes which were the same: eyes which had once again the gleam of hope where despair had too long held sway. Things were going to be "fine."

It was a memorable, terrifying experience—this faith of the people of Britain's second city. "Foreigners" south of the Border called it a revolutionary fervour. It was something deeper than that: the fierce, patriotic pride of the Scots in their race, their faith in themselves and their destiny. I think that all of us who had been dubbed the "wild men of the Clyde" were chastened by that demonstration. We had been elected because it was believed we could perform miracles, and miracles were needed to relieve the tragedy of Clydeside in 1922. But miracles and politics do not mix, and the hopes we had as the train pulled out that night have since been adjusted, altered, augmented. Thirty-two years have passed since that wintry night. Much has been done, and more remains to be done by those of us who have survived and by those who follow. My hopes, at least, have never been abandoned, nor do I believe that the fiery faith which swept through Glasgow in those days has been quenched. It still burns: to make this report of my experiences merely a facet of the whole, a stage of progress.

The background to the 1922 election had elements of intrigue, which has always marked the hierarchy of the Tory Party when it feels that its leader has served his purpose. A meeting was arranged at the Carlton Club on 22 October, 1922, for Tory members of the Coalition in both Houses. In a matter of hours Lloyd George was refusing to see a deputation because he knew he was no longer Prime Minister. Thanks largely to the clever work of Stanley Baldwin, hitherto an obscure, taciturn and self-described "plain man," Bonar Law was persuaded to become Prime Minister. This charming and sincere man, one of the greatest of parliamentary debaters, already marked with the signs of the death that took him a year later, was an old adversary of mine. In 1906, as a young man of twenty-two, I had interrupted one of his meetings in Glasgow when he was speaking on tariff reform—and had been thrown out for my pains. I can also claim to have been thrown out of a meeting held some years later during the Grayson trouble when his then political opponent, George Barnes, was the speaker, so that this did not affect my admiration for Law as a man.

After a brief period of the Bonar Law administration, the Tory machine reported that an appeal to the country would bring a resounding victory. Not for the last time, the machine was in error. The Labour Party put up 414 candidates and won 142 seats, polling nearly two million more votes than in the 1918 election. It was an historic milestone in the onward march of British Socialism.

It was with this background of Britain's political scene that we set off for London. There was no question of sleeping on the train. For one thing we were too excited, and for the second, most of us had found it difficult enough to scrape together the train fare, let alone the fee for a sleeper. Most of us managed to cram ourselves into one compartment and all night we discussed our plans. That was no problem; we had done it long before. For months we had talked as if we were certain to form the next Government. Most of the men in that compartment have since gained a niche in the country's political history. There was John Wheatley, leader of the Labour group on the Glasgow Town Council. John was a portly, stocky individual with the physical appearance of Mr. Pickwick, but none of his characteristics. He was the leader of the Scottish Socialists, a man of tremendous honesty and unflinching resolve, but his character was marred by a vindictive streak through which imagined or real slights were remembered and revenged. Wheatley was always regarded as an extreme Left-winger, but when he was leader of the Labour Group on the Glasgow Town Council he wanted to expel me. I was, in his view, too far to the "Left."

In complete contrast by both temperament and appearance was James Maxton, regarded as something approaching a saint by the electors of Bridgeton. Jimmy was a spellbinder as an orator, knowing how to combine sentiment with hard fact, and with a charm that nullified the most bitter of adversaries. His intellectual powers were such that he could have reaped the greatest rewards of politics but for his indolence—a defect about which he was perfectly frank. Jimmy was just unable to get up in the mornings, but he would explain away his laziness with such charm, and remedy dilatoriness with such brilliant common sense, that his most exasperating actions had to be forgiven. No constituency ever had a representative who felt its troubles so personally. I have often seen Jimmy Maxton weep as he read some letter of appeal for help. His subsequent slow and haphazard effort to remedy the wrong belied the fervid resolve which he felt. He was a man with great capacity for love, and he always spoke straight from his heart so that I have watched him sweep a hostile audience on to his side in a matter of minutes. This oratory, full of Celtic fire and sound sentiment, served him well on the hustings. In the calmer, more cynical atmosphere of parliamentary debate it failed him, although he was always listened to with the greatest respect by his colleagues.

George Buchanan represented the Gorbals, a district quite unjustifiably notorious in outsiders' eyes—the Gorbals gave Bonar Law his first representation as a Tory M.P., which belies its reputation as a hot-bed of anarchy. George was by trade a pattern-maker and none knew better than he the bitterness of prolonged unemployment. Plain of speech, direct, and single-minded about his work on behalf of the men, women, and children he had pledged himself to help, Buchanan was admired by his Tory adversaries and later was to be a great success in the Ministry of Pensions.

Sitting beside him was a man who made me smile as an example of the revolutionary menace crossing the Border *en route* for London. The Reverend Campbell Stephen was a benign and kindly looking clergyman, the holder of various degrees of which, like most Scots who regard education as a priceless asset, he was quietly proud. Stephen was no hell-fire ascetic, but a plump, happy man whose eyes were a-twinkle with the fun of being alive. He was a brilliant wit, and made his point without cruelty or rancour. His political creed was primarily a simple one; a living wage policy. Any charge that the Scots group took itself too seriously may be nullified by the fact that we always regarded Maxton and Stephen as living specimens of the Socialist wage policy—the hungry leanness of Jimmy being the "before" and the jovial rotundity of Campbell the "after."

Two others of the group I can still see vividly. There was Tom Johnston, quiet and serious. Tom was unlike most of us in that he was not really happy as a political speaker. Words came awkwardly at a political meeting, and heckling put him off his stroke. But with a pen in his hand he was brilliant. As editor of *Forward* he was a power throughout Scotland and an adversary previous governments had feared.

Equally formidable was David Kirkwood. He was at this time the most notorious of the "wild men" and had, of course, frequently clashed with authority during the war years. Only Churchill, as Minister of Munitions, had been big enough to recognize the honest purpose of Davie. When he went to London he had an interview with Churchill. He expected the usual pomposity about criticism being sabotage and efforts to ameliorate workers' wrongs being unpatriotic. Instead Churchill, as a preliminary, said "Let's have a cup of tea and a bit of cake together."

They talked, and three days later Kirkwood, a skilled engineer forbidden to work in a munitions plant, was manager of one of Beardmore's shell factories. Within six weeks a factory built to produce a maximum of 12,000 shells a week topped 24,000. The factory led the output race for every munitions plant in the country and never lost it till the war ended. Kirkwood never forgot the far-sightedness of the man who had made this possible, even if they often clashed in the Commons during the years that followed. But I am still convinced that if I had told him on that train that he would one day be Lord Kirkwood he would have fainted!

There was no sleep for us that night. We talked and planned. Much of it was over old ground, but there was a greater sense of urgency. Of one thing we were all convinced. The seventeen of us who represented Socialism in Scotland would maintain the closest unity irrespective of anything the Labour Party might do. With all the efficiency of new brooms we intended to make instant and great changes. We were bloodless revolutionaries, but revolutionaries for all that.

CHAPTER NINE

PARLIAMENTARY SUCCESS

THE immediate and physical needs of existence were our problem as soon as we arrived in London. We had to find somewhere to live. In the twilight of a foggy morning London seemed inhospitable and quite unaware of the momentous group which had come to set the Thames on fire. I knew London from regular visits as a representative on the Trades Board of the clothing workers to which I had been appointed as far back as 1909. While some of my friends went to look for lodgings near St. Pancras Station I kept in mind that proximity to Westminster would save bus fares. I went to Pimlico and in the one-time maisonettes turned into tenements I found some lodgings. There were two furnished rooms for rent, and I invited George Hardie, brother of Keir Hardie, to share them. The larger bedroom had a table and a decrepit armchair. It cost 21s. a week with breakfast. The smaller was on the top floor and just had room for a bed and wash-stand. Its price was 15s. We tossed, and George won the bigger room. Finally we agreed to pay half the total amount each so that we had a better individual bargain and each had the chance of sitting down now and then.

I remember that at the time I had a little more than £5. An M.P.'s salary was then £400 a year. In my case this was supplemented by a grant from my trade union. There were no free railway passes, and most of us had families and homes to maintain in Scotland. Making ends meet was a problem with which we were all familiar, but doing so in those first few months in London was difficult indeed. Meals in the House were quite beyond the means of most of the Scottish Labour members, and we used to walk miles to discover cheap and clean food. At that time I had an expert knowledge of those excellent eating-places where sausages, onions, tomatoes, and chips sizzled in gleaming white pans in the window invariably presided over by an Italian whose girth was an excellent advertisement for his food. Many a pleasant hour I have spent in those places, enjoying the food and the warmth when it was too cold to sit in our lodgings or even to lie in the bed to keep warm.

I am sorry to say that much of the harmony of those first few days soon evaporated. Within a few months there were jealousies which grew like a slow cancer to the later tragedies which split the group asunder. In those early days, so full of promise and resolve, it was fortunate perhaps that the future was hidden. Our earliest move was to attend a meeting of the Independent Labour Party at Johnson's Court, Fleet Street. Although we were affiliated to the Labour Party we retained an independent propaganda existence. Further, though the I.L.P. had, of course, members among M.P.s from England and Wales, the Clydeside group was by far the most influential. Our decisions on policy, propaganda, and parliamentary procedure were to guide the I.L.P. and ultimately the cause of Socialism in Britain.

Maxton and I had discussed the question of the leadership of the Opposition before we left Glasgow. He was suspicious of Ramsay MacDonald and preferred Wheatley. He had nothing to say in favour of the existing leader, J. R. Clynes. I told him that Wheatley would be quite unacceptable to the others. I preferred Ramsay MacDonald as a man with House of Commons experience, a personality which would gain attention, and a name which was known. I agreed that Clynes, as a trade unionist rather than a politician, was not our man.

At the meeting I proposed MacDonald. It was opposed by Maxton with all the vehemence at his command, and it was as well that MacDonald was not there to hear him. It was also opposed by Snowden with the cold fury of which the little man was a master. But it was seconded by MacNeill Weir and carried.

There was still the meeting of the Parliamentary Labour Party. This was held in the large Committee Room of the House of Commons, on 21 November, 1922. Clynes was in the chair. He was quiet, almost self-effacing as he explained what he had done to combat the Speaker's proposal that Labour should share the places on the Opposition Front Bench with the Liberals of

83

Asquith and Lloyd George. His integrity forbade him to embellish his statement with excuses. He had, in fact, done little, and although the matter was really quite footling, Clynes's tolerance about it upset the 122 members present, most of them newly elected, and imbued with the desire to grab every atom of prestige and advantage for the skirmishes that lay ahead. In any event, though most of the members present did not realize it, the Speaker's word was law, and nothing that Clynes could have said would have changed it.

MacDonald, perfectly aware of this, nevertheless made a fiery speech of protest in which disapproval of Clynes was thinly veiled. He knew, of course, that he was making his election more certain by so doing. I wondered then how many of those present —they included Clem Attlee, though he took no part in the discussion—knew for what they were voting.

Two people at least realized that we were not merely about to elect the Leader of the Opposition but the future Socialist Prime Minister. In honesty I can say that I myself believed this to be true. I sensed that the miscalculation of strategy by the Tories in throwing over the Liberals would quickly lose them the reins of government. In candour I would say that only one other person seemed to realize this fact. And he was Ramsay MacDonald.

Clynes was supported by Arthur Henderson, J. H. Thomas, and, with very faint praise as the lesser of the two evils, by Snowden. I again proposed MacDonald. He won by the narrow margin of five votes, and on being proposed as a substantive motion, was elected *nem con.* In later years I have been criticized for my actions which finally resulted in MacDonald becoming Prime Minister and, as some would have it, the greatest traitor to his party the Labour movement has ever had to endure. My reply is that in 1922 there was no one else either worthy or capable. Socialism in the Palace of Westminster was robust, energetic, but still an infant. It needed an experienced guiding hand. Then, and for at least six years, that hand had to be MacDonald's.

The need for guidance became evident when the new Parliament met. Some of my colleagues sought to tear away the thousand-year ritual and routine of Parliament with ill-tempered remarks and brash criticism. Kirkwood was the first to assert himself, on that first day of the new Parliament, as we stared at what was to us an incongruous anachronism of the pomp of the State opening, when he said in a loud aside to John Wheatley: "John, we'll soon change all this." The remark did not shock those who heard it. It was merely brushed aside as an infantile annoyance of no consequence.

We had still to learn that Parliament was all-powerful, that through its machinery we could achieve everything that was in our hearts and hopes; without its aid we were useless. I am myself sensitive to atmosphere and I caught a sense of this power of the House as I sat in there for the first time listening to the Address.

During the subsequent debate seventeen Labour members made their maiden speeches. Many of them were excited and fiery. In pre-election days they would have aroused cheers from the electors. In the House they fell flat. No one, Socialist, Liberal, or Tory could doubt the sincerity which impelled my friends to demand immediate social improvements, to bring about the instant end of capitalism, and to eradicate the evils of unemployment then and there. Yet they failed because of their appeal to emotions instead of the mind. The machinery of government was ready to obey if it was told how to act rather than what to do. One gallery reporter summed up those maiden speeches as "sound and fury." He was kind enough to leave the quotation incomplete.

When I caught the Speaker's eye and embarked on what is the greatest ordeal a politician can have I felt in my mind that I was in some way failing my constituents with my maiden speech. My words lacked emotion. There was no zeal about them. I seemed to be regarding the members opposite as opponents instead of enemies. That night I went to bed miserable, wondering what the people of Linlithgow would be saying the next morning when they read the parliamentary reports in the Press.

I was out before dawn and grabbed a newspaper from a newsagent's in the Vauxhall Bridge Road. Under a street lamp I read:

"Shortly afterwards a speech from the Labour Benches was made which renders it necessary to qualify the general criticisms given above. Mr. Shinwell was the speaker, and to the surprise of the House he devoted himself solely to answering two speeches made from the Government Benches by Lady Astor and Mr. Esmond Harmsworth. Point by point he dealt with them, using all the mannerisms and conventions of parliamentary debate, as if he had been in the House for years instead of hours, and displaying all the qualities that go to make a debater of some weight and ingenuity."

So I had mastered the most difficult obstacle. I may be forgiven my elation at such comments tucked away in a long parliamentary report. For me it seemed to make the trials and tribulations of the past worth while.

CHAPTER TEN

I BECOME A MINISTER

M Y financial difficulties, as I have explained, were acute during my early days at Westminster. My wife never complained, but I knew that things were even more difficult for her than for me. Housing shortages were not so severe after the First World War as after 1945—there had been no bombing, of course—but rents were very high. I was, however, lucky enough to rent a house on the Becontree estate in Essex, then one of the biggest developments of its kind in the country. Our four children quickly settled down in the new environment, as did my wife, who had the gift of making friends easily all her life.

Very soon, we were in the throes of a General Election. The onrush of events in Europe had to some extent minimized the crisis at home. In the autumn of 1923 some of my colleagues saw the signs of the world revolution they expected. The Rhine Republic was proclaimed; Bavaria defied the Reich's authority; Turkey became a republic. The whole of Europe east of the Meuse was seething.

Then quite suddenly, Baldwin, who had become Premier on the resignation of Bonar Law through ill-health, announced that he intended to demand a mandate to introduce Tariff Protection as the principal weapon against unemployment. Incidentally, the emergence of this obscure private member into the limelight of premiership is an incident which all prophets of political advancement should keep in mind.

There can hardly be a member of any Cabinet in twentieth-century governments who has not been tipped for the job of Prime Minister—I have even had this experience myself—but history shows that circumstance creates the man, and not the man the opportunity. Lloyd George and Winston Churchill would not,

I suggest, have become tenants of No. 10, Downing Street, except through the pressure of war. MacDonald, as I have shown, received the vote in 1922 which set him on the path to premiership because a number of his enemies were delayed from attending a meeting of the Parliamentary Labour Party. Campbell-Bannerman and Baldwin emerged because of bickerings within their own party. It may be possible to forecast other ministers because of their particular flair for the job in question. But the office of Prime Minister is often the gift of an erratic and capricious fate.

Baldwin, already adopting the rôle of the simple country gentleman—"I am not a clever man," he explained in a sensational speech at Plymouth when he gave a hint on the policy he proposed to follow—proceeded to set Bonar Law's policy aside. Parliament was dissolved on 13 November and the general election fixed for 6 December. I had three weeks of hectic electioneering in West Lothian. I had first become prospective Labour candidate there in 1917 and I knew the people and places of this, my first constituency, with experience, and through that, with affection. The county town, Linlithgow, was the birthplace of Mary Queen of Scots, and nearby is Dalmeny, the seat of the Rosebery family. The fifth earl, Archibald Primrose (who I remember seeing as a boy when he attended an international football match between England and Scotland in Celtic Park with the Scottish team wearing the Rosebery colours), was, of course, a hero to many of the people of West Lothian, largely because of his devotion to Scottish interests. When he first came into political prominence in the eighteen-seventies, he was among the leading voices for a separate ministry for Scotland. My opponent before this election and afterwards was James Kidd, a Unionist who led the first attack on Lloyd George and started the break-up of the Coalition Government. He was the secretary of the Brewers' Association, but got the temperance vote although at the time I was in favour of prohibition. There was Liberal opposition, of course. In 1922 I polled 12,625 votes against Kidd's 8,993. At this, my third contest, I increased my vote by nearly another thousand, and I sensed favourable reaction throughout that hurried three-week campaign.

West Lothian is largely agricultural, but there are a few coal mines, and it is the most important zone of the shale industry. In the manner with which Scottish contribution to the industrial wealth of the United Kingdom is often treated few people south of the Border had any conception at that time of the importance of this industry. In the years up to the outbreak of war in 1914 annual production of shale reached 3½ million tons, but the expansion of the American and Middle Eastern oil wells nearly caused the trade's extinction in West Lothian. Tax reliefs on home-produced oil later brought back some semblance of prosperity. To-day Scottish shale oil runs a good many of the bus services north of the Border, and the shale also yields a mass of by-products, including wax, sulphate of ammonia, and the chief ingredient in soapless detergents. Some 4,000 men are employed in the industry. There is still a mass of shale untapped but unfortunately it lies between 2,000 and 4,000 feet below the surface. A planned economy would certainly investigate the possibility of tapping the enormous source of fuel and other raw materials which exist in the 200 square miles of shale extending from Airdrie to West Lothian.

Because my constituency was the centre of the shale industry I got to know (now Sir) William Fraser, at that time chairman of the Scottish Oils and now chief of the parent company, Anglo-Iranian. He was—and is—a doughty political adversary of mine, but we both found a meeting point in a feeling of respect for one another. He is one of the shrewdest men in British industry, and a good friend of Scotland. He did his utmost to keep me out of the division but he fought a clean fight, and even if he did not take the defeat of his candidate easily he never acted in any way to harm the well-being of the people and their sources of work just for the sake of political tactics.

My election agent when I fought West Lothian was James Lamond, a railway fireman who was earning 22s. a week when I first knew him. He was one of the finest men I have ever known, typical of the enthusiastic members of the rank and file of the old I.L.P. He had taught himself shorthand so that he could act as branch secretary of the Railwaymen's Union in Bathgate. He lived with his wife in a small council house which was always my headquarters at election time. Jamie lived and breathed Socialism; he killed himself with overwork in its cause.

When I went to Bo'ness, the largest town in West Lothian, my host was always Angus Livingstone, headmaster at the local school. For centuries Scotland has exported youngsters to every part of the world uniquely well trained to seek their fortune. There is no industry or profession without its stories of the poor lad from the Highland crofter's cottage or the slum of a Lowland city who rose to the heights. The intellectual life of the nation has always been strong and admired, and in theory at least any lad with brains and determination could obtain a good education, even though he might almost starve in the process. The inspiration of this intellectual wealth in Scotland was the village schoolmaster, who was a good friend long after schooldays were over. Angus was such a man. I could count him among the few men who have become my intimate friends, and the help he gave me cannot be calculated in ordinary terms.

There were many in the Labour Party who had high hopes of the 1923 election. Then, for the first time I think, we had becomes conscious of the fact that we were one of the three great political parties of the nation—and not merely political agitators. At the annual party conference held in the previous June there had been 929 delegates and they represented four million affiliated members. We were not merely one of the three great parties, but on these figures the largest political organization in Britain—and the poorest. That Labour could govern was at least partially proved by the fact that in the government of the local authorities there were some 10,000 elected Labour representatives.

Even with these facts to encourage us, most of us were quite surprised when we found ourselves with 191 seats in the new Parliament. New members included men who were to shape Labour's policy in the years to come: Arthur Greenwood, Albert Alexander, Clem Attlee, and F. W. Pethick-Lawrence.

The Tories had 258 seats, but the Liberals with 158 held the balance of power—and their leader, Asquith, had made it clear where his party stood: "We would not lift a finger to keep the Tories in office."

The decision that Labour should form the Government was taken by MacDonald, Henderson, Snowden, Thomas, Clynes, and Sidney Webb. The party as a whole had considerable doubts about the wisdom of doing so, but MacDonald was eager to attempt it. His Cabinet-making was entirely his own effort— carried out at Lossiemouth over the Christmas holidays. When

his list appeared we saw the first signs of MacDonald's contempt
for the abilities of his own colleagues and his sneaking admiration
for his adversaries. Lord Haldane, Lord Chelmsford, and Lord
Parmoor were in the Cabinet, not one of whom was suspected
of Labour sympathies until that moment.

I had some insight into the workings of MacDonald's mind a
few days later as I walked through the Lobby. He was chatting
to Patrick Hastings. He called me over and Hastings walked off.

"I want you in the Government and can offer you a post in
the Mines Department," he said loftily. "Nominally you will be
under Webb at the Board of Trade, but it's an executive position
and you will have your own department."

I pointed out that I was not a miner, and that surely a miner
should have the post. MacDonald had included very few trade
unionists in his Cabinet ministry—only five; of whom Thomas,
Clynes, and Henderson were first and foremost of parliamentary
prominence. His answer indicated that he had little time for
trade-union experts in political office.

"It would be wrong to put a man in the job who could not
take an impartial view," he replied.

This specious argument did not convince me that I should
accept the offer and I was given time to make up my mind. I
talked to a number of miners' M.P.s, including my intimate
friends Duncan Graham and James Welsh, the miner-poet. They
said that they thought the miners would be delighted to have
me represent their industry. I gained the impression later that
some of the South Wales M.P.s were unhappy that one of their
number should not have got the job.

It was a gloomy and rainy January morning when I walked
along Dean Stanley Street to my new office. The weather was one
reason why I carried an umbrella, and I rather fancy that many
of the clerks were relieved to see that a representative of the
"wild men of the Clyde" was, after all, a harmless-looking fellow
and attached to the emblem of propriety carried by all good civil
servants.

The office of the Permanent Under-Secretary to which I was
shown was chilly in more than one sense. Sir Ernest Gowers
greeted me with courtesy but little enthusiasm. Very soon I
recognized him as one of the most able of civil servants and I

had every assistance from him during my brief stay in the Mines Department. With him was William Brace, a labour adviser to the department, and a one-time miner. He was most formidable looking, with a large moustache that transformed him from his really quite mild character into a bristling martinet. Strangely, or perhaps not so strangely, it was Brace who spread the disapproval of my appointment in the department. When I was alone with Gowers the latter became more friendly, and as he left me in my office I felt that I need not walk out and resign then and there after all.

My first action was to call for a memorandum explaining my powers and the department's activities. The information satisfied me that I was perfectly capable of handling the job.

An early visitor was John (now Lord) Hyndley, at the time honorary commercial adviser to the Mines Department. He was associated with a number of coal distribution concerns and had assisted the Government on coal problems during the war. I liked him as soon as I met him and he has remained my good friend ever since. There are few men who can combine mental shrewdness and a large heart as he does. In the history of the coal industry Hyndley's name is prominent and deserving of praise. He has served both the industry and the miners well. With more Hyndleys in the past there would not have been the bitterness of many years.

To my regret I have not always taken his sound advice. I lack his patience and diplomacy. He once smilingly told me: "You know, if I could always sit beside you and jerk your coat when you are about to speak in haste something you'll repent at leisure you could go very far in the affairs of our country."

Trouble soon came my way. In March, 1921, the Government had returned the mines to private control. The miners refused to take wage cuts and were locked out, according to them; or they struck, according to the owners. They held out until the autumn. Now, with a Labour Government in power, they wanted the cuts partially restored by an increased percentage on their earnings. The owners, led by Evan Williams who was bitterly hated by the miners of South Wales, rejected the demand. Another strike seemed very near.

MacDonald was anxious that no strike should occur during Labour's term of office, and he paid me the doubtful compliment of telling me to handle the negotiations instead of the Minister of Labour. Nor was my chief, Sidney Webb, any more anxious to dabble in something which looked like ending in failure.

I tried what was frankly bluff with the owners. I told them if they refused to give way or at least to compromise I would " use drastic measures." What these were I did not know, but in the imagination of the owners they were infinitely worse than anything I could have planned. They sulkily issued a press announcement that "Mr. Shinwell held a pistol at our heads," and there was much head-shaking among my staff at this uncivil method of carrying out the civil-service procedure. But it worked. The owners agreed to a 13 per cent increase on miners' earnings and commensurate increases for the day-wage men. MacDonald was delighted—but my satisfaction was not because of the plaudits of the Cabinet but from the thanks of the miners. My action established me as their friend and for a long time afterwards I was busy speaking at their demonstrations and invited to inaugurate various welfare schemes. In regard to the latter I had the pleasure of promoting a Bill for compulsory pithead baths during this Government.

A lively memory of the period is of my meetings with Lord Haldane, the greatest Liberal War Minister, who had become Lord Chancellor at MacDonald's invitation. Why he liked me I never discovered, and when he openly stated that I was one of the ablest men in the party with which he was now serving, though still unconverted, he did not ameliorate my position among my colleagues. Politicians are a jealous breed, and a reference of this kind will invariably cause much heartburning among the careerists who are to be found in every party.

Haldane used on occasion to invite me to dinner. Once his sister was there and the only other guest was Lord Buckmaster. Haldane had a pawky sense of humour and artfully led the after-dinner discussion to the topic of the nationalization of the mines so as deliberately to start an argument between Buckmaster and myself. Haldane was obviously on my side, and I think I can claim a victory over Buckmaster in this battle of words.

A little later there came a delicate time in the House. The

miners' group of M.P.s promoted a private Bill for the transfer of the mines to the State, the administration to be by a group of Government nominees sharing the work with representatives of the Miners' Federation. There was more enthusiasm than common sense in its aims, and the Government refused to accept responsibility for it. However, it had to state its case, and I was told to give the Cabinet view, along with Sidney Webb. Neither of us shone in that debate, and Lloyd George gave us both a frightful verbal hiding.

The fact that we were really a Government without power, hamstrung by the threat of the Liberal balance of power, was ignored by the country and by our own party members. Criticism grew steadily. I remember the minor sensation when Hannen Swaffer wrote a personal and somewhat unethical attack on MacDonald. The story was a circumstantial one—though doubtless true enough—that the Prime Minister had been seen to leave Downing Street by a back door, walk along the Embankment and turn into the Adelphi where he rang a bell and was instantly admitted to a discreet little flat there. The vagueness of the motive ascribed to this incident heightened the gossipy flavour, and we junior members resented both the suggestions inherent in the story and the intrusion into privacy. I called a meeting and we all agreed to ask Swaffer to print an apology. But William Leech, Under-Secretary for Air and one of MacDonald's intimate friends, told his chief, and the Premier sternly warned us against doing anything about it.

MacDonald was a worried man. His sensitivity made the constant sniping of the Back Benchers a bugbear to him. Although their targets included everybody on the Front Bench except John Wheatley, Minister of Health, MacDonald took it as a personal affront. I often told him to dismiss the whole business as of little consequence, but he was deeply hurt by the enmity of his onetime principal supporters, the Scottish group.

"It's treachery," he told me.

He was, however, at that time obstinate enough to stick it out. During the summer recess he was planning for the months ahead, and from Lossiemouth I received a note from him which indicated the way his thoughts were leading him, with no suspicion of catastrophe around the corner.

ymouth, 1923. Some of the delegates to the T.U.C. enjoying a game of bowls on Plymouth
oe, during a break in the conference. In this group are J. Bromley (extreme left), the author
econd from left), F. O. Roberts, M.P. (fifth from left), J. Hill (sixth from left), T. Groves
eventh from left), A. A. H. Findlay (second from right), and Bob Smillie (extreme right).

gathering of Socialists. British Socialists acted as hosts to a group of German Socialists at
aston Lodge when the latter visited Britain in 1923. The above photograph shows (left to
ght, standing): Otto Wells, Canon Adderley, Mrs. Emanuel Shinwell, Emanuel Shinwell,
Vill Thorne; (sitting): Arthur Henderson, the Countess of Warwick, Ramsay MacDonald,
Rudolph Breitscheid.

The author, about 1925.

29th August, 1924.

My dear Shinwell,

How are things going in connexion with Mining legislation for next year? I am writing to Webb putting the same question to him, but I should like you to know that my thoughts are turning in that direction.

Although it is rather late, I must tell you how much I have enjoyed watching you doing your work. Everybody with whom I discuss the Government agrees that you have been splendid, and if I could give you any opportunities of showing yourself to better advantage, you can depend upon my doing so.

With kindest regards,

Yours very sincerely,

J. RAMSAY MACDONALD

The proverbial final straw came with the Campbell case. At this distance the whole business seems like a storm in a teacup, as indeed it was. MacDonald hated Communism. He made no protest when the Attorney-General, Sir Patrick Hastings, prosecuted J. R. Campbell, editor of the Communist *Workers' Weekly*, for a "don't shoot" article. There is no doubt that the article was a fatuous and deliberately provocative piece of writing, designed by its author to stress the Communist line that the Socialists were reactionary and corrupted by the capitalists. As there were no strikers for the soldiers to mow down what danger the article had cannot be envisaged. However, Sir Patrick—it is strange that lawyers seldom make good politicians—dug up the old Mutiny Act of 1795 and comforted a few Tory blimps by announcing that a prosecution would be put in hand. On top of that he raided the *Workers' Weekly* offices and arrested the editor. Many of the general public were undoubtedly disturbed at these moves, for Campbell had served with distinction throughout the war and had been badly wounded. Further he was merely the acting editor and therefore just a scapegoat. Labour members, who had a short time before said precisely the same things as did the article at street corners in a hundred towns, started an uproar in the House. The merest hint of the suppression of freedom of speech is a danger signal to British people of every political colour—and always may it be so.

The Cabinet agreed to withdraw the charge. This made a

bad business worse. Both Tories and Liberals then charged the Prime Minister with interfering with the course of justice. In the midst of the controversy MacDonald sent for me. I found him in the large drawing-room at No. 10. He was pacing up and down in a welter of indecision and excitement. Finally he turned to me and said that he intended to resign.

I told him that there was no need for that. Asquith intended to propose a Liberal amendment to the Tory vote of censure, demanding an inquiry. If the Government agreed to the inquiry all would be well. In any event, as Hastings had already told me, the blunder was his and he wanted to resign.

From MacDonald's reaction to all these comforting words I realized that he was really bothered but little about the Campbell case. He was worried over the Government's position with its hopeless minority. Again he repeated: "I can't stand the constant criticism from the Back Benchers."

I tried to calm him with the explanation that most of it was to placate their constituents. Their interruptions and captious criticism looked very well in the local newspapers. He remained unconvinced.

Before I could discover new arguments a message was delivered from Ben Spoor, the Chief Whip, that the Liberals were annoyed at MacDonald's delay in acceding to their request for an inquiry.

"Asquith's putting down a motion of censure. That settles it," said the Prime Minister.

The vote against the Government was carried by 364 to 198. The first Labour Government was over, buried by its leader—a man who could no longer stand the strain of criticism from his own side. It was not the Campbell affair that brought him down. MacDonald knew that the case was an unfortunate incident that could have been erased, but he could not obliterate the words of his one-time friends and comrades from his sensitive, vain, yet brilliant mind.

CHAPTER ELEVEN

DEFEAT—AND RETURN TO OFFICE

THE tawdry sensationalism of the Campbell case continued in a fresh guise at the election. The form it took was the notorious Zinoviev letter. Whether this was a forgery, or just a copy of a genuine document, is a matter on which myriads of words have been written without proving the case one way or the other. The main interest in the letter was of course MacDonald's reaction. He was at the time in the midst of a spectacular electioneering campaign throughout the country. Late on 15 October, after a tiring but successful day of speech making, he retired to his bedroom and went through his dispatch boxes. In one of them, marked "Foreign Office," was included, without any covering memorandum, a letter headed "Executive Committee of the Third International (Communist)," which was signed by Zinoviev, President of the Presidium, and by McManus without initial or Christian name. It should be realized that the Foreign Office secretariat probably considered there was no need to write any explanatory note, for the document was really in no way sensational. White Russian organizations produced scores of such letters; others of a more genuine nature were forwarded by Secret Service agents to Whitehall. Fleet Street was offered—and normally rejected—all sorts of notes signed by Zinoviev and hawked around the newspaper offices by shady characters desirous of earning a dishonest guinea.

MacDonald had an almost pathological hatred of Communism. He was the type of man who saw Reds under the bed, and Russian conspiracy in the slightest anti-British sentiment. He forthwith wrote a note of protest to the Soviet Government and had both the letter and protest published. Yet his queer trait of hesitation and fear influenced him to keep a tiny escape route from blame for himself. The protest was corrected by him in his own handwriting; it was not initialled by him.

The basic controversy of the election was the question of a loan to Russia. MacDonald's protest left Labour candidates bewildered and without leadership. They had been advocating the loan as of value to Britain's trade and as an easement of the international situation, and in the light of subsequent events there are certainly some arguments in favour of the view that the refusal to grant the loan was a major blunder. MacDonald was virtually repudiating the views of his own party. The inevitable result was that the Tories gained 152 seats; Labour lost 42, and the Liberals 119. I was among the defeated.

There was a certain amount of personal satisfaction in realizing that the party leaders genuinely regretted my absence from the new Parliament. Many of them wrote letters of regret, and two of them I am quoting, not because of any sympathy therein, but as significant of the private thoughts of the two men whose names were, for good or for ill, to be the most important in the party's parliamentary activities for some years to come.

My dear Shinwell,

There is no result of the Election that has given me more sorrow than yours. You were doing so well and there were such fine opportunities for you in the Opposition. I hope that our Party will be more alive than it has been up to now, in taking steps to get essential men back, and that your absence will only be short. The nature of the Election, however, goes far to justify the sneers that our Communist friends throw at parliamentary action.

With all best wishes,
Yours very sincerely,
J. RAMSAY MACDONALD

My dear Shinwell,

Your defeat—so utterly unexpected—is a great blow to me. I am quite unable to put into words my sorrow. Your loss to the Parliamentary Labour Party is irreparable and the serious aspect is that I see no immediate prospect of your return. But I do hope some accident will soon bring you back again.

I am terribly distressed at the whole business of this General Election. I get no satisfaction from the increased Labour vote. It only throws into great prominence the magnificent opportunities we have wantonly and recklessly thrown away by the most incompetent political leadership which ever brought a government to disaster.

Believe me,

Yours very sincerely,

PHILIP SNOWDEN

My union was still in existence so that there was a job for me to do, although as I explain in Chapter Five the struggle with Havelock Wilson was more intense. The lean years had come again to my family and myself. We were only one family of many sufferers. I saw the stagnation of life which seeped steadily over the working classes—particularly among the miners. Conditions in the coalfields were tragic and appalling. The situation wore down the obstinate loyalty of the miners to the political creeds of their fathers, and many of them, both Liberal and to a lesser extent Tory till then, swung to Socialism. By the summer of 1925 the crisis was very near. The owners issued lock-out orders. The T.U.C. retaliated with instructions to the railway and transport unions to stop all movement of coal. Baldwin contrived a breathing space by announcing a Royal Commission to inquire into the mining industry and promised a Government subsidy while it sat to prevent the owners' proposed cuts in wages and increase of working time. The Tories knew that it was merely a truce; it was spent in piling up coal reserves. The miners as a whole did not see the omens. The only leader who warned them of the trouble to come was A. J. Cook, a Welshman with wonderful oratorical powers and a burning sincerity in all he said. But he was intolerant of opposition or even competition. Immensely popular with the miners, he brooked no rival. I once spoke with him at a miners' demonstration in Fifeshire. I felt in good form and delivered some really red-hot stuff. It was quite in the Cook style, but he disliked the applause I was getting. Suddenly he stood up and interrupted me, apparently because he regarded himself as the solo star of the meeting. Such a man was of priceless value to the miners' cause but was not the most suitable for negotiating with the T.U.C. nor, for that matter, with the Labour Opposition in the Commons.

The nine months' respite ended. The lock-out notices were issued on 30 April, 1926. Next morning, May Day, a special

99

conference of trade-union executives voted for a General Strike, with 3½ million votes for, 300,000 awaiting instructions, and 50,000 against. Notices went out to strike at midnight on 3 May. A lightning stoppage in the *Daily Mail* composing plant twenty-four hours earlier brought an ultimatum from Baldwin. He did not even wait for an answer to it, gambling instead on a break-down of unity among the unions. By Monday morning he knew that the only union which had disobeyed orders to strike was Havelock Wilson's Sailors' and Firemen's Union; even here Wilson had been unsuccessful on Tyne- and Tees-side, in the Lancashire ports, and in part of the Port of London, where shipping was brought to a standstill.

I was in the East End docks area of London during the General Strike. I worked in the Settlement with which Clem Attlee had been associated, though I cannot recall seeing him there during this period. Despite the forebodings of Churchill, Joynson Hicks, and Birkenhead, who were the principal men behind Baldwin, the strikers were peaceable and there was no real violence. Troops poured in to protect the food convoys (which the General Council of the T.U.C. had arranged, along with the continuation of the health and sanitary services). Police, soldiers, and strikers settled down amicably enough. A few officers took action when the troops fraternized in cafés or by playing in football matches, but there was no real trouble.

The strike, of course, collapsed. Leadership had been almost non-existent in T.U.C. headquarters. Not once in the House of Commons had MacDonald said he approved of the strike.

The miners continued the struggle for eight months. I held many meetings in the coalfields, notably in County Durham where my personal prestige increased considerably. In referring to the General Strike I criticized the T.U.C. leaders strongly and claimed that they had gone into the fight half-heartedly, worrying more about the draining of their financial reserves than about the outcome of the fight or the welfare of their members. I also said that a General Strike was a useless weapon in any event because it was bound to become political in character. It would always develop into a war against the Government, and that was alien to the British character.

Unexpectedly, through the sudden death of the sitting member

for West Lothian, James Kidd, I found myself in the throes of a
by-election early in 1928. My opponents were Mr. Kidd's daughter, and Douglas Young, standing as a Liberal. The election was
of considerable importance to the party leaders for it was the
first since the mining lock-out in a mining area. Snowden was
among those who came up and spoke for me. Lloyd George made
a much-heralded speech for Young, which was in fact a bitter
attack on myself, and proved a complete flop. Locally, the
Government's policy had made itself severely felt. Two coal mines
and five shale mines had closed in the previous twelve months,
throwing about 1,400 men out of work. They were just part of the
24,000 miners recently made workless in Scotland alone. There
were also many hundreds of unemployed oil workers. My campaign was fought on the question of the betrayal of the miners,
the neglect of the unemployed and of local industry, and the
failure to improve social conditions. In practice, the main point
of contention became the Mines Eight Hours Act which, of course,
helped me, but gave Miss Kidd some terrible heckling when she
tried to speak in the mining villages. The outcome was inevitable.
I was again in Parliament.

It was a short parliamentary session for me. The wily Baldwin,
armed with a Budget designed to catch votes but not to ward off
the aggravation of the nation's ailing economy, dissolved Parliament and came out with his infamous "Safety First" slogan. For
once he had miscalculated badly. The Tories found themselves
with 296 seats as compared with Labour's 287, with a further
59 Liberals against them. MacDonald had not lost the trust of
the Socialist electorate. The cries of "treachery" in the 1926
strike had been forgotten, his ineffectual efforts on their behalf
forgiven. His promise of a remedy for unemployment by increasing
production had been accepted. As the Liberals had said much the
same thing it seemed reasonable to hope that MacDonald would
this time have more support from them than he had in 1924.

For the first time the number of M.P.s backed by local parties
outnumbered trade-union nominees. This was, I think, the
reward of the years of public speaking carried on by many people
like myself, and of the vigorous activity of the I.L.P. The trend
did not please some of the people at Transport House. My criticism
of T.U.C. lethargy during the General Strike had duly been noted

by the T.U.C. top leaders and MacDonald received a broad hint that my presence in his new Government would not be acceptable. I had stayed in my constituency for a few days after the election. I had been told that the Prime Minister was having trouble in forming his Cabinet, and one morning I received a letter from him ordering me to come to London as quickly as possible as he was under pressure to keep me out.

When I arrived at Downing Street I told him that he should not trouble about me, but he insisted that I should wait a day or two before saying anything. He then sent for me again and told me that, despite the demands he was receiving to include some trade-union leaders who had been returned in preference to others, he was determined to have me in the Government, even if temporarily I had to live in comparative obscurity and out of harm's way. The office he had in mind was Financial Secretary to the War Office.

I declined immediately. The remarkable charm of the man then showed itself as he put his arm around my shoulders and said: "Now, don't refuse an old friend, Manny. I want some people in the Government on whom I can depend."

I still would not agree, but temporized my refusal by promising to defer my final decision until I had had time to think it over dispassionately. Straight from that meeting I went to a meeting of the National Council of the I.L.P. Maxton was chairman, and when I arrived they were angrily discussing the fact that no member of the I.L.P. executive was included in the Government— not even Jowett, or Wheatley, who had both been in the Cabinet in 1924. I told them what MacDonald had said to me. Pat Dollan and most of the others were in favour, but Maxton was wholly against my acceptance. "If you keep out, we shall have a real fight," he said.

There was, of course, great personal animosity between Maxton and MacDonald. At the beginning of the year I had received two letters from MacDonald which might have involved me in the personal intrigues which beset him. The first, sent while the Prime Minister was at Lossiemouth, said:

My dear Shinwell,

    The Aberdeen paper this morning states that an attempt is to be made to extend Maxton's chairmanship of the I.L.P. Surely this is not true. If it is, cannot it be defeated? Are you going to stand? If you are the most careful preparations should be made to secure your return. You might let me know what is doing.

J. RAMSAY MACDONALD

I replied, giving him the brief facts and not committing myself in any way, and immediately another letter came which graphically showed his disquiet and suspicion—and not only about Maxton:

My dear Shinwell,

Bradford and other branches want me to stand for the chairmanship but it is quite impracticable. I hope you will stand and that there will be a concentration upon you. If you think it is too risky, you ought to take care that you are on the N.A.C. whatever happens. But I think that by organization you could be elected chairman. The others will do their best to poll their maximum vote and will do their best not to split.

If Maxton stands it will be scandalous after what has happened, but there is no lack of pure artfulness in him. He loves to be a figure in the Press and is affording them fine chances of using him to the detriment of the movement. In the Aberdeen Tory paper there is something every day about him, and the point always is that he is a great and important figure and influence in the Party. Vanity unsupported by a capacity for work is at the root of the trouble they give.

The loyalty to me which they professed in the meeting in the House was a necessary piece of defensive armour. I have never regarded them as being of any consequence on this side of an election if we did not let them palm themselves off on the Party. Their real danger is if we need their loyal support, e.g. votes if we try again to carry on a Government. Our only insurance against them then is a good grip on their constituencies. I have just had an interesting and significant letter from the I.L.P. of Dumbarton.

Yours very sincerely,

J. RAMSAY MACDONALD

At the end of the I.L.P. meeting over my appointment it was decided that I should take the post, and so I told MacDonald. He arranged for me to see the new Secretary of State for War, Tom Shaw, a leading man in the cotton unions and an old friend of mine.

103

He was evidently expecting me, for he said: "So you've come after all!" I explained that I had done so with some reluctance but now that I was there I intended to work. I was not the type to act as a minor figure-head. Shaw agreed that there was little doubt about this.

There was plenty for me to do. Snowden, who had shown some animus to the Party's demand for revision to the Unemployment Insurance Act which he estimated would cost the country £20 millions and had insisted on restricting the increase to £12 millions, was insisting on heavy cuts in military expenditure for his Budget in April, 1930. He was admittedly faced with a difficult situation for the Churchill estimates made when he was Chancellor the previous year had failed to reach his expectations by £18½ millions.

Naturally the service chiefs fought hard to prevent any cuts in their own branch of the Army and Shaw left me to counter-attack. My brief from him was that I must cut no matter what the generals said. Strangely, I did not find myself unpopular as a result of my obstinacy to all their explanations and protests. I recall that Sir George (later Lord) Milne, the C.I.G.S., asked me to conduct an inquiry into the expenditure on the maintenance of mechanically propelled vehicles. He suggested that I form a committee. I retorted that I had no love of committees, and if the job was to be done there would be a one-man committee consisting of myself. I think that it appealed to his military mind.

It was extremely difficult to get the service chiefs to discuss the problem. I discovered that there was tremendous overlapping of responsibility as mechanization developed in one branch of the service after another and each section produced its own plan without any consideration of co-operation with another. When, for example, the heads of the Army Service Branch and the Ordnance Department met in my office they were ready enough to talk to me but were barely on speaking terms with one another. I forced some semblance of rationalization into the whole set-up of Army mechanization and achieved considerable economies which, so far from jeopardizing the efficiency of the service actually enhanced it—or so Milne told me when he formally thanked me. I smilingly suggested that it must be unwise to mention my name among his colleagues. "Not at all," he replied, "it's the first breath of air we've had from the politicians in the War House for a long time."

I enjoyed my stay at the War Office. It is a conventional attitude to decry the intelligence of the high-ranking officers of the Army. My experience then and in 1950 taught me that they are more co-operative and more intelligent than many other permanent Government officials who are lauded for their brilliance. I dislike Commons' attacks on our generals by people who know nothing about them, and I have said so in the House on more than one occasion.

CHAPTER TWELVE

THE 1931 CRISIS

M Y stay at the War Office ended because of the Government's
quandary on who to send to a conference of the International
Labour Office at Geneva. MacDonald and Jimmy Thomas told
me that I must return to the Ministry of Mines so that I could go
to Geneva. Thomas had always had a certain admiration for me,
and in his forthright and picturesque language I remember him
once telling me "What we need are brains, and we prefer working-
class brains." In spite of his close association with MacDonald
he had little time for the intellectuals who came into the party
straight from the universities; who treated their activities as a
sort of political slumming in which they were constantly indicating
their superiority by birth and intellect over the working-class
member of the party. These men seemed according to Thomas to
keep one goal in mind: the Treasury Bench. It was the pre-
ordained destiny in their own minds—but not in Thomas's.
Despite his carefully contrived speech, liberally larded with
homely expletives and with the aspirates added or omitted in
direct contravention of the dictionary, Thomas had a keen and
common-sense brain. He was a first-class negotiator, achieving his
aim by temporizing until the next time. This had been the secret
of his great success with his railway unions. Where negotiators in
the other unions ran up against a brick wall because they refused
to diverge from an ultimatum, Thomas would settle for an hour
less when he asked for two, for sixpence on the rate when he had
been briefed to get a shilling. He would bide his time and get the
remainder later.

Ben Turner was the Minister for Mines and not making much
of a success in the job. He had no wish to tackle the tricky problem
of the Geneva conference which was to get international agree-

ment to a 7-hour day for mine-workers. Thomas told me that Britain, with a Socialist Government, must weigh in with some force. I did not relish the almost impossible task presented and repeated that MacDonald had sent me to the War Office in 1929 against my wishes, that I had been treated badly when the Government was formed and that now I had found the War Office a pleasant place in which to work—and more important there was some useful work to do there.

But eventually he persuaded me to agree, and my transfer to the Secretaryship of the Mines Department was announced the following day. Forty-eight hours later I was on the boat train for Geneva. Before I went I had the chance of a brief chat with Willie Graham, President of the Board of Trade, my chief, and one of the financial experts of the party. He was the back-room boy for Snowden during his Chancellorships, and a personal friend of his until the crisis when he remained loyal to Labour. Graham readily agreed that I should have a free hand to run things at Geneva without constant reference to London. He was also reasonably agreeable that I should run things my way in the department. "Give me a report on what you're doing," he said, "so that I can let the Cabinet know what's happening. Otherwise the problems are yours. I'll wear the feathers and you can do the scratching."

It suited me very well.

Although on a brief visit to Downing Street MacDonald told me that he regarded my presence at the Geneva conference as merely a gesture of goodwill from Britain and that there was virtually no chance of getting agreement, I told him that I was confident that something could be done. I felt it futile to go with a defeatist attitude. Most of the famous European Socialist leaders were at Geneva, including Albert Thomas, the former French workers' leader who was now Director-General of the International Labour Office, with whom I was very friendly.

Hospitality during the conference was on a lavish scale. The result was that I felt extremely unwell on the morning that I had to make my speech to the convention and had no time to prepare any notes. I spoke without any—and that was possibly the reason why the speech was enthusiastically received. The motion was passed by a majority.

This success enhanced my prestige considerably. I received

congratulations from the T.U.C. and from the miners' unions. Even the mine-owners were quite pleased for the convention would remove a competitive element in the export trade in coal. A little later I got to know some of the owners' representatives still better. The Coal Mines Bill was still being discussed in Parliament. It ultimately reduced hours and made arrangements for amalgamations, but its real vigour was cut away in the House of Lords. At that time the owners were fighting every clause bitterly—a genuine motive along with the rest being the decrease in exports. The world slump had broken out, but part of the more serious drop in overseas coal business came through competition from the Polish and German mines, which were supplying better and cheaper coal than Britain to Scandinavia. I suggested that we should go and study the problem on the spot. At first the owners declined, so I told them I would go myself. Eventually some of them came with me, and on our return we issued a report which proved so helpful to the industry that they gave me a dinner to celebrate it.

MacDonald was still at this time quite friendly towards me, but the suspicion of anyone's move unless he had inspired it showed itself in a note he sent me. First came a sentence of praise —and then the indirect and vaguely worded reproach for showing initiative. The letter read:

My dear Shinwell,

I was very glad to see at last in the *Daily Herald* a paragraph which appreciated the work you are doing, and I am just dropping you this note to assure you that it expressed my sentiments.

It has been reported to me that you had an interview with Norman* regarding the Mines Amalgamation Committee, during which you stated you had been approaching people and had received their consent, and also that you had made up your mind regarding the duties of the chairman. I hope this has been done after consultation with Graham. The rule is that all committees of such importance are appointed only after a minister has submitted his proposals to me and has talked over his intentions. I was put in a fix to-day, because I knew nothing about it.

Believe me,

Yours very sincerely,

J. RAMSAY MacDONALD

* Montagu Norman, Governor of the Bank of England, had taken offence when I told him I would have nothing to do with a suggested chairman who was a member of the House of Lords.

Personal triumphs and interests were soon eclipsed by the onward march of political tragedy. The world depression began in spectacular fashion in the United States with the Wall Street crash. In Britain disaster came more slowly and insidiously. The people had grown so accustomed to the queues for unemployment benefit that it was hardly noticed that each Tuesday and Thursday the lines of men signing on were becoming longer. The British political crisis which resulted in 1930-31 from conditions which pervaded the whole world was a parallel but separate development. It need not have happened. As Labour members like myself watched the strange proceedings of our Government we suspected and hoped that the scene was being set for an election, after which an uncompromising policy could be followed. We were wrong.

MacDonald, with his love of compromise and coalition, was privately approaching the Tories and Liberals on the unemployment question, using his characteristic terms of a "Council of State," "Common pool of ideas," "A measure of agreement," and so on. Baldwin was at least honest enough to refuse co-operation. Lloyd George said he accepted the offer not only in principle but with all the conditions laid down by the Labour Party. I felt then—and claim now—that Lloyd George was the villain of the piece. He had an almost pathological hatred of MacDonald, an emotion to which he added the weight of intelligent contempt. Both feelings were reciprocated by the Prime Minister, but this did not prevent him wishfully believing Lloyd George's words and refusing to reckon on his flair for making political mischief. Conferences took place at Downing Street. The only men present on the Labour side were Snowden and Vernon Hartshorn, a Welsh miners' leader who had resigned in June from the office of Lord Privy Seal because of criticism of his failure to alleviate unemployment.

In fairness to MacDonald it must be said that Liberal co-operation was essential if he did not wish to risk an election. Lloyd George held the balance of power. But nothing came of this Labour-Liberal search for a miracle, and by the end of the year the first hints of the disaster were there for all to see. Faced with a Budget deficit of £50 millions Snowden took a Tory vote of censure in February, 1931, as the opportunity to sound the alarm. Afterwards he appointed the May Committee headed by an insurance company chief recently retired, and consisting of two members from each party. The May Committee issued its report in July, 1931. The result is part of history. The Labour Government offered its biggest economy cut in unemployment benefit, saving £22 millions by limiting benefit to twenty-six weeks, imposing the means test, removing "anomalies," and increasing the contribution rate. The next biggest cut, of £10 millions, was on education and teachers' salaries. Arthur Henderson was one man who retained a sane attitude during this momentous and tragic time. His cool attitude saved the Labour Party from disintegration. We junior ministers never had a chance to intervene; the Cabinet was a closed reserve. Ernest Bevin and Walter Citrine, representing the T.U.C., tried to persuade MacDonald and Snowden to have second thoughts. It was, of course, useless. Snowden was not a man to change his mind, MacDonald for once had the tenacious obstinacy of a cornered and frightened man. But he at least felt the desolation of lost friendships. When I went home after he formed his National Government I almost immediately received a telephone call from MacDonald. "I want you to stay," he told me. "You can carry on with your policy."

"No," I told him firmly. "You needn't have done this. You could have gone into Opposition and the Party would have stood by you."

In explanation of his action in the crisis MacDonald sent me a letter on 24 August.

My dear Shinwell,

I need not say how deeply I regret the necessity for the resignation of the Government, but I wish to thank you most sincerely for the assistance you have given and the pleasure I have had in working with you. It is a very painful decision that has had to be taken, and I wish you to have no doubt at all about what it was. We were on the verge of a financial crisis which if not dealt with within the space of days, would have meant not cuts of ten per cent, or anything of that kind, in unemployment pay, but would have disorganized the whole of our financial system, with the most dire results to the mass of the working classes. It may take a little time for people to understand what are the issues and the alternatives to what I have done with some colleagues, but the events of to-day have shown that, but for the step which has been taken, before this week had well begun we should have been in the midst of a crushing calamity. The Government that has been formed is not a Coalition but a co-operation between individuals who are banded together to avoid the disaster. No parties are involved in it, and as soon as the country gets on an even keel again, the Government will cease to exist.

While the trouble lasted no other question could overshadow it, and no action which did not directly meet it, and which took time in coming into operation, was of the least use. We should have been fiddling beautiful music whilst Rome was burning. We had to follow what we considered to be a line necessary for the maintenance—even if in a temporarily limited form—of everything we stand for. I know it is hard to understand this, but I am certain that its truth will be seen as the days go on when the Party will have to stand impotently by whilst its work is being undone by others. Having failed to meet the immediate situation we should have been swept away in ignominy before the end of this week by popular clamour, so that it can be proved later on, whatever offence we have caused at this moment, we have created the conditions under which the Party can continue as an Opposition and allow the public, saved from panic, to consider a return of our general policy when things have become more normal.

I am,

Yours very sincerely,

J. RAMSAY MACDONALD

I had seen the phenomenon of a Socialist Chancellor of the Exchequer being cheered by Tories and Liberals, waving handkerchiefs and order papers in hysterical enthusiasm for an increase in taxation. There had been no jeering from the Socialist benches. We were too dumbfounded by Snowden's greatest hour. . . .

CHAPTER THIRTEEN

RAMSAY MACDONALD

JAMES RAMSAY MACDONALD had finally and irrevocably severed his connexion with the Labour movement in those tragic and historic days of 1931. He cannot be dismissed in a few words of condemnation for his actions near the end of his life. The pattern of Labour when it took office in 1945, and indeed the basis of the party's present policy, stem from the activities of several men, but both the hero and villain of the drama of twentieth-century Socialism in Britain is Ramsay MacDonald. It must not be forgotten that he led the Labour Party for a total of seventeen momentous years and was Prime Minister in two Labour Governments.

We can pay tribute to his early influence; we can deprecate the tragedy of his final years, but we cannot ignore him. I knew this remarkable man as intimately as most in the years of his triumph, and I later had to analyse his character when we were bitter opponents.

For many years I was a frequent visitor to his home, calling at his request many times when he felt in need of a confidant. I used to sit and listen to him in his modest semi-detached house in Belsize Park, North London, and afterwards in the more roomy house, Frognal Lodge. He could be most expansive in conversation when he conceived a liking for anyone, and he then loved to talk from the heart about policy, about his colleagues and about the future of the Party. Often he was critical of some of his colleagues. I remember particularly his dislike for Snowden who, he stated, was no orator and no Socialist, but a Liberal, both in thought and action.

It was somewhat embarrassing to have to listen to the same sort of criticism from Snowden, who would ask me to tea with his wife Ethel at their Golders Green home. Snowden had neither admiration nor affection for MacDonald. I have little doubt that this flattering position of being a repository for the confidences of both was because each wanted to attach me, as one of the younger men of the party, to his strings. Such was the self-interest and mutual animosity of the two main figures of the 1931 political disaster.

To dismiss MacDonald as a traitor to Labour is nonsense. His contribution in the early years was of incalculable value. His qualities as a protagonist of Socialism were of a rare standard. There has probably never been an orator with such natural magnetism combined with impeccable technique in speaking in the party's history. Before the First World War his reputation in international Labour circles brooked no comparison. Keir Hardie, idolized by the theorists in the movement, did not have the appeal to European and American Socialists that MacDonald had. There is no doubt that his international prestige equalled that of such men as Jaurès and Adler. Among his people in Scotland he could exert almost mesmeric influence.

No one has ever completely explained the magnetism of MacDonald as a young man. He was the most handsome man I have ever known, and his face and bearing can best be described by the conventional term "princely." Partly this was due to the spiritual qualities which are so often found in the real Northern Scottish strain, with its admixture of Celtic and Norse blood. Some of it probably came from the paternal ancestry which gave him aristocratic characteristics and marked him as a leader of men. Lesser men might despise this suggestion of heredity; the people who loved him in those early days recognized it as an inborn quality. It also put him in Parliament. Leicester was intrigued about this Labour candidate who was the sole opponent of the Tory in 1906. If he had been an uncouth firebrand it is unlikely that he would have found much favour. The immense Liberal vote was his from the start. The Liberals and sentimentalists were utterly charmed by this handsome idealist whose musical voice wove gently round their spell-bound hearts. He won that election by emotionalism rather than intellect—as others before and since have won elections.

Success solely on such a basis is transitory. MacDonald showed that he had qualities greater than the ability to dress facts in a cloud of metaphors. Four years later, in 1910, he retained Leicester in two elections with an increased majority.

These years represented the zenith of MacDonald's physical and mental powers. It is tragic to realize that his subsequent deterioration was almost wholly brought about by overwork, and by the sheer inability to maintain himself and his family without relying on occasional subsidies which came his way.

I saw him during the worst of his financial troubles in 1918, when he had lost his seat. An article every week for *Forward* at two guineas, a series of week-end meetings for a total of three guineas—these were his sole means of livelihood. He never charged an excessive fee for speaking, unlike several others I have known. Some widowers with a family to maintain might have managed on the money he had by dint of scraping and watching every penny, but it was not a characteristic of MacDonald to devote himself to mundane detail.

This long period of struggle and overwork had a profound effect on his health and a permanent bearing on his outlook. I realized the nagging effect of his ailments when I first met him. Ramsay MacDonald was a name to conjure with in my formative years. I often heard him speak at meetings in Glasgow, but the first meeting with him was disappointing. I was at the time prospective Labour candidate for West Lothian and was to preside over a meeting at which MacDonald intended to speak on peace by negotiation. When I met him at the railway station in Bathgate his face was drawn and he winced when he lifted his suitcase. As I took it from him he said that his neuritis was troubling him. This was, I think, a physical symptom of nervous frustration.

His confidence in his oratorical powers—this more than his personal vanity—had persuaded him right up to the declaration of war that Britain's participation could be avoided. On 30 July, 1914, as Chairman of the Labour Party, he had sent a resolution to the Prime Minister opposing participation. On 2 August (a Sunday), when a huge peace demonstration was held in Trafalgar Square, MacDonald had remained at home preparing what he believed would be the most momentous Commons speech of his life. It was magnificent in its delivery and its rhetoric, and it was meaningless. In the final brief calm before the storm he could have been heard and admired by the mass of people whose interests he represented. He threw away the chance, and the silence of the House which greeted him at the end told him so.

He compromised. He was neither for the war nor against it. Personal considerations undoubtedly influenced this characteristic waywardness. The Labour Party was supporting the war; the I.L.P. was strongly pacifist. His only serious rival for leadership of the Party, Snowden, was ardently anti-war, and the possibility of Snowden taking a line which would prove popular with the Party was undoubtedly one reason why MacDonald followed a semi-pacifist policy. In his estimation he could swing either way.

Despite the moderation with which he expressed his views MacDonald was singled out by the Press for a campaign of vituperation. While his colleagues in the Independent Labour Party still suspected him for his mildness on the war question and were dismayed at his vacillation, the Press campaign turned him into a hero to the working people of such areas as Clydeside. It was in this area that he demonstrated his powers of oratory the like of which I have seldom heard. I remember his speech at the "in memoriam" meeting on the death of Keir Hardie. The two men had not been friends for some time before. Hardie was uncompromisingly against war for any cause; MacDonald was not. Yet he captivated the immense crowd with verbal magnetism which artfully avoided the topics he considered dangerous.

The audience expected to hear MacDonald, the man who was called "traitor" for his unswerving fight against the warmongers in every country. They heard a man who loathed past wars, regarded future wars with abhorrence, but carefully evaded giving his opinion on the basic question of the current one. Only a fractional number of his huge audience—the members of the I.L.P. who knew the real facts about him—realized how the narrow and tricky ledge had been so cunningly negotiated. Even more clever was the way that he drew a parallel between his own life and that of the man he had come to honour.

Closer contact with MacDonald came with a conference at Charing Cross Hall in Glasgow, to discuss the protection of civil liberties after the promulgation of the Defence of the Realm Act. MacDonald was to be the principal speaker. I was then President of the Glasgow Trades Council and was usually called upon to take the chair at meetings organized by the Labour movement irrespective of subject or speaker.

The Glasgow Press reported that an organization called the Scottish Patriotic Federation, led by Neil Jamieson, intended to break up the meeting. When I arrived at the hall there was a large crowd outside. The stewards had closed the glass doors to prevent a sudden rush, but there was no real difficulty about getting in, and I easily pushed through the crowd, was recognized, and admitted. MacDonald was uneasy about trouble, but I assured him that there was no need to be alarmed.

"You'll get a great reception," I told him.

As I escorted him to the platform I heard that the stewards were tackling Jamieson and his gang, and having a hard time to curb a sudden onrush. I went to the top of the landing and saw that Jamieson had managed to force the door open sufficiently to get his head through, so I ran down and punched him between the eyes. The door was closed and I returned to the platform, where I made a short introductory speech in favour of peace by negotiation. MacDonald made his speech, which was received with tumultuous applause, and the meeting ended.

To my surprise, when walking through the hall on the way out, a plain-clothes police officer I knew approached me and said: "Councillor Shinwell, I'm afraid there is going to be trouble about this afternoon. Jamieson had to go to the infirmary for treatment."

I was surprised but not unduly worried. Rough and tumble in Glasgow politics were part of the game, and I knew no instance of colleagues or adversaries making any legal fuss about a bruise or two. But the following Tuesday I was summoned for assault, the evidence being that I had attacked Jamieson with a piece of lead piping.

Whether Jamieson was hit with a piece of piping I do not know. I explained to the magistrate that Jamieson had boasted that he was going to break up the meeting, had tried to get into the hall for that purpose, and I had assisted the stewards in preventing him from doing so. The magistrate, after hearing the evidence, dismissed the case as "a grotesque and fantastic charge."

MacDonald never referred to this incident. I think he strongly deprecated even the suspicion of violence. This is not to suggest that he lacked courage. He would face a hostile audience when necessary though he did not relish a bout even of words with an audience not already sympathetic to his beliefs.

In 1917 I tasted something of the exasperation which his friends so often felt. The war had reached stalemate, with armies dying to capture a few yards of Flanders mud, only to lose it again a few days later. War weariness pervaded all sections of the community in all countries. Consequently, when a group of Socialists in neutral Scandinavia proposed an international conference to discuss peace by negotiation, it was grasped as a lifebelt by millions of ordinary people. At the August Labour Party Conference the proposal to send delegates was adopted by 1,840,000 votes to 550,000.

In Germany Socialists were given permission to go by the Imperial Government because it urgently wanted a negotiated peace; France was not enthusiastic. The decision of the British Labour Party was due, not to the lead of MacDonald, but of Henderson. Almost immediately Henderson was put out of the War Cabinet and the Government let it be known that it disapproved of the Stockholm project. The adjourned Labour Conference voted again, and though the original decision was affirmed the majority had dropped to 3,000. This decrease in enthusiasm influenced the Government to announce that no passports would be issued for delegates to Stockholm.

I knew with what enthusiasm MacDonald had looked forward to this conference. He was correct in believing that his great international prestige would give him a leading rôle in the deliberations. He genuinely believed that negotiation was a possible method of solution, and if he were the leading negotiator, a probable one. The power of words was unlimited in his estimation.

I determined to outwit the Foreign Office on his behalf. Havelock Wilson of the Seamen's and Firemen's Union had been the most vociferous of the anti-peace group, and it was certain that he would do his best to see that no ship officially sailed for

Scandinavia with an unofficial passenger. I telegraphed Mac-
Donald that I would collect a crew and find a ship for him.
Without waiting for a reply I actually collected the crew on
Clydeside—a not difficult effort in view of the disappointment of
ordinary people at the prohibition of delegates to Stockholm, and
I had news of a small ship which was then lying at Aberdeen.
Everything was prepared and all I needed was MacDonald's
reply giving the date when he wished to sail. No reply ever came.
He ignored this possibly melodramatic but genuine gesture with
contempt.

Yet such was the man's charm and ability to arouse sympathetic friendliness and devoted loyalty that never did I tax
him with his cavalier treatment of my offer.

It was not until his return from a visit to the United States
some time later that the toll of the lean years began to make its
mark. He was then about sixty years of age and one part of him
was longing for the chimney corner, the peace of Lossiemouth, the
position of father of the Party. Yet the movement he had done so
much to build up had all the heady intolerance and impatience of
youth. It regarded novelty as a virtue and suspected the familiar
as reactionary.

Here was the fundamental paradox of the man and the Party
as I knew them in those historic years: a man with the mental
attitude of late maturity was bewitched by the emotional appeal
of youth; a political movement which was impatient for the golden
age of the morrow yearned for the wisdom and leadership of the
veteran in the political arena.

Clashes were inevitable. They came over tiny, unimportant
matters which nevertheless rankled both sides. I remember how,
in the first Labour Government, we received the usual invitation
for dinner with the Speaker, then J. H. Whitley. Some junior
ministers, Jack Lawson (now Lord Lawson), Albert Alexander
(now Lord Alexander of Hillsborough), George Hall (now Viscount Hall), and myself (I am the only one of the quartet still
outside the House of Lords) resolved that we would not dress up
in the formal and outmoded attire hitherto essential for this
function. MacDonald was curiously infuriated and incensed at
our obstinacy.

"We must do what other people do," he ordered, and offered

no help even in getting agreement that we should give way so far as to put on dinner jackets instead of lounge suits.

The Speaker, rightly jealous of the traditions of the House, took some time to agree to our decision either to come in dinner jackets or to ignore the invitation. Eventually he gave way, and the occasion broke the convention for good. But MacDonald and some other ministers did not miss the opportunity to dress up. To us a formal and pleasurable opportunity to meet colleagues and opponents "off duty" was turned into a hilariously comic occasion by the sight of our fellow ministers. Ramsay MacDonald stood looking very nautical in a blue uniform which I believe had something to do with the cinque ports. He at least was tall enough to wear his shining sword with some semblance of fitness. Unfortunately he was standing next to the small and rotund Stephen Walsh, Minister for War, whose weapon touched the floor and continually got between his legs. Tom Shaw (Minister of Labour) was doing his best to look as if the breeches and stockings of court dress were his normal attire, but he was extremely self-conscious. Not so Sidney Webb (Board of Trade), who was entirely oblivious of the ridiculous appearance he presented with spindly legs and a short little body. It was perhaps very childish to burst into guffaws.

MacDonald had not merely acquiesced in the rule of court dress on that occasion. He had eagerly accepted it as one of the fruits of office. It was symptomatic of the topsy-turvy situation to come, one which was aggravated by these quirks of vanity and the larger and more reasonable problems which he allowed to ferment and nag at him.

The toll of the years and the burden of office made things steadily worse. I recall a message asking me to visit him at Frognal Lodge during the second Labour Government. We walked up and down the garden while he moaned about his problems—both public and private. He was a tired, old man. His back was bent, and the characteristic upright gait was gone. I tried to encourage and cheer him up with my own optimism about the Party's future. Its effect soon evaporated. By the time I left him he was again insisting that all was dark and the game hardly worth the candle.

This was the man as I knew him, and I think I can claim to

have known him well. Not even long friendship could find an excuse for what he had done to solve the crisis; dispassionate judgment could not find any hope that the Ramsay MacDonald of 1931, tired, dispirited, helpless, corrupted by flattery and adulation, would contrive a magical answer or shoulder the fantastic burden he himself piled up.

CHAPTER FOURTEEN

IN THE WILDERNESS

O N 7 October, 1931, the climax of this tragi-comedy was reached. MacDonald dissolved Parliament and appealed to the nation for "a Doctor's Mandate." The patient was carefully reduced to a state of hysteria so that the recommended treatment should be taken without thought or judgment. MacDonald was quickly off the mark with a manifesto to the nation issued on the evening of the day Parliament was dissolved. It was broadcast, and incidentally marks the first occasion when the B.B.C. played a leading part in an election campaign. Snowden gave one of the radio talks and attacked his late colleagues with all the venom of which he was capable. He had earlier said gloatingly in a debate that after the election "the House would see the Labour M.P.s no more."

He was nearly right. The wild warnings of the "National" candidates were heeded by a panic-stricken electorate which had neither time nor guidance to think objectively. There was still a steady and loyal kernel of more than $6\frac{1}{2}$ million Labour votes, but they returned only 49 members to Parliament; of the Front Bench leaders only Attlee, Cripps, and Lansbury remained.

I was defeated in West Lothian by only 600 votes, a close result which many opponents and some friends said would not have happened if I had followed MacDonald. I became one more cipher in the figure of 2,900,000 unemployed. My financial position was serious, and some friends suggested that I should take a post with an industrial concern. I was not very enthusiastic, but an interview was arranged for me. The firm was a subsidiary of a large chemical combine and the job I could have had was a good one. The managing director did not, however, take kindly to my statement that I could not abandon politics, as I was again the prospective candidate for West Lothian. That, he told me, was "awkward." Four years later I noticed his name as a successful candidate in the election, and he did not find it necessary to resign his position.

He told me to think things over. Afterwards, as I walked down Millbank where the firm's headquarters then were, I met Willie (now Lord) Henderson, an old and devoted friend, son of "Uncle Arthur" and a member of the Labour Party H.Q. staff. He was—and is—one of the shrewdest and kindest men in the Party. He asked me how things were, and I explained that the economic factors were tempting me away from politics to industry. Soon afterwards Arthur Henderson sent for me and offered me a £250-a-year job doing propaganda for the Party, and there would be no expenses provided by Transport House. I would be expected to address meetings all over the country; local parties were required to help with travelling and hotel expenses when they could afford it.

I held more than a thousand meetings during the next four years, travelling the length and breadth of the country. Meetings often took place on seven consecutive days, involving awkward cross-country journeys to get to them. Maurice Webb, in charge of propaganda at the time, and later Minister of Food in the post-war Government, was most helpful and worked out a schedule so that now and then I had a few days at home—my daughter was married during this period and I was indeed grateful that I could help a little with the wedding arrangements. In my home area and in the large towns I visited I used to inquire about the chances of a job. Not only were there very few vacancies going, but I also learned that no firm would employ me because of my reputation as a Socialist agitator—although I had been a Minister in two Labour Governments. I was, in fact, quite fortunate compared with my colleagues. There were many ex-M.P.s who had given up good jobs when elected to the Commons. After losing their seats in the 1931 debacle they had to go on the dole. Many of them abandoned political life, and if it had not been for my propaganda job I might have been compelled to do so too.

Those years of travelling about Britain taught me how

generous is the heart of the ordinary British man and his wife. In the depressed areas of South Wales and the North-East, in the dreary industrial towns of Lancashire and Yorkshire, in Scotland and many other places in the country, some member of the local party would as a matter of course invite me to his home after the meeting. His wife would always have something tasty for me to eat, often at the sacrifice of their own meals. When I stayed in such a home overnight and came down to a neat attractive table, I knew all too often that I was having "father's Sunday breakfast."

Many a time I slept in a bed vacated by the children despite my protestations, and on more than one occasion I shared the best bed with the lodger. The hospitality was generously and unquestioningly given, but as time went on I realized it was quite unfair of me to take it, so I scraped together the money to stay in the cheapest commercial hotel I could find, keeping the bill to bed-and-breakfast, buying a high tea in the evening, and making do with two meals a day.

The local parties for which I spoke were more often than not just as hard up as I was, and both they and I depended on the collection for our expenses of hiring the hall in their case and the night's lodging money and the train fare in mine. A cold, wet night or some special event in the town could bring disaster for both of us. I remember in a South Wales tour the Labour Party, learning that a prominent speaker from London was coming down, duly showed what they thought was the necessary respect by booking me a room at the best hotel in Newport. I fervently hoped the collection would be a good one, for I had only a shilling or two and my return ticket to London in my pocket. Whatever the collection was I had none of it. I did not worry unduly as I thought my bill would be paid at the hotel, as invariably happened when a booking was made in that way. But next morning no official arrived to ask me how I had slept, and the young woman at the reception desk smiled sweetly and held out the bill. I muttered that I was not leaving till later and hurried round to the post office, where I spent a shilling to telegraph my wife: "Send £2."

She was not unaccustomed to signals of this kind. How she managed to keep a little reserve for emergencies I don't know, but she rarely let me down. This time, however, no reply came, and my endeavours to sit nonchalantly in the hotel vestibule under the watchful eye of the receptionist were getting more and more pathetic. I decided the only solution was to pawn my overcoat. Newport is singularly short of pawnbrokers, or else their premises are tucked away in obscure corners of the town, for I found none. I returned to the hotel with a carefully rehearsed story about lost money and the offer of my overcoat as security. I did not need the excuse. The telegraph boy and I walked up the hotel steps together.

I spoke on every subject under the sun: social and economic matters, foreign affairs, agricultural problems, industrial relations—anything which I sensed would interest the audience. It was wonderful training. In the morning and afternoon I would seek out the public library and read through the day's newspapers. Any subject which appealed to me as a likely topic for discussion I would read up in the encyclopædias and in the books under the subject headings. The value of this was that I read all opinions on a question; too many Labour propagandists rely on party material and restrict their interest to subjects of direct political import as if nothing else mattered to the audience.

My good opinion of a town or village was based largely on the existence of two facilities for its inhabitants and visitors: public libraries and public conveniences. For an itinerant orator both are vitally important. Perhaps things have by now improved, but it was depressing how frequently the local authority had ignored the provision of these essential facilities for the mental and physical well-being of the public, and even if they had rather unwillingly provided them, had hidden them away in obscure side streets as if equally ashamed of both. This peculiarity forced me to find alternatives; both have their substitutes for the earnest seeker.

There was plenty of fun in this work. Prospective Labour candidates provided much of it. At one meeting in the North a candidate failed to arrive in time for the meeting to introduce him to his prospective constituents. I saw the crowd was getting restless so I spoke first, getting them in a good mood. When he arrived I cut my speech short to give him a chance. His first and only remark to his audience was: "I don't know what the hell to talk about."

At another meeting on the coast where over-fishing was depriving the local men of their livelihood, the prospective candidate was asked what could be done about it. I had rather expected this sort of question and had spent a goodly time that day reading up international trawling regulations, the legal aspects of the three-mile limit, distribution methods in the fish trade, and so on. The prospective candidate had a much simpler solution, however. "What we must do about inshore fishing is to nationalize it," he said, and sat down. The effect of this statement on an audience composed almost entirely of very independent one-man self-employed fishermen may be imagined. In the end I managed to satisfy them.

But such men were exceptional. Most of the prospective candidates and all the local officials for whom I spoke were worthy of their audiences—keen, sincere, and blessed with that asset no education can give: common sense.

I told of my experiences in an article in *The Labour Magazine* in August, 1932, under the title of "Ain't it Grand to be Temporarily Dead?" I said that if I had listened before I started to some experts in pessimism it was extremely doubtful whether I would have any audiences to speak to at all.

"But I need not have felt afraid," I continued, "for my first audiences—they were in the Midlands—were not only large, but exceedingly responsive. . . . But my triumphal march was rudely disturbed when I ran into a few places and found our people listless and making no kind of effort to stir things up. 'What was the Head Office doing?' they asked. 'Are we going to have a lead?' 'What's doing in other places?' 'What about our policy?' Strangely enough I rarely found the audience in dejected mood. There was no evidence of the defeatist spirit there; it was nearly always confined to the local leaders. . . .

"Of course, meetings have varied considerably both as regards attendance and the response to our message. In Durham, South Wales, and in some parts of the Midlands they have been exceptionally good; in Lancashire, Yorkshire, and North Wales fair; while in what are described as backward areas, East Anglia, Cambridgeshire, Devonshire, and Cornwall, meetings have varied from good to moderate. The variable nature of the gatherings sometimes assumes strange forms: in a constituency we have never won I had a meeting of over 1,000 eager and enthusiastic; in a safe area about 150 people attended and were hard to move."

At this time, too, the Press began to be of some importance to me. For one thing I found journalism a useful source of extra income. One week-end when I came home I collected the really urgent bills and found that they totalled £30. I sat down and wrote two articles and sent them to the *Daily Herald* and *John Bull*. They were accepted and this helped to square the account. The strangest writing job from which I made a few useful guineas was for an article about gold in Wales. I did a lot of walking in those days to the benefit of both health and pocket. My only pair of shoes were badly worn and in a small North Welsh village I asked a cobbler if he would mend them while I waited. He eventually agreed to put his other work aside and while he cobbled he told me the gold story. The district was, of course, an important gold-mining area in Roman and Celtic times. Repair of my shoes cost 2s. 9d.; I received five guineas for the article.

The other value of the Press to me was really much greater than financial gain. Local newspapers gave far more space to political matters in those days than they do now, and long extracts from my speeches would appear. The reports invariably described me as ex-Secretary for Mines and this lent some kudos to my remarks. Local devotees to the habit of writing to the editor would follow with some attack in the following issue, to which my local comrades would reply, so that there was quite a snowball effect, and the publicity extended far and wide.

But I was, and am, convinced that the spoken word is far more valuable than the written. Even if people read they do not remember so clearly as when they hear. Time after time in my life strangers have approached me and said: "I remember hearing you speak in Glasgow," and the date is twenty-five or thirty years ago. They can invariably tell me what I said, though frankly I cannot confirm the reliability of their statements for I have not a lively memory for such things. As I suppose I have spoken in public at least 10,000 times since those days in Gaol

Election campaign at Seaham, 1935. Emanuel Shinwell
with two Labour Councillors.

Election campaign at
S e a h a m , 1 9 3 5 .
Emanuel Shinwell wav-
ing his hat at the crowd
after the announcement
of his victory over
Ramsay MacDonald.

Square, Glasgow, nearly fifty years ago perhaps I may be forgiven for this.

The men who had "the gift of the gab" in the years between the wars deserve more gratitude from the Party than they get. The names of men whose oratory I have admired at street corners, in public halls, and at various conferences too often mean little to the hierarchy of to-day. They include men like Dick Wallhead, W. C. Anderson, J. W. Kneeshaw, O. G. Willey, Fred Montagu, E. Fairchild, Bill Gee, Tom Mann, Ben Tillett, George Lansbury, Bruce Glasier, James Maxton, Sir Pat Dollan, O'Connor Kessack, and Neil McLean—the list ends there, omitting so many others deserving of mention only because lists can mean but little. Of these spade-workers only Lansbury and Montagu ever found their way into the pre-war Labour Governments. The excuse was, I believe, that propagandists make poor administrators. That is nonsense. Most of these men had great organizational experience. Many had served long and well in local government.

During this propagandist campaign I was approached by Ebby Edwards, M.P. for Morpeth, who wanted to retire, with a tentative invitation to become the Labour candidate there. However, the chance came to be selected for Seaham, the Prime Minister's division. There were several nominees, nearly all local men. Rather to my surprise, I was unanimously adopted on 10 September, 1932. The news was given national coverage, and I challenged MacDonald to resign then and there to test the truth of my statement that the previous election was not a true reflection of Labour strength in the Seaham Division.

The challenge was, of course, ignored. In this and his subsequent attitude MacDonald was both unwise and ungenerous to his constituents. The Durham miner is a fanatically loyal man to his ideals and also to anyone in whom, after his slow and deliberate decision has been made, he has placed his trust. That loyalty enabled MacDonald to retain his seat in 1931. It still existed when I was nominated as Labour candidate. I marvelled at this unswerving trust as I got to know the area better. Poverty and unemployment were as bad as they had ever been since the Industrial Revolution. Only unemployment benefit and the dole minimized starvation and made it malnutrition. The manner in which some patiently endured such conditions made me say that "the people have become so used to poverty that they hate to give it up." I was also disturbed at the conditions in which the people lived, not only in County Durham but in every industrial area. There was no reason for the ugly slag heaps, the mine refuse dumps, the appalling sanitary conditions, and the slums. The whole of industrial Britain needed—as I often said at the time—a national spring cleaning.

My propaganda job, of course, had first call on my time, although I spent every possible week-end in the constituency, and with the knowledge born of many ups-and-downs in election-eering I saw that I was gradually swinging the workers to my side. Elsewhere in the country I had as hard a fight. The poverty of the depression had seeped into men's minds. They were listless with the hopelessness of their lives, demoralized by the prolonged period of unemployment. It is of interest that I have always found people more receptive to new social concepts when they are above the borderline of poverty.

There were many adversaries in the field. The Communists were very busy; the misery of the workless produced fertile soil for their revolutionary propaganda; and Transport House used to send me to the trouble spots—invariably in South Wales and Scotland. They, like the Fascists, had no time for restrained debate, and it was futile to heckle their speakers. Nor did they believe in the customary heckling at mine. Both of these parties put implicit faith in rough stuff, intimidating the audience and trying to intimidate me by persistent interjections. I can honestly claim, however, that no meeting of mine was ever broken up or suspended. If superior lung power failed to quieten them I could always win by ridicule.

MacDonald continued to neglect Seaham while I continued to nurse it. There were many who, reading of his delight in the drawing-rooms of Mayfair and the country houses along the Thames Valley, solved the mystery of this neglect by confidently stating that the House of Lords would be his home after the next dissolution. It was a reasonable attitude. MacDonald had won the seat in 1931 against Will Coxon, a local schoolmaster, with Socialist votes. The Tory and Liberal element were of little importance—about 12,000 out of the 52,000 who went to the polls. There was every indication that this time his Socialist vote was in dire jeopardy. I knew it, and so did he. Yet he visited his constituency on only two occasions during the period of the 1931-35 Government.

Even the glossy society magazine the *Bystander* was amused at the situation. On 17 January, 1934, its *Westminster Whispers* feature stated:

> "Next time will be a different matter. Mr. Shinwell has appeared on the scene—a man of brains, of personality and of experience. He has been carefully nursing the place. Nothing is too much trouble. The Socialists are determined to get Mr. Macdonald out. Will they have the opportunity?
>
> The Premier is an example to the keen young men. How has he shown his gratitude to those 17,000 Socialists and Independents who voted for him? How has he thanked those 12,000 Liberals and Conservatives who dutifully put him in? Once, and once only, has he been in his constituency since October, 1931. One speech he has made. One personal appearance, if we exclude his Hollywood habits. They should be proud. He has put his trust in them. He has left them to carry on the fight alone. . . ."

He continued to neglect them. But the fight was carried on by every speaker that the Tories and the MacDonald group could find. The hotels did a roaring business. Halls were booked simply to keep me out. Even the local bookmakers were laying odds of 2 to 1 against me. But I had the crowds—at street corners, in miners' institutes, at the pithead. Convoys of cars made their glittering way through the November mud and around the streets of Seaham on election day. They moved among the taciturn people who preferred to walk, for neither I nor my helpers had many cars to offer.

But there had been less tangible but much more powerful influences at work on my behalf than those exemplified by the "National" car convoys. A letter I received from Ernest Bevin is typical of the anger at MacDonald and the quiet, determined resolution to aid me which came from all sides of the movement:

Dear Mr. Shinwell,
   All the trade unionists in the country are particularly anxious that you should be returned to the House from Seaham Harbour with an overwhelming majority.

No organized body of men ever gave to a Prime Minister more loyal and whole-hearted support and help than we gave during the regime of the Labour Government, and nobody was more wickedly treated afterwards. When the crisis arose he did not even call the Party together to advise them the facts or to place the situation before them and give them a chance to help, and any suggestions that were made by trade unionists were turned down without any serious consideration having been given to them.

You will know that the Trades Union Congress are deeply interested in the miners' position. They are one of the largest bodies affiliated to our Congress. For over ten years now the miners have been promised reorganization and, whilst a beginning was made by the late Willie Graham, his work has been held up ever since by the National Government. Now, at the 11th hour, they come along with a promise with the sole reason of winning votes, but from one's experience of this Government it would be extremely unwise for anyone to place any reliance upon their promises. I would urge our members and others not to be misled.

The Trades Union Congress and the Labour Party have been considering preparing methods to deal with the Coal Industry on a comprehensive basis, and if a Labour majority is returned in this Parliament—and I believe it can be—the schemes are ready. They can be dealt with promptly, and the stigma of mining being a sweated industry can for ever be removed.

The same principles which the Labour Party applied to great Transport Undertakings in London can be applied to the Mining Industry, and the consumer can gain by receiving an adequate supply of fuel at reasonable prices whilst, at the same time, the miners can be given a proper living wage, pensions can be established and displacement funds created. All the misery and starvation which has gone on in the past can be obliterated.

We all hope that the miners, their wives and families, and every working man and woman in your division will vote solidly for you and say to the world—

We will not be intimidated by the threats of Mr. Neville Chamberlain and the great City Interests, neither will we be deluded by the last minute promises of your opponent.

All best wishes,

Yours sincerely,

ERNEST BEVIN

General Secretary, Transport and General Workers' Union.

Right up to the morning of Polling Day the political experts of the Press were forecasting a narrow margin between victor and vanquished.

I won by a majority of 21,000 votes. MacDonald did not stay to hear the result. By the time it was announced he was back in London.

CHAPTER FIFTEEN

PARLIAMENT IN 1935

A DAY or so after the Abyssinian War broke out in 1935 the Labour Party Conference began at Brighton. Arthur Henderson, who might have given the delegates the heartening lead on the international policy they needed, was on his death-bed. Lansbury was a sick and tired old man. Hugh Dalton moved a resolution calling on the Government, in co-operation with the League of Nations members, to take the necessary steps to curb Italy's attack. It was opposed by Cripps and by Lansbury, the former because he suspected the League of being a weapon of the Great Powers and the latter because of his uncompromising pacifism. The resolution was carried by an overwhelming majority, but the schism was there. Lansbury resigned the leadership, and the public were encouraged to believe that the Labour Party lacked policy or cohesion.

Less than three weeks later Baldwin dissolved Parliament. He fought the election under the old tag of a "National" Government, but he had satisfied himself that MacDonald and his group could be dropped without the loss of many votes.

I returned to the House and was among the fortunate minority who did so. Labour held 154 seats against the 420 National members—a majority which enabled the Government almost immediately to go back on its election pledges and to run the country steadily to the debacles of 1938 and 1939. First and foremost, the spirit of the country as shown in the famous Peace Ballot with its 11,000,000 out of 11,500,000 votes in favour of the League, was traduced by a steady drawing away from the League, thus giving the "all clear" to Hitler, Mussolini, and lesser lights of the Fascist-Nazi creed.

Among the notable personalities on the Opposition benches

were Attlee, Greenwood, Morrison, Bevan, Dalton, and Alexander. One of the earliest incidents of that Parliament which I recall was at a meeting of the Parliamentary Labour Party. Attlee was in the chair, as was his right in view of his election in 1931 and the fact that he had acted as leader during Lansbury's illness during the previous Parliament. The question of the election of officers for the first year was the first item on the agenda.

Attlee's name was put forward. I suggested that as most of us had been out of the House during the 1931-35 period and had had no opportunity of seeing Attlee in action it might be sensible to defer the election for a time. This was heavily defeated. Some hinted that my motive, because I had defeated MacDonald, was that I hoped to get the post myself. I certainly had no such idea, and my only intention was to make certain that the Party took every precaution to elect the best man. Only two-thirds of the members were present, and there was a certain aura about the whole affair which gave the impression that there was a stage manager in the wings. Certainly I would not suggest that Attlee had anything to do with this; he is above intrigue, although there have been at least three major conspiracies against him since he took over the leading rôle in the Party after the 1935 election.

One occurred in 1937 when the discontent about him came into the open. I remember taking Ellen Wilkinson to task at a Party meeting for her attack on Attlee. Her diatribe was merely the culmination of considerable plotting by some members of the Party who intended to remove him in favour of Greenwood or Morrison. At the original voting for the leader after the 1935 election Attlee received 58 votes on the first ballot against 44 for Morrison and 32 for Greenwood. On the second ballot, when Greenwood dropped out, the voting was 88 for Attlee and still 44 for Morrison.

The 1937 plot came to nothing, and when another attempt was made during Attlee's illness in 1939 it was also abortive. I was approached to lend my help, but declined. I should stress that to the best of my knowledge neither Greenwood nor Morrison had played any part in these intrigues. Plots of this kind are a natural part of the political game, common to all parties. The Lloyd George Liberals played their cards well in 1916 when the Welsh Wizard took over from Asquith. The Tories intrigued with brilliant success in 1922 in removing Lloyd George in favour of Bonar Law, but the men behind the scenes were not so successful in shifting Baldwin, on whom several attempts were made.

Incidentally, the last big effort to remove Attlee occurred during the post-war Labour Government. The idea was to persuade Ernest Bevin to stand against him, but to his credit he declined and the scheme fell through. Not long afterwards a number of the plotters were given jobs in the Government by Attlee. I mentioned this to him one day. Attlee laughed. He was perfectly aware of what had been going on. It is not bad tactics to make one's enemies one's servants.

To return to 1935, we were not only weak in Parliament but there was some division of thought about policy. At the Party Conference prior to the election I told the delegates rather impatiently that I had become a little tired of listening to the pedantries and complaints about comrades who had sinned against policy by failing to toe the line.

"What does it matter if men change their minds?" I asked. "Inconsistency is a prerogative of men. It is a disease from which none of us are immune. Therefore let not too much be said on that issue. It might go hard with many of us. Neither are we concerned with those high moral altitudes which for many of us are quite unattainable. The nearer we approach ideals the further they appear to recede. . . . There has always been room in our party for variations of opinion."

All the same, I felt it needful to warn the delegates that the Socialist League was virtually in opposition to the Party. This League was inspired and led by Sir Stafford Cripps. It began life some three years earlier as a "ginger group" called the Society for Socialist Inquiry and Propaganda, but was soon pursuing its own policy instead of moulding the Party's. The ultimate result was that Cripps, George Strauss, and Aneurin Bevan were expelled from the Party. Strauss and Bevan soon returned, but Cripps, despite steady persuasion by Attlee, did not return until the war had been in progress for some time.

Meanwhile Cripps had sought the aid of Alfred Barnes, then the leader of the Co-operative Party, and myself. He had prepared a statement which he intended to circulate. We tried to persuade him to modify it and to show it to the Party Executive before it was issued. Cripps was a great advocate, and he made us feel that we had won him over. In a court of law such methods are undoubtedly good tactics, but they are poor politics and when he then went ahead and issued his statement without a word to either of us it indicated a lack of political judgment. Both Barnes and I were extremely annoyed about this: we were just as anxious as Cripps to promote a forward policy in the Party. He was expelled as a result—an action which I am certain he had not envisaged.

Associated with this statement was Cripps's grandiose plan to form a United Front. It was to consist of Labour, the I.L.P., and the Communists. The last had gained quite formidable public support during the depression. The Labour Party reaffirmed in 1936 its refusal to accept Communist support, and I, as a member of the I.L.P., and Alfred Barnes, representing the Co-operative Party, were also adamant about Communist aid. It was this factor which we both thought we had persuaded Cripps to accept. We were wrong.

The members of the United Front made strange bedfellows, and not only among the rank-and-file. I was told of a meeting arranged at a small hotel in Southampton between Cripps, Fenner Brockway, and Willie Gallagher. The landlord, unaccustomed to notables in his hotel, prepared a dinner of the real old English type, with a fine sirloin of beef and plenty to drink. Cripps and Brockway were vegetarians and abstemious. Gallagher was also an abstainer but made excellent play with the sirloin; he told me that he had the time of his life.

But behind the façade of the United Front, with its what I might call militant pacifism, were ugly developments. Mosley's Fascists were marching up and down, and there was a totalitarian atmosphere of intolerance on both sides which was quite uncharacteristic of Britain.

I have never been able to understand why Mosley turned his back on the Labour Party. He entered the House of Commons as a Tory, then crossed the floor and sat among the Liberals and Labour men on the Bench below the gangway from where he criticized the Baldwin Government. Soon afterwards he joined the I.L.P., at the time affiliated to the Labour Party. It is strange how the I.L.P. has always had an attraction for members of the so-called upper classes. In that organization Mosley was treated with far more consideration than those who had been associated with it for many years and had worked hard to build it into a strong organization.

There was a glamour about him and his first wife Cynthia—a most charming woman—which appealed to the dilettantes who for some years were in control. Then he became a member of the National Executive of the Labour Party—through trade-union votes, before the conference decided to prevent trade unions intervening in the election of representatives of the constituency parties.

I recall a speech he made at Llandudno when the whole conference—with the sole exception, I think, of myself—rose and cheered him. His supporters sitting on the same bench with me were furious at my attitude, though it is interesting to note that in 1931 some of them joined MacDonald. I admired Mosley's debating ability and courage but I have always been a little afraid of sudden conversions. During the lifetime of the 1929 Government Mosley had the ball at his feet. The failure of the Government to deal with unemployment gave him his chance to shine, but he eventually resigned and afterwards formed his organization known as the "New Party." At this time he was still a member of the Labour Party, and if he had shown some restraint he might easily have gained a position of leadership. But impatience at the slow turn of events combined with, I have no doubt, the desire to run a show for himself drove him in a direction which soon associated him with the Fascists of Italy, Spain, and Germany.

Those of us who were in Parliament had a busy time. When there is a weak Opposition M.P.s have to be ready to speak often and on a variety of subjects. I confined most of my activities to the shipping question, but I recall one speech which I made on the White Fishing Industry. I will be the first to admit that the day before I rose to speak I knew nothing about the subject; but my flair, born of long-time experience, to absorb facts quickly, resulted in it being very well received.

I recall also a motion on the feeding of schoolchildren which the party asked me to move. I referred to the disquieting reports regarding the physical condition of the nation's children, and asked that provision should be made for supplying, in addition to milk, at least one meal per day to every child attending an elementary or secondary school.

I have often thought how much labour and money would have been saved if the facilities had been provided then instead of at the height of the war, as of course they had to be. But the motion was defeated by 178 votes to 126. It was opposed by Miss Thelma Cazalet, Tory member of a wealthy family. I was shocked that a woman could oppose such a welfare service.

The growing tension in the world and the obvious mismanagement of Britain's affairs both at home and abroad were reflected in the growing acerbity in the House. Lord Winterton once said that in the heyday of the Baldwin régime the House was like a tea-party with the "dear vicar" in the chair. That atmosphere rapidly disappeared in the last months of his premiership before Chamberlain took over. And it was in the following year—1938—that I was guilty of un-parliamentary behaviour though I felt it justified from the standpoint of personal honour.

On the whole, debates in the House of Commons are free from personalities. There is plenty of hard hitting and occasionally M.P.s make use of invective. References of an offensive nature to the personal character of a colleague are frowned on though sometimes tolerated when the heat of the moment and the anger of the speaker makes it a human and understandable error. But this abuse is not permitted to go beyond the limits: every speaker is normally careful to avoid reference to an opponent's personal affairs or his origin.

The Mother of Parliaments is very rarely shocked by any worse examples of bad behaviour than these verbal infringements. Physical measures are so occasional that they become historic. I was not present when Ronald McNeill, one of the Ulster M.P.s, threw a book at Churchill, but I was there when Leopold Amery, one of the most brilliant and sincere Tory leaders, crossed the floor of the House to slap George Buchanan, and I remember Neil McLean engaging in a bout of fisticuffs with a Tory M.P. In 1938 I was involved in a physical clash myself.

The occasion was question time, and from the Opposition Front Bench I was asking about the privileges and facilities accorded by the Government to General Franco's agent in London. Commander Bower, then M.P. for Cleveland, shouted out: "Go back to Poland."; the relevance of this comment on my question escaped me, but I thought that his intention was to be offensive. I have never been to Poland, but presumably my Polish ancestry was suggested as a reason for my returning there. It should be remembered that this was 1938; a short time later the world knew that to have Polish blood in one's veins was something to be proud of; at the time of Commander Bower's interjection Poland was to many unthinking people just another country in Eastern Europe.

John McGovern drew the attention of the Speaker to what seemed to be an intentional insult. I felt that my fellow-members would regard my acquiescence to be a sign of cowardice. I was not aware that Bower had been a boxer in the Navy, but in my frame of mind this would not have intimidated me. I crossed the floor and struck him on the face. Immediately the House was in confusion, and I walked to the Bar of the House, realizing that what I had done was a serious infringement of the House's code of behaviour, whatever extenuating circumstances there might be. Friends on the Opposition benches, however, called me back. I returned and apologized to the House. Bower also rose and made an apology, which was taken badly by members on our side of the House. Officially the matter had ended.

To my great regret I learned a little later that Commander Bower had suffered damage to the ear drum and he had to stay away for some time. It was a worrying period, and some of my Front Bench colleagues gave me the cold shoulder. On his return I felt quite certain that he would have the matter out, and in view of his fighting ability and the injury he had suffered I thought there might be trouble. But nothing happened until one day, after I had delivered a speech which had been well received in the House, he approached me in the Lobby. I braced myself up and really thought that the show-down had come at last; instead he warmly congratulated me on my speech, and so the dispute between us ended—though the incident disturbs me even now.

We were, of course, fighting for hopeless causes in that Parliament. But there is some satisfaction that many of them were transformed into reality due to the need for "fair shares" in the war and when Labour came to power. From the same period my files show a brief comment I made in the debate on the King's Address concerning the mines. "I come to the conclusion," I told the House, "that nothing short of public ownership of this industry will suffice. . . . (We suffer because of) the recalcitrant, ill-advised, mischievous, avaricious, and short-sighted mine-owners." The House was amused. More than ten years were to pass before I could inform it that public ownership of the mines was a fact.

I admit that during this period many of my speeches were harsh. The tone came from the long tours I had made of the country doing propaganda work. I had seen such squalor, poverty, and hopelessness that I had to let myself go. Between the wars, both in Parliament and out of it, my speeches ran into many thousands. I was also given the opportunity of speaking in the United States, but could never find the time. I had no illusions that America desired to see and hear me for any really serious reason. Speech-making in America is a profitable and popular form of entertainment. Rhys Davies, one of our active members in the between-the-wars era, and Under-Secretary of the Home Office in the 1924 Government, told me of his experience in a small Mid-West township. He was introduced by the chairman as Ramsay MacDonald's right-hand man. Afterwards Davies, when about to receive his fee, told the chairman: "You know, it was very flattering of you to say I was the Prime Minister's right-hand man, but hardly true. I am just an ordinary Member of Parliament."

"Never you mind," advised the chairman. "Before you arrived no one had ever heard of you. After you leave they will have forgotten you. Sign on the dotted line."

But one overseas tour I was able to make had little junketing about it. It was to ascertain the facts about the Spanish Civil War.

CHAPTER SIXTEEN

THE SPANISH CIVIL WAR

WHEN the Spanish Republican Government was formed in 1936 the news was received enthusiastically by Socialists in Britain. Many of the new Government members were well known in the international Socialist movement. The emergence of a democratic régime in Spain was a bright light in a gloomy period when war had raped Abyssinia, and Germany had repudiated the Locarno Treaty. On the sudden outbreak of civil war in July, 1936, Socialist movements in all those European countries where they were allowed to exist immediately took steps to consider whether intervention should be demanded.

The Fascist attack was regarded as aggression by the majority of thinking people. Leon Blum, at the time Prime Minister of France, was greatly concerned in this matter. As political head of a nation which was bordered by Spain he had to consider the danger of some of the belligerents being forced over the border; as a Socialist he had a duty to go to the help of his comrades, members of a legally elected Government, who had been attacked by men organized and financed from outside Spanish home territory.

In Britain, although the Government was against intervention, the Labour Party had to face the strong demands from the rank-and-file for concrete action. The three executives met at Transport House to consider the next move, and I was present as a member of the Parliamentary Executive. We were largely influenced by Blum's policy. He had decided that he could not risk committing his country to intervention. Germany and Italy were supplying arms, aircraft, and men to the Spanish Fascists, and Blum considered that any action on the Franco-Spanish border on behalf of the Republican Government would bring imminent danger of retaliatory moves by Fascist Italy and Nazi Germany on France's eastern flank. As a result of this French attitude Herbert Morrison's appeal in favour of intervention received little support. Although, like him, I was inclined towards action I pointed out that if France failed to intervene it would be a futile gesture to advise that Britain should do so. We had the recent farce of sanctions against Italy as a warning.

While the war was at its height several of us were invited to visit Spain to see how things were going with the Republican Army. The fiery little Ellen Wilkinson met us in Paris, and was full of excitement and assurance that the Government would win. Included in the party were Jack (now Lord) Lawson, George Strauss, Aneurin Bevan, Sydney Silverman, and Hannen Swaffer. We went by train to the border at Perpignan, and thence by car to Barcelona where Bevan left for another part of the front.

The reception we received from both officials and the people was pathetic in its enthusiasm. I had the disturbing impression that they thought it only needed the gesture of a few visits by foreign Socialists to make victory certain. Conditions in the city were bad. Food was very scarce and the people were severely rationed. We were given rooms in the best hotel in the city, but with all the luxury of the accommodation there was hardly any food. The municipal authorities in Barcelona invited us to a dinner attended by all the prominent people of the town. They did their best with the food, though it consisted, of course, of the traditional Spanish dish of fish, shellfish, and vegetables mixed with rice and cooked in oil. In normal times a modest amount is quite palatable, but they were short of oil, and what they had was rancid. Wherever we went it was the same, and I lived most of the time on oranges and water with what bread I could get. I must say that Jack Lawson consumed everything laid before him. How he managed it I don't know. The most eatable meals were, as is invariably the case during wars, in the military messes.

We drove along the Mediterranean coast through scenery of unsurpassed beauty, marred by the appalling poverty of the villagers, obviously in need of food and dressed in rags. This was not so much a symptom of war as the normal condition of the people. In the larger cities, such as Valencia, the stench of the slums was worse than anything I have met in the Middle East.

I considered that the dangers from disease were far greater for our party than the occasional air-raids.

It soon became clear to me that the bravery of the Republican soldiers was not going to be enough. Ill-equipped, only partially trained, lacking arms (I was always asking to see heavy artillery and was always promised that I should see it—later), the Army seemed to me to be doomed to defeat unless a miracle happened or the democracies intervened.

We travelled to Madrid—a distance of three hundred miles over the sierras—by night for security reasons as the road passed through hostile or doubtful territory. It was winter-time and snowing hard. Although our car had skid chains we had many anxious moments before we arrived in the capital just after dawn. The capital was suffering badly from war wounds. The University City had been almost destroyed by shell fire during the earlier and most bitter fighting of the war.

We walked along the miles of trenches which surrounded the city. At the end of the communicating trenches came the actual defence lines, dug within a few feet of the enemy's trenches. We could hear the conversation of the Fascist troops crouching down in their trench across the narrow street. Desultory firing continued everywhere, with snipers on both sides trying to pick off the enemy as he crossed exposed areas. We had little need to obey the orders to duck when we had to traverse the same areas. At night the Fascist artillery would open up, and what with the physical effects of the food and the expectation of a shell exploding in the bedroom I did not find my nights in Madrid particularly pleasant.

The famous and gallant defender of Madrid, General Miaja, invited us to dinner at his headquarters in a vault well below the ground. Most of his staff was there, with their wives. I was struck by the Semitic appearance of many of the women and mentioned to the Chief-of-Staff, who was my neighbour, that exactly similar women could be seen any day in London's East End. He told me that in the days of the Spanish Inquisition large numbers of Jews were given the choice of the stake or conversion, and many preferred the latter. Christopher Columbus, who was of Jewish ancestry, sailed on his voyage of discovery of America on the same day as the Government order that Jewish people should either get out, be converted, or take the consequences. He chose that momentous day in October, 1492, as a symbol of hope in new lands and better conditions for the people of his ancestral race. Truly, the intolerance and inequality which had fomented the civil war of 1936 was no new situation for Spain. And regrettably no gesture of help or mediation came from the great nation which the explorer's voyage caused to be born.

We were asked to make many speeches to large audiences of soldiers and civilians to encourage them in their struggle. The enthusiasm was there, but I could not help but feel that arms and food would have been of greater value than words if we had only been able to provide them. The most popular speaker was Hannen Swaffer who had years before reported the marriage of Alfonso and Isabella. He invariably took as his theme the contrast between the opulence of the royal court as he saw it then and the miserable poverty of the ordinary people as he now observed it for the first time. The Latin temperament found this type of generalization much more to their taste than a mundane but factual recital of the true facts about the military and political situation.

The words of our speeches were translated to the audience and the only time my less colourful remarks received more plaudits than Swaffer's rhetoric was at a training school for officers. I stood up and exclaimed, before continuing in English: "A bas el Fascismo." This delighted the audience and they were my devotees from then on.

It is sad and tragic to realize that most of the splendid men and women, fighting so obstinately in a hopeless battle, whom we met have since been executed, killed in action—or still linger in prison and in exile. The reason for the defeat of the Spanish Government was not in the hearts and minds of the Spanish people. They had a few brief weeks of democracy with a glimpse of all that it might mean for the country they loved. The disaster came because the Great Powers of the West preferred to see in Spain a dictatorial Government of the right rather than a legally elected body chosen by the people. The Spanish War encouraged the Nazis both politically and as a proof of the efficiency of their newly devised methods of waging war. In the blitzkrieg of Guernica and the victory by the well-armed Fascists over the helpless People's Army were sown the seeds for a still greater

Nazi experiment which began when German armies swooped into Poland on 1 September, 1939.

It has been said that the Spanish Civil War was in any event an experimental battle between Communist Russia and Nazi Germany. My own careful observations suggest that the Soviet Union gave no help of any real value to the Republicans. They had observers there and were eager enough to study the Nazi methods. But they had no intention of helping a Government which was controlled by Socialists and Liberals. If Hitler and Mussolini fought in the arena of Spain as a try-out for world war Stalin remained in the audience. The former were brutal; the latter was callous. Unfortunately the latter charge must also be laid at the feet of the capitalist countries as well.

So the Spanish War dragged on to its inevitable end. The slithering down the slope to war was now far advanced. Baldwin retired. Chamberlain took over. The whole ugly picture of maladministration was revealed when so-called preparations were made for war in September, 1938, and Chamberlain sold out Czechoslovakia at Munich. Labour could wield no power except those of words. But neither these, nor even the crescendo of invective which came from the lonely and despised Winston Churchill, could sway the Tories from their chosen course. We had merely to sit and wait for the sacrifice which a nation would have to make to purge itself of those evil times.

CHAPTER SEVENTEEN

WAR-TIME ACTIVITIES
IN THE HOUSE

O N Friday, 10 May, 1940, I was on my way to Bournemouth to attend the annual conference of the Labour Party.

It was a beautiful spring evening, and the scene from the carriage window gave no hint that this was one of the darkest days in the nation's history. That morning the Nazi armies had swept into Holland, Belgium, and Luxembourg. A few optimists still talked of the impregnability of the Maginot Line; far more hopefully believed that the British and French forces would dam the flood of men and machines sweeping westwards.

One thing was certain: the period of hypocrisy and lies was over. The lone figure of Winston Churchill I had seen morose and despised by his own party in the House during the pre-war years was even then moving from the Admiralty to 10, Downing Street.

The Labour Conference was to have shaped the war policy for the Opposition. Now it was obvious that it would have to decide its policy as part of the Government. Coalition was a certainty. When the majority of the delegates arrived the air of excitement was intense. We knew that Churchill had begun to form his National Government; that immediately after he had seen the King he had asked Attlee that he and other leaders of the Labour Party should join. Despite the ominous news from the Western front I could not help but find some amusement in the effects of the changed political situation on some of the more prominent delegates. They seemed to be in a state of nervous prostration; whether this was anxiety for the welfare of the country or came from feelings of personal ambition it is not for me to judge. On this occasion I was not staying at the same hotel as the principal figures of the Party and the rumours became more fantastic the less contact there was with the hierarchy. But it was a fact, I was told, that my name had been on the list of prospective Ministers put before Churchill by Attlee and Greenwood.

On the first day of the conference Attlee spoke to the full assembly of delegates. He wanted the conference's approval of the Executive's decision to join the Coalition, which was readily granted. On the second day a message was brought to me that Churchill wanted me to speak to him by telephone. It was impossible to leave the hall at the time so I arranged to talk to him at 6 p.m.

He came straight to the point. "I want you to join my Government. I want you to take charge of the Ministry of Food— in the Commons." By this time I knew that Lord Woolton had been appointed Minister of Food.

"I am sorry: I'm not interested," I replied.

The Prime Minister was surprised. "What? I understand your colleagues want you in."

"I'm sorry," I repeated; "I can't accept; but I assure you that I don't intend to embarrass the Government in the prosecution of the war."

I think that I fulfilled that promise. In the many stormy interludes which occurred in the next six years my attitude can best be summed up in the remark I made during a debate in Parliament on a motion of confidence.

"There ought to be two motions: one of confidence in the Prime Minister and one of censure of the Government." Churchill in my view became the architect of victory in spite of his friends, and too rarely because of their help.

During the rest of the programme of the Bournemouth Conference there were some who regarded me as an extremely foolish man; some who suspected a Machiavellian intrigue behind my refusal. They failed to accept the far simpler truth that I had consistently, through many years of parliamentary life, expressed my dislike of Coalitions.

The House of Commons met the following week, and I was approached by the late Arthur Jenkins, who was Attlee's Parliamentary Private Secretary. He told me that his chief wanted to see me. Despite Churchill's hint that Attlee wanted me in the

Government he had not mentioned the matter to me. I believe that he called me to the room he used as Lord Privy Seal through curiosity about my refusal to accept office. "Why didn't you accept Churchill's offer?" he asked, and added: "If the post he had in mind didn't suit you might have gone to the Ministry of Shipping."

I answered that I had no wish for "arrangements to be made" merely on personal considerations. I repeated the reason which must have been familiar to him. "I don't like Coalitions. My constituents don't like them. I refused to take office in such a Government in 1931, and I refused on 13 August for just that reason." But I recognized that in the circumstances the Labour Party had no alternative.

Looking back, I must confess that my refusal of office might not have been so immediate if Churchill had suggested the Ministry of Shipping. My forebodings on this matter were so great that the end would have been justified by the possible means. Further, on maritime matters I would doubtless have been able to gain the help of Churchill himself, who would not have hesitated to ride rough-shod over the conservatism which was strangling our life-lines of food and raw materials.

If in the thirties Churchill had been a lonely and obstinate fighter for the power of the Royal Navy I think I may claim that I had to some extent filled the same rôle on behalf of the mercantile marine. Soon after the rise of Nazi Germany had projected the shadow of future war I had agitated for a Ministry of Shipping. It was resisted tenaciously by both Baldwin and Chamberlain. No one who knew Clydeside and other shipping centres could have been unaware of the tragic position into which our shipping and shipbuilding had been allowed to slide.

Even when under pressure the Ministry of Shipping was set up under Sir John Gilmour the old attitude continued. This was essentially a Government fault, for both the shipping and shipbuilding industries had the brains and ability to tackle the problem. True, financial greed and share manipulation had besmirched their good name and their resources, but the sea engenders a loyalty and probity among the men who matter which transcends even the injuries inflicted by financiers who regard a ship and her crew merely as a business proposition. On the Clyde, the Tyne, and Tees, on the Mersey and in all our great seaports were men sickened and worried by the conditions into which this vital industry had been allowed to fall.

From the outbreak of war, I had access to much secret information about our shipping. Ship-owners, shipbuilders, and the seamen's unions willingly gave me the real facts or voluntarily came to me with their fears and difficulties. The keynote of the situation was the building policy on cargo ships. While Germany and Italy, apart from European allies and neutrals, had been building fast cargo vessels—and in the case of our enemies, ships with reinforced decks for gun emplacements—the almost standard design for a British ocean tramp made for a maximum speed of nine knots. Extra knots are very expensive to produce, and our traditional world trade routes had been built up on this low speed. This had almost brought Britain to her knees in 1914-18. Seamen, shipping magnates, and designers repeatedly told me that the tragedy would occur again.

As early as March, 1940, the shipping position became serious. In a Commons debate on the subject the atmosphere was unreal, for we had been told that we had 18 million tons of effective shipping. From my own sources of information I was able to startle the more thoughtful members of the House with some real facts. Our effective food and raw material carrying ships I estimated at no more than 10 million tons. In giving these figures I commented that the First Lord of the Admiralty (Mr. Churchill) had presented a balance sheet to the House which indicated that on balance we had lost in the first six months of the war about 200,000 tons. "If the Right Hon. Gentleman ever decided to give up politics and go in for company promoting," I observed, "and issued a balance sheet of that kind, he would find himself in one of His Majesty's institutions."

The remark was a political barb. I gained no pleasure from the giggling approval of the Chamberlain clique which delighted in discomfiture of Churchill no matter what the source. In fact, I knew that Churchill was privately as alarmed as I was. I had led a deputation to the Admiralty regarding the arming of merchant vessels, and he had received me with great cordiality. He was still playing a solitary game, and with the cards stacked against him, in those spring days of 1940.

In terms of parliamentary greatness the pre-war years were Churchill's finest. His own party, the Liberals with whom he had once sat, and most of the Labour members who had never forgotten his jibes that "Labour was unfit to govern," regarded this as the twilight of an already long political day for him. But his speeches were memorable as he fought for rearmament. The Labour Opposition did not agree with him, but at least they treated his speeches with the respect that their authority and zeal merited; not so his own ex-chief Baldwin nor the Tories who sat behind the rather sullen-looking outcast: they delighted in persistently interjecting, and in treating his warnings with derision.

I have some experience of feeling alone in the House, and it is not a pleasant thing. But never have I been spurned by my party as Churchill was in those years. The attitude of the majority of Tories was as childish as it was disgraceful. Along the stone corridor he used to walk, with many Tories ostentatiously turning their backs. In the smoking-room, where political feuds invariably get a brief truce, there were a few friends: Brendan Bracken, Robert Boothby, Anthony Eden; very few others. How many of those jeering members must have whimpered at the memory of their jibes when he was proved right and he became their leader! Unlike them, he was too big in heart and mind to bear malice for the aggravations they had delighted in making for him.

The whole Labour movement expectantly awaited the influence of its representatives in the Government. It had given its unanimous support to the Coalition agreement. It had, as a matter of fact, worried rather less than advisable about the mandate under which it should work. Attlee had said at Bournemouth that the decision was on behalf of Labour all over the world, for the freedom of the human spirit. No one could quarrel with the goal; the strategy of getting there had been left all too vague.

Criticism in the House was sparse. On the Front Bench there were F. W. Pethick-Lawrence, Arthur Woodburn, Jim Griffiths, and myself. Bevan was a back-bencher and later on became prominent in debate. Sometimes he used his debating ability and mastery of invective in a somewhat personal manner and resentment often marred the efficacy of his criticism.

My impression was that Labour members of the Government found those early days bewildering. Attlee made many speeches, but there seemed some doubt as to whether he was consulted on many points before they were to all intents and purposes settled. Ernest Bevin brought his great ability for organization into play as soon as he took office, but he was not at home in the House in those first few months, disliking the fact that it was impossible to treat M.P.s like subordinate officials of Transport House; but he had great personal courage and tenacity; my admiration for him grew as the war went on. Dalton disappeared into the mysterious by-ways of Economic Warfare and had to bear the brunt of criticism of his Ministry's consistently erroneous and optimistic surveys of Germany's supply crises. Greenwood had even more mysterious duties, and I subsequently shared the interest of members as to why he was dismissed from office.

I felt that loyalty to Labour principles overrode loyalty to Party leaders. I was a member of a democratic party. If my colleagues were being hamstrung by the remnants of the Old Guard then criticism must be made.

On 4 August, 1940, when invasion seemed to be merely a question of where rather than when, Arthur Greenwood spoke on economic policy.

Once again came an oft-repeated promise: "The Government do not intend to allow the limit of its prosecution of the war to be anything less than the whole of the resources of manpower, industrial capacity, finance, and foreign assets at our disposal."

In my reply I complained that the intentions were noble, but the methods remained mysterious. There was no clue whatever of a coherent plan. I then took the first opportunity I had had of welcoming Mr. Bevin in his position of Minister of Labour. The formalities over, I asked him about the training programme for war factories. "I think he said that he envisaged the possibility of 40,000 persons being trained in the course of this year. It is estimated on the most reliable authority that 780,000 men and women are undergoing training in Germany. The Minister of Labour agrees. Then what nonsense is this! How futile, how childish in comparison!"

Bevin was very angry with me. He outlined at length his difficulties and then added: "Please do not say there is no planning, and that the danger is being dealt with in a half-hearted way."

This, I thought, was a little unfair and I rose to correct him. "My whole case," I explained, "was designed to show that there must be an economic policy."

I had aroused Ernest Bevin's capacity for ill-temper. Perhaps to soften the impact I hastened to inquire about the activities of Arthur Greenwood. I asked about priorities of men and materials for war industry which come under his control as Minister without Portfolio. He interrupted me with a certain amount of unnecessary acerbity.

"The discussion has so far been conducted on friendly lines," I said. "The Minister without Portfolio still remains my Rt. Hon. Friend. I do not want to convert him into a Rt. Hon. Gentleman."

The position was to my mind serious. Miners, I knew from the conditions in my own constituency, were working only three or four shifts a week. Large numbers of people, evacuated from defence areas, had nothing to do. While the B.B.C. broadcast constant Government appeals for men to go into the aircraft industry I received a letter—a copy of one sent to the Prime Minister—which reported the dismissal of 350 skilled men from an aircraft factory in Castle Bromwich. The great steelworks of Ebbw Vale was not in full production. Men were being stood off in motor factories at Oxford and Dagenham.

It was an early round in a fight which was to last for five years. In November I returned to the fray. On the third day of the debate on the King's Speech the subject was war production. I asked the Ministers not to be over-sensitive.

"Generally speaking," I said, "ministers are far too prone to regard criticism as opposition, when its sole purpose is to stimulate. I beg of them, at least for the duration of the war, to be tolerant and responsive, and to open their minds to fresh ideas."

I went on to charge the Government with bewildering the country by failing to speak with one voice. "A close examination of ministerial speeches would disclose the fact that some ministers are as mercurial as prima donnas," I continued. "There is a danger of complacency when ministers indulge in fairy tales."

I stressed that the Government was not using its powers, and I cited the polite appeals to owners of machine-tools and high-powered cars, instead of acquiring them by order.

Hore-Belisha was another of the members who castigated the

Government on the same lines, and then Ernest Bevin rose to reply. There was no doubt that he was furious.

"When I took office," he said, "whatever may be my other weaknesses I think I can claim that I understand the working classes of this country, I had to determine whether I would be a leader or dictator. I preferred, and still prefer, to be a leader, and if my Hon. Friend the Member for Seaham Harbour had taken office, having regard to the speech he made this morning, I assume that he would have taken the other road, that of being a dictator."

Less than two months later, on 21 January, 1941, I said: "Instead of active and unified policy, we have seen the Government resorting to a series of makeshifts, futile expedients, and trifling devices, improvising without the vestige of a plan, living from hand to mouth, and what is worse, constantly waiting to be stimulated by the House and by pressure of public opinion."

I reminded Attlee of his statement soon after the Government was formed that it was the Government's intention to exercise effective control over all our resources—wealth, land, property, and labour. The position as I outlined it was that we were content to run a war for survival with £1,000 millions less than the enemy regarded as the minimum. We still had incomplete rationing. Prices were not rigidly controlled. More than 700,000 were unemployed. I challenged the Government to charge me with overstatement or views unrelated to the facts by asking: ". . . whether it is true or not that we have so far failed to mobilize more than 60 or 70 per cent of the nation's resources in labour and material which can be made available for the war effort. That is the test."

In May, 1941, during a dark period of the war—heavy air attacks had laid waste Portsmouth and Plymouth; Greece had been evacuated, and enemy tanks were within the defence perimeter of Tobruk—Churchill demanded a vote of confidence. I told the House that I thought there was no need for the motion. "Those who criticize do not seek the Government's downfall. Nor are they unduly concerned about personnel. It is in the field of policy that criticism rightly emerges."

"Why does the Prime Minister challenge us with this Motion?

Does he regard criticism as unseemly? Would he prefer a collection of Yes-men?"

The Address in November, 1941, gave me another opportunity to arouse the House. I reminded the Minister of Labour (Ernest Bevin) that more than a year before he had said: "Give us another six months' intensive production, and we shall have passed Germany, and the ugly Nazi régime will crumble up in Hitler's hands."

But after six months, so far from crumbling, Germany had been able to launch her attack on Russia. Since Bevin had made that rosy promise Hitler's " crumbling régime" had found the material and men to occupy Yugoslavia, Greece, and Crete apart from countries which had succumbed without resistance. Two days before I spoke the expanding German Navy had sunk H.M.S. *Cossack*; the day after the *Ark Royal* was lost.

I assailed the Government on the subject of rationing. On reflection it is amazing to realize that even at this stage of the war only basic foods were rationed. Not until a fortnight after this debate did the points rationing system come into operation.

The House was amused by my image of the Government ship. I suggested that she was carrying too much ballast. "Ballast may be useful: it keeps the ship steady. The trouble about the Government ship is that it is too steady. It seldom moves. In the words of the poet Coleridge it is like 'A painted ship on a painted ocean'."

Parliamentary give-and-take of this kind upset many Ministers, although I doubt very much whether the Premier himself minded. I wondered, for example, if he would have approved of the voluntary efforts on his behalf which Brigadier Harvie Watt, at the time his P.P.S., saw fit to make. I had been indulging in some cut-and-thrust with the Prime Minister and afterwards, in the Commons' tea-room, Harvie Watt, who came from Linlithgow and was a friend of mine, approached me and said: "You know, the Chief has a lot of worry and trouble just now. He doesn't deserve to be annoyed and aggravated by attacks in the House. After all," he continued, waxing eloquent on hereditary matters, "you mustn't forget the P.M. has great military gifts. His ancestor was the Duke of Marlborough."

"If military genius can be handed down like that," I replied, "then I should be a good critic. My ancestor was Moses."

I felt that Marlborough's victories at Ramillies and Blenheim really could not compare with the masterly campaign for forty years in the wilderness if we were to base our capabilities on that count. . . .

But Churchill knew, if his colleagues did not, that I had no quarrel with him except where he was restricted by exterior influences. I summed up my attitude at a meeting in Cardiff. "The Government needs a good outside-left," I told my audience, "but I've no quarrel with the centre-forward of the team." Later, when Albert Alexander, who was by then First Lord of the Admiralty, challenged me in a debate to say which rôle in the team I sought my immediate response was: "not that of goal-keeper like the Rt. Hon. Gentleman."

Some of the most bitter clashes I had with Churchill concerned the opening of a Second Front. In his history of the war Churchill has explained the impossibility with characteristic brilliance and conviction. This has perhaps disguised the fact that he was an obstinate and solitary adversary of an early adventure in Western Europe. Since Gallipoli he had been a great advocate of the right hook for political rather than military reasons.

Seldom in military history can a campaign have been so frequently postponed. The invasion of North Africa was originally planned for March, 1942. It eventually came off as an alternative to the American plan for invasion of Western Europe in July, 1943. Before this, with signs of imminent collapse of the Russian front, a diversionary landing in France was planned for April, 1942. This small-scale invasion was to have taken place on 15 September, 1942 (which actually marked the turning point of the war in Russia with the halt of the Nazi armies at Stalingrad). It would have been followed in the spring of 1943 by an attack on a larger scale. By the time of the Casablanca meeting in January, 1943, the Americans were persuaded by Churchill that this must be delayed until the autumn.

I was perfectly aware of the obstacles that were being con-trived to avoid a Second Front. I knew also the country's feelings about it. They pervaded far more sections of the community than those extremists who daubed "Second Front Now" on walls. I addressed scores of meetings in the middle years of the war and it was easy to sense the anxiety of all classes of people that Russia should be rescued from what many thought were her death throes. I sometimes spoke on behalf of the "Save Russia Fund," and it was quite usual for a collection of £200 to come from a meeting of about 500 people.

In the war I gained an unenviable but genuine reputation as the M.P. who received a larger postbag than any other. This was true, certainly at the time of the Second Front agitation. Letters averaged 500 a week. They came from servicemen, factory workers, professional people. Far too many of them gave an alarming picture of incompetence and buck-passing. Lack of equipment was due to production bottlenecks; the bottlenecks were there because of lack of raw materials; the raw materials existed but lack of co-ordination failed to get them in the right place at the right time. It was a sorry picture and though I upset many people in high places by saying so, ordinary people seemed grateful. Moreover, I had some reason to believe that Churchill's annoyance with me in public was not altogether borne out in the views he expressed in private.

In the closing weeks of 1943 Churchill had his momentous conferences with Roosevelt, Stalin, and Chiang Kai-shek in North Africa. It was, I think, after this conference that Brendan Bracken, Churchill's private secretary, came up to me in the smoking-room of the House and asked whether "I was in the mood," as he put it, to join the Government.

Without awaiting my reply he explained that the job he had in mind was in the Ministry of Fuel and Power. Major Gwilym Lloyd George was to be moved; changes were in the air. The only stipulation was that while the war lasted I was not to press for Nationalization.

The proposition frankly surprised me and I asked on what authority he approached me. I gathered that it was on the direct order of the Prime Minister. Obviously, the whole business was *sub rosa* and I could therefore indicate a tentative interest without formal acceptance or rejection. I told Brendan Bracken that if I did accept I would have to be given an entirely free hand, and that the Treasury must be more forthcoming about miners' pay.

These stipulations were evidently no obstacle to my appointment, and I was told that I should hear further news within forty-eight hours. Two days later Brendan Bracken told me that the proposed transfer of Lloyd George to the Ministry of Food had proved abortive, and nothing could be done about it. I frankly felt that this was a rather specious excuse but as it fitted in with my own lack of desire to join the Coalition Government, which, on reflection, had been my final reaction I was not disturbed—until I was told in the course of conversation and quite accidentally that Churchill had wanted me in the Government, but that some of my Labour colleagues had demurred.

This needed looking into, and I asked Attlee about it. He hotly denied that he or any of his Labour colleagues had opposed my appointment. Then he added the curious statement that "nobody had any authority to ask me to join."

If, as I presumed, he meant that no individual member of the Government could make such an inquiry as Brendan Bracken had done without general approval he was denying Churchill's right to do what I believed he had done. The mystery deepened some weeks later when the Prime Minister—who was always well-disposed to me and rarely failed to stop and chat—encountered me in the Lobby. He knew nothing of my interview with Attlee. He said he was sorry I was not in the Government.

"It's not my fault," he added. "I wanted you in, but your colleagues objected."

I took little note of this remark nor of several similar comments Churchill made—one as late as the time when I was Minister of Fuel and Power in 1945. I accepted it as a friendly piece of flattery which his instinctive kindliness is often impelled to show. But more than five years later, when lunching with Lord Beaverbrook, he repeated the story that Churchill had wanted me in the Government.

According to Beaverbrook he had not forced the issue because he did not want any dispute with his Labour Ministers. They let it be known that they regarded my refusal of a post in 1940 as a slight on them and they disliked my alleged aspersions on themselves and my criticism of Government policy afterwards.

That lunch with Beaverbrook was an entertaining and candid occasion. We both believed in the Empire but disagreed on almost every detail in our creed. But there is joy in disagreeing with this exciting man, if only because it stimulates his mind and loosens his tongue to voice those keen analyses of the people around him. I had first met Lord Beaverbrook during the war through Hannen Swaffer. He told me that the Beaver was curious to see what sort of man I was. The conversation turned to ships, and I told him of my agitation to get a building programme of speedier vessels. He was at the time grappling with a similar problem as Minister of Aircraft Production, and he thoughtfully observed: "You know, if you solve a problem you always get a second one."

How true this was I was beginning to realize. My refusal to join the Government in 1940 was not based solely on any emotional dislike of my political opponents nor of a rigid intolerance—and certainly not through any desire to make matters awkward for my Labour colleagues. In the self-examination which I think everyone indulged in after our sins of omission and commission as a nation caught up with us on 3 September, 1939, I formed two objectives which I believed my privilege as an M.P. and my duty as a citizen made needful.

The first was to press the Government to wage war with all the vigour the nation demanded and to use the full resources of the country. The problem of achieving this really simple end was one reason for my activities.

As the victory of our arms, if not of our aims, became more certain the second objective loomed larger in my mind. I could recall the travesty of the "land fit for heroes" I had known in my thirties. I intended to play what part I could in seeing that the men and women who had won through to victory would not find history repeating itself.

Beaverbrook's "second problem" was suddenly on top of us, though I myself had attempted to foresee the problems throughout the war. To my mind it seemed that opposition would be as obstinate and formidable as it had been over the winning of the war. Winning the peace was a task indeed. My contribution to it was sincere; it brought me a lot of enemies.

CHAPTER EIGHTEEN

CONTEMPLATION OF POST-WAR PROBLEMS

THE problem of winning the peace after the victory of our arms was one which had been well to the fore in my mind, and whenever the situation permitted it I endeavoured to speak and act in this regard. My position in the House gave me a considerable amount of freedom to do this even if it appeared to be contrary to Government policy and was criticized as a digression from the main objective. After 1940 there was, of course, no official Opposition in Parliament. But I felt myself free to sit in the traditional place of a Government opponent even if it meant forming a one-man Opposition. This was not an endeavour to obtain political notoriety; indeed many of my colleagues warned me that it was a certain road to political eclipse. I felt, however, having declined office in Churchill's Government, that I could best serve our country in this way.

My policy brought many misunderstandings. There was the occasion in May, 1941, when I refused to support the Government on a vote of confidence. There were others who abstained, but I received the most criticism. Attlee stated that the gesture was different in my case as "You are more prominent." A month later I was again in trouble with my friends for refusing to attend a secret session concerned with shipping losses. This was during the period when H.M.S. *Hood* was sunk and the *Bismarck* had only just been eradicated as a terrible menace to our shipping. I felt that the public should know the facts and I also believed that the Government was not without blame for the position. The difficulty was aggravated because I had been chosen by the party to speak. They selected Ben Smith in my place.

Probably the most serious row behind the scenes in which I

Off to Spain, 1938. With the author (extreme left) are Aneurin Bevan, Jack Lawson (now Lord Lawson), Tom Williams, John Jagger (concealed) and Ted Williams (later High Commissioner in Australia).

Labour Government, 1945. Front row (left to right): Lord Addison, Lord Jowitt, Sir Stafford Cripps, Arthur Greenwood, Ernest Bevin, Clement Attlee, Herbert Morrison, Hugh Dalton, Lord Alexander, Chuter Ede, Ellen Wilkinson; back row (left to right): Aneurin Bevan, George Isaacs, Wedgwood Benn, George Hall, Lord Pethick-Lawrence, James Lawson, Joseph Westwood, Emanuel Shinwell, Ted Williams, Tom Williams.

Nationalization of the coal mines. The author and Lord Hyndley at Murton Colliery, Co. Durham, on Vesting Day.

was involved occurred in February, 1943, when the Beveridge Report was out. Several Labour members were complaining about the Government's attitude to the report and we told our colleagues in the Cabinet that we must insist on an official view of their intentions. The arguments were long and at times somewhat bitter; they continued until the Government was forced to say that the report would be implemented at least in part. This did not go down too well in the Labour group, particularly when Herbert Morrison made a speech in which he said that he considered the report went too far.

This critical attitude to matters which concerned the post-war situation was not adopted because I enjoyed making niggling complaints in the middle of war. My motive was to ensure the better world to which so much lip-service was being paid. I had no doubt that, given a proper direction of the war, the British people would win. I knew from the letters I received and the crowds I addressed that victory did not merely mean the defeat of Nazism and Fascism abroad, but victory over the bad old ways and days in their own country. Without some proof that their leaders could be trusted in this regard I had misgivings about the unquestioned continuation of the will to win during the weary years of war which lay ahead.

I was kept very busy speaking and writing on this subject. As early as December, 1941, *The Fortnightly*, an old-established periodical of considerable international influence, asked me to write an article on "Design for Victory." In this I commented:

"It is important to remember that our failure to establish something like an equalitarian mode of living, to banish every evidence of preferential treatment for business interests or for individuals, is noted outside our own boundaries. Isolationist and anti-British agitation in the United States is quick to profit by any fact that appears to discount our enthusiasm for democracy. We can best dispel this type of propaganda by being completely democratic. In these critical times no one is more anxious than I am to preserve national unity. With the enemy at the gate it would be madness to indulge in futile internecine political squabbles. But this does not mean that we must accord automatic endorsement of every act of the Government, and sit in mute acceptance of every Ministerial statement. . . . Protestations about reconstruction of our national life at some distant date will not do. . . . The things to be done are obvious. The whole power and influence of the great interests—land, finance, coal, transport, and the rest—must be made the instruments of public well-being."

Late in 1943, the Government's plan for reconstruction was issued. On 30 November I spoke in the House on this plan, which had met with a mixed reception. I opened my remarks by pointing out that real reconstruction was hardly mentioned. Apart from an attempt to nibble at the problem of land reform there were no specific proposals about coal, no mention about steel, no plan for agriculture, and no reference to the need when the war was over for expanding exports.

I complained that nothing was said about road and rail transport, nor the future of the mercantile marine and civil aviation. I deprecated the absence of proposals for the economic development of relations within the British Commonwealth, for new industries based on discoveries of synthetic products like plastics, of scientific research, of full employment.

The Government programme talked much about pensions, unemployment benefit, and workmen's compensation. I said that these, though desirable, were not reconstruction, but the fruits of it. They depended on a vast expansion of our national income.

Not long before I spoke the Chancellor of the Exchequer had declared in the House that it would not be in the public interest to give his estimate of our current assets and of the amount that would be available at the end of the war. I guessed that by the time victory came our foreign assets would not amount to more than £400 millions, but I stressed that our internal resources, in terms of skill, technical ability, and so on, were very great.

I asked the House to ponder on the policy of Britain at peace. I warned it of the dangers of attachment to the United States economically, and of the dissension in the Commonwealth if we forged strong economic links with the Soviet Union. "Independence is, in my judgment, the integral element in our survival as a great nation. In my view—and I am not speaking as a first-class Imperialist—the strength of Great Britain in the future *vis-à-vis* Soviet Russia and *vis-à-vis* the United States, in order to enable us to play our full part and perhaps enter into co-operative relationships with these great nations, lies in an even better economic understanding with the countries of the British Commonwealth."

This went down quite well with the Tories. They were not as pleased, however, when I asked if they had considered whether it was possible for even a vestige of capitalism to survive unless it adopted new methods. The small man was being swallowed up by the monopolies. If we were going to have monopolies it was far better that they should be governed by State policy.

"I believe the solution lies in a measure of State ownership so far as the key industries are concerned, and in a large measure of State direction," I told them. "Unless we are prepared to adopt these devices there will be much peril for this country in the future."

All through this debate members were urging the Government to get on with post-war plans. There was only a half-hearted response. Sir William (now Earl) Jowitt, Minister without Portfolio, promised a White Paper on the Beveridge Report early in 1944, to be followed by others on a medical service and workmen's compensation. Jowitt had rather a rough time of it. He had to face interruptions as he tried to placate the House with assurances that all was well. He had a most unenviable task in answering queries about the functions of Lord Woolton, Minister of Reconstruction. What they were did not become particularly clear, except that his lordship had no intention of making any plans himself, but would have them prepared by the Ministries concerned. No one, not even the Tories, were particularly happy about this explanation.

Concern regarding the position following the end of hostilities was not confined to members of the Labour Party. Several Tory and Liberal members continued to press upon the Government the need for the preparation of plans for constructive development, notably Lord Winterton, Robert Boothby, Lord Hinchingbrooke, Quintin Hogg, and Alexander Spearman. Clem Davies was active for the Liberals. Fred Bellenger associated himself on more than one occasion with our activities. We met at Spearman's house and elsewhere and concocted plans which formed the subject of debate. On general political issues we were poles apart, but on the need for economic planning, Commonwealth development, the rehabilitation of industry, and on social welfare we were largely in agreement.

We decided to ask Lord Woolton, who had become Minister of Reconstruction, to see us. At first he declined, but when we threatened to make a row in the House he agreed. I shall never forget that deputation. I was asked to be the spokesman, and after I had put our case, and some of the others had spoken, we waited for Woolton's reply. All he did was to twiddle his thumbs and utter a few platitudes. The Tories were disgusted with the show one of their own ministers made.

I know that after the war few of those who were Tories and were associated with this group did much to help, but perhaps that was to be expected because Labour was in power; they considered that their duty was to oppose. Of them all I liked the honesty of purpose of Winterton. Much as I have disagreed with him I have admired his forthrightness. During the war he gave up his house in Eccleston Square for the care of refugees. He is, whatever one may think of his politics, a very generous man. Our association caused much amusement, and we were nicknamed "Arsenic and Old Lace," the name of a successful London play at the time. My comment was that I was prepared to associate with anybody who could help to further the policy in which I sincerely believed.

Among those on the Labour side who took an active part in our debates were Aneurin Bevan, Ellis Smith (a typical representative of the industrial workers: sincere and thoughtful in all his activities), Richard Stokes, one of the Labour Party's business men, who concentrated his attack on the Government's handling of the tank position, and lost no opportunity of riding his hobby horse of the taxation of land values; and Sydney Silverman, who always showed considerable debating ability, and kept up a persistent offensive. These men sought to impress upon the Government the need for a vigorous prosecution of the war, and to prepare for the aftermath of hostilities. Within the Labour Party they, with myself and several others, maintained a constant pressure on the Labour members of the Coalition—which frequently caused much excitement and acerbity. Much as my colleagues in the Government resented criticism I will maintain that even when the argument was conducted in harsh terms considerable service was given to the country by having men in the House who refused to regard a Government as infallible.

At this period my book *The Britain I Want* was causing nation-wide interest. Somewhat to my surprise it became a best-seller; a significant indication of the trend of public thought at the time. Despite the delay to the Second Front there was a quiet feeling of confidence in the country that we were over the worst and that victory was eventually certain. I addressed my book "to all men and women of good will." There was an unbounding supply of this virtue among the ordinary people of Britain. I hoped that it would not be wasted. The large number of letters I received on this book came from an amazingly wide cross-section of the community—young and old, rich and poor, of many shades of political opinion. One letter is worth quoting as an insight into the character of a man whose writings had exerted such a profound influence on thought during the previous forty or fifty years, and though he was then in his seventy-seventh year, was still pre-occupied with the Shape of Things to Come.

My dear Shinwell,
> I'm very pleased that you've sent me your book with which I am in almost complete agreement. I suppose you were asked to write it and that you had to write to the title, *Britain I Want*. That seems to have prevented your saying as plainly as you might otherwise have done, that there isn't going to be a Britain except as a part of a unified Socialist world. More strength to your elbow.
> Yours for the Revolution,
> H. G. WELLS

The thoughtful character of the mass of British people in the Second World War was an outstanding factor of the national picture—one that is unique in time of war. It was reflected in the tremendous popularity of the B.B.C. features designed to appeal to the intellect rather than the emotions, and notably in the case of the Brains Trust programmes. The principal speakers were Dr. Cyril Joad, Commander Campbell, Lt.-Commander Gould, and Julian Huxley, but I was on several occasions a member of the team. I found it most interesting. It also provided me with much publicity. There is no doubt that broadcasting, television, or the column in a daily or weekly newspaper give the person concerned considerable publicity and often help him to gain a position of importance in his own political party. This is certainly the case in the Labour Party.

Joad regarded himself as the most important member of the Brains Trust, although he was not so profound or knowledgeable as Huxley. I knew Joad as a member of the Labour Party: he had at one time been a candidate for Parliament, and before his adoption I remember him asking me if it was a wise move, as he himself had some doubts about it. He thought that it might affect his reputation. He rightly said that Parliament is a very critical assembly. But I persuaded him to run, though he never succeeded in becoming a member.

Campbell was the most colourful character of all the Brains Trusters. He rarely gave a direct answer to the question but managed to switch to some adventure derived from his experiences in a varied career. Many of them were bizarre—true sailors' stories best taken with a pinch of salt. The Express Newspapers ran their own Brains Trust as an ancillary to the B.B.C. feature and I took part in many of them with Campbell. At one of them a member of the audience asked a question about health. Campbell followed his usual habit of reminiscing. He told us that when he was a ship's officer he once served aboard a vessel which had no doctor. The medical equipment consisted of a medicine chest and an anatomical chart. On the chart the body was marked off by numbers from one to thirteen: one for the heart, two for the kidneys, three for the liver, and so on. One night, according to Campbell, when he was on sick watch, a member of the crew came to him and from his symptoms it appeared that he was ailing in section thirteen. Unfortunately the divisions in the medicine chest went only from one to twelve, so Campbell gave him a dose of medicine consisting of half of the liquid in section six and a half from section seven.

Campbell's anecdotes, and Gould's controversial evidence of the existence of the Loch Ness monster, provided some light relief in a war-time feature which was fundamentally a valuable and thought-provoking source of inspiration and interest to millions of people.

With the opening of the Second Front my sense of urgency about peace-time planning increased. Shortly after D-Day the heartening news from France put the House in a receptive mood for a contemplation of post-war Britain. This brought a prolonged duel between the Chancellor, Sir John Anderson, and myself. My view was that it was all very well for the Government to make airy statements about a vastly increased export programme. I asked about the policy when competition slowed down the expansionist policy. Would the solution be lower wages, or would we prepare for this situation by a national spring-cleaning and internal expansion involving the development of Commonwealth trade and the modernization of the transport and basic industries of the country?

The best that I could extract from the Chancellor on the wages question was: "We contemplate stabilizing wages on an inclined plane if productive efficiency justifies it."

During this debate I referred to the dangers of the monetary plan to stabilize currency which Lord Keynes was then formulating in Washington.

"I am not going to accept Lord Keynes as my mentor," was my comment. A little before this I had talked over the war and post-war plans with Lloyd George at Churt. My old enemy of 1915 had become placid with the years, but I always enjoyed his comments on the Government's prosecution of the war. He found much for amusement and reflection as he watched history repeating itself, except that he was in the grandstand and not trying to captain the team. He was not seen in the House very often during the dark days of the war, and I gained the impression that, while his moral courage was as strong as ever, increasing age had weakened physical resilience so that he had some fear of air-raids. Despite the comparative security of his country home he had provided himself and staff with quite formidable protection. I thought, however, that his prestige as the war leader of twenty years before and his experience as a politician were of value and I suggested that he should come up to Westminster and lend a hand in the Opposition.

He shook those silvery locks of his vigorously. "No," he protested. "This is Winnie's war. I have had mine." I count those war-time visits to Churt as among the most pleasant and profitable experiences of my life. His views ranged over many topics. On one visit he evinced a great interest in the food problem, and Churt was, of course, an example of a practical experiment in increasing agricultural output, though I fear it was achieved at prohibitive expense. When I mentioned to him that my wife was staying in Cumberland, my children were away in the forces or on war work, and I was living a bachelor existence in a bomb-damaged bungalow at Ewell, he said: "Ah, then you must nourish yourself with Churt soups."

He had two recipes typed out for me. On a later visit he asked if I had been making them. Although no cook, I was able to tell him honestly that I had. My younger daughter Rose, who like her elder sister Lucy has inherited her mother's love and flair for cooking, took care of those recipes, and they now exist in a scrap-book she kept, mostly full of one of my family's favourite hobbies: collecting cartoons of Father.

Here they are:

Cabbage Soup: 1½ pints of milk, half a cabbage shredded, 1 tea-spoonful seed tapioca, one bay leaf, salt and pepper to taste. Cook all together very slowly for about 1½ hours.

Vegetable soup: One pint of stock, any vegetables shredded or chopped, salt and pepper to taste, some herbs if liked. Cook very slowly for 1½ hours.

This digression of Lloyd George's did not prevent him from some pointed and lively comments on the political doings of the day. Of Lord Keynes he said: "He dashes into conclusions with acrobatic ease and rushes into opposite conclusions with the same agility."

I quoted this remark in my debate with Sir John Anderson.

Only a few members saw any need to goad the Government into action. Coalition makes for lethargy. It was fortunate for Britain that the Prime Minister has a personal sense of urgency in military matters, or the same dilatory attitude would have affected the current war efforts as they were already threatening the future peace plans. It was significant that the two most dangerous incidents to the Government's life in the latter part of the war concerned policy designed to improve the national situation at the expense of the well-to-do classes.

One revolt came when 116 Conservatives refused to vote for the Catering Bill designed to improve conditions in eating-places; the second, involving 112 Conservatives, would have brought the Government down at a critical period of the war if it had not been for Liberal and Labour support. These Tory members were prepared to risk disaster in order to retain the extra vote for business men due for abolition under the Parliament (Elections and Meeting) Bill.

To me every indication of the Tory attitude proved that when V-Day came they would contrive the negation of every promise just as they had done when they abandoned Lloyd George after 1919. Just before then he had made a statement of national needs and national policy which was in effect his own political death warrant. He said: "It should be the sublime duty of all, without thought of partisanship, to help in building up the new works, where labour shall have its just reward and indolence alone shall suffer want."

It was turned into a vain hope in 1919. I feared that we were now hearing much the same empty promises in 1944. I said as much in a little book *When the Men Come Home* which was published in September, 1944. Once again, the number of readers proved how thoughtful and full of misgivings the mass of people were becoming.

The Labour Party Conference of 1944 gave the nation proof of the things I had been saying over and over again from the B.B.C. studios, in magazine articles and newspaper interviews, in factory canteens and lecture halls, and before some dubious colleagues and cynical adversaries in the House. At that conference the National Executive suffered defeat over several issues, notably on the need to pursue a more vigorous Socialist policy. The conference delegates were in no mood to indulge in compromise. The accent of criticism was from youth. Young Army and Navy officers, many of them now in Parliament, artisans from the factory bench, doctors, lawyers, and teachers vied with one another in mounting the rostrum to give their views on a new approach with new ideas to their particular calling, industry, or profession.

Political prophecy can be dangerous. I have been mistaken more than once. There are always many ready to make one eat one's words. But by the winter of 1944 I felt confident enough to write:

"Labour will govern. The party is preparing itself for the next electoral struggle; it will for the first time produce a majority Labour Government."

I was right this time.

CHAPTER NINETEEN

MINISTER OF FUEL AND POWER

AFTER the victory in Europe there were significant signs that the political truce which had existed during the war would soon end. The Prime Minister undoubtedly hoped that the Coalition would continue. He had been the architect of victory, now he wished to be the designer of peace. Equally, there were some Labour members in the Cabinet who were not opposed to the continuance of a situation which, even if it delayed the application of Socialist policy as set out in the Party programme, would give them personal prestige.

Some had a misguided belief that the retention of the Coalition might be of advantage to the nation. They were hypnotized by a picture which as subsequent events proved did not deceive millions of ordinary men and women. The Tory Party was still the same organization as that which produced the guilty men of the nineteen-thirties. Its backers and organizers were the same men who had sneered at Churchill then, just as they had with indecent haste fawned upon him when the march of history brought them within an ace of disaster. The Tory Party never seems to learn. It continued contemptuously to underrate the intelligence of the people of Britain, and imagined it had a glorious chance to grab the reins of peace-time Government. Its coach was decked out in nice new colours, and the coachman was to be the familiar and admired figure of Churchill, though less prominent and less admirable persons would wield the whip.

In fairness to my Labour colleagues in the war-time Government it must be said that the strong influences at work to continue the Coalition were inspired by a desire to give people a chance to consider the issues and to bring the war in the Far East to an end. Although no one knew that atomic bombs on Nagasaki and Hiroshima would finish hostilities within two months, it was suspected that Japan was in her death throes, and there was a justifiable belief that the real war was over.

It was with these doubts about an election that the Labour Party's conference at Blackpool opened. I went there convinced we must fight as a party. This was not wishful thinking, but the result of evidence. Hannen Swaffer wrote in October, 1944: "Shinwell's war-time experience on the platform—certainly it has been greater than any other man's—has convinced him that the country is waiting for a change, and if Labour challenges the old-time ideas boldly it should win next year's election."

That conviction was stronger as the result of my experience since Swaffer made that comment. It was not only the workers who were thinking about a change. Employers were realizing that the nation could never return to the conditions that prevailed in 1939. I received invitations to address all kinds of employer groups on post-war policy—from Kentish farmers to Manchester industrialists. Far more significant was the increasing volume of mail I received from men and women in the forces—calm, intelligent, but sometimes cynical comments on the shape of things to come. These views invariably included the remark that the writer was giving the opinion of his comrades. The letters were also a pointer to the trend of thought of their parents and wives. Millions of people, if they did not expect an immediate paradise fit for heroes to live in, were going to demand in no uncertain voice an end of the evil things which had brought misery after 1918 and had helped to produce the situation of 1939.

On the Saturday night, when the conference delegates were arriving, I met Nye Bevan. We had both heard rumours about a recommendation for a joint appeal to the country. We found that we were of one accord: Labour in our opinion could win an election on its own.

Later we sought out Herbert Morrison, whose attitude was unknown to us. My impression was that he had a fairly open mind about the problem, but we convinced him that our chances were good and our duty to the party was certain.*

* It is only fair to mention that Herbert Morrison, when he was made aware of this reference to himself, stated that he had in fact strongly opposed the proposal for another coalition. This, of course, was unknown to me.

During other conversations it was suggested that Attlee was not the ideal personality to appeal to the elector. This attitude was, I thought, absurd. I recalled a meeting during the war in Workington, Cumberland, when Attlee gave a factual but not very exciting address. I followed him. My first words were: "We have just heard the speech of an honest man."

The cheers of the audience were as great and as prolonged as any I heard during all my hundreds of meetings during the war. They confirmed what I had said on more than one occasion when talking about the leadership of the Party and its future premiership if we formed the Government. "We have chosen Labour's leader," I said. "His political integrity is far preferable to the so-called glamour of the MacDonalds and the Snowdens." When the time came the electorate confirmed my views on a Labour victory, but I had little confidence, when I went to bed on that pre-conference night, that all my colleagues were so convinced. My forebodings were well justified next day when the National Executive met the Parliamentary Committee. Clem Attlee was, of course, there, and Ernest Bevin attended as an *ex-officio* member. There was some acerbity in the long discussion which followed, although it would be quite wrong to suggest that arguments became acrimonious. History shows that the best-laid plans of politicians can go awry in gauging the outcome of elections, and it was right that the decision should be arrived at sanely and slowly. In the event, the motion to fight the election as an independent party was carried by a large majority. Whatever my arguments may have done to influence the decision it is not my place to say, but I know that the matter was clinched when Will Whiteley, the Labour Chief Whip, told the committee that his own opinion was that the rank-and-file of the Parliamentary Party would strongly oppose a Coalition in peace-time.

Next day the conference met in general session. The news that the Labour Party had finished with the Coalition and was going to fight was received with tumultuous applause. I am satisfied that if the proposal had been otherwise it would have been rejected and would have quickly led to an irreparable split among the leaders of Labour at the time.

All doubts were banished when we got out to the country. When I was speaking in Lancashire and Yorkshire I had meetings where the enthusiasm compared with the fervour of Clydeside in the early twenties. My principal colleagues experienced the same thing, and when our itineraries enabled us to have a brief meeting I found them very optimistic indeed. We were, of course, aided by our adversaries. Churchill tarnished his splendid record as an upholder of parliamentary democracy with his broadcast insinuations of the Gestapo aims of his opponents and his resurrection of the dear old canard about savings bank deposits being swallowed up. Years before, this bogy had strutted around with great success. Now an intelligent and thoughtful electorate were amused —and exasperated. They gave their answer on 26 July, when 393 Labour members were returned.

The country gasped at the size of the majority, and it was intrigued on the question of whether Labour could govern. The convention that executive ability and leadership is a hereditary factor dies hard. I do not believe that many people, apart from "old ladies" of both sexes, expected bloody revolution overnight, despite the whispering campaign of our opponents, which began the moment they knew they had been rejected by the country. But undoubtedly many observers wondered whether the hierarchy of the party, after six years of superhuman effort in office where, in the final concept, they were on the sufferance of their normal political enemies, had been able to draw up any blue-prints of government. The aims were there, said these critics, but were the methods available too?

In honesty I must admit that they were not always in every instance as complete as they might have been. I wrote for the London *Evening Standard* during the election campaign: "Some confusion exists in Labour circles on the measures to revive export trade and on international economic relations. The party is inclined to be sloganish, and is disposed to rely too much on international terms which do credit to the idealism of Labour adherents, but may prove disappointing in practice."

But Labour was the Government and a task of government in many ways as formidable as that of 1940 had to be handled without delay. I returned from the jubilation in my constituency to London and was sent for by the Prime Minister. "I want you to take the Ministry of Fuel and Power," he told me, "and the job will include nationalizing the mines. You will be in the Cabinet."

It was a nightmare period, this transition from war to peace. There was no political controversy about the fact that for Britain the war had been a gigantic economic and financial disaster. Sir John Anderson (later Lord Waverley) summed up the views of the economists of all shades of political opinion when he stated some years before that after victory the country would be faced with bankruptcy. The price we paid was willingly met by a free people defending their freedom, but the extent of the crisis was greater than many thought. It was aggravated by the abrupt cessation of Lease-Lend and by disasters in other areas of the world.

The 1945 Labour Government possibly failed itself by modestly doing considerable good by stealth. For example, few people in this country, Europe, or America knew of the sacrifices which were made in order to feed India and her neighbouring states. Famine on a cataclysmic scale hovered over the Far East. Cargo after cargo of grain were diverted from Britain to the Asiatic area to stave off the misery—a gesture of human decency which merely resulted in jibes about bread rationing as compared with the absence of such rationing in the actual war period. Considerations of humanity apart, the rationing of Britain's bread consumption by a tolerant and modest system undoubtedly prevented political unrest in areas which had been under Japanese conquest —and I often wonder what our critics are saying now that aid is a basic weapon in staving off Oriental Communism.

In those first months of Government I recall many consultations when we were deeply anxious about our food supply—and it is an appropriate moment to pay tribute to Sir Ben Smith, Minister of Food, who quietly worked without rest or relaxation to feed the nation.

My own problems were not simple or easy to solve. I immediately took up the task of preparing the legislation for nationalization of the mines. The miners expected it almost at a wave of a ministerial wand. The owners were hardly less anxious to get out of the pits—on terms. For the whole of my political life I had listened to the Party speakers advocating state ownership and control of the coal mines, and I had myself spoken of it as a primary task once the Labour Party was in power. I had believed, as other members had, that in the Party archives a blue-print was ready. Now, as Minister of Fuel and Power, I found that nothing practical and tangible existed. There were some pamphlets, some memoranda produced for private circulation, and nothing else. I had to start on a clear desk.

My officials suggested that I should prepare the headings of the legislation, and for these I had to take many problems into consideration: methods of compensation; the composition of the Board and the composition, or even existence, of area Boards; the assets we should take over—the pits themselves, of course, and also the varied and bewildering enterprises which ranked as activities of the coal companies.

Compensation was a difficult problem. The owners' organizations were astute and resourceful negotiators, and it was a tremendous task to make an honest and equitable estimate of the value of an individual company's assets. Many pits had for years been worked without regard for the future, and a large number, through badly planned working, were nearing a stage where they would be unprofitable. Even in the case of the better pits the demands for coal during the war had brought about much the same situation. Consequently I saw that the discussion with the owners revolved almost entirely on the question of compensation. The Labour Party was in favour of compensation and not, as has been said, of confiscating the mines. The miners themselves did, of course, include many whose bitter experiences precluded any feeling of sympathy for the owners, but in this regard I may say that Arthur Horner, in my many discussions with him, never put the ideological precepts of his Communist affiliations before the welfare of the men he represented. He never made demands "on the Party line" nor did I seek his comments so that I could ascertain the Communist attitude. Nationalization of the mines was a Labour Party plan. I kept it as such, and Horner accepted the fact. We were unanimous in our aim to make it a success. Both Horner and Will Lawther agreed with me that the matter of compensation should go to arbitration.

The miners' demands were summarized in a Twelve Point Charter. The rank-and-file in the pits were getting anxious, and there were many small strikes at the period. But on the whole they were patient and reasonable. All they stressed was that they expected something from nationalization. "So do I," was my reply to their leaders. "Nationalization is not of very much value unless the workers in the industry concerned gain something." Unfortunately there were some colleagues who, while willing to pay lip-service to this statement, thought I was much too ready to comply with the miners' demands.

I have not a reputation for gentle diplomacy, but I had to exert every ounce of tolerance and persuasion at this period. For the sake of production at the time and for the well-being of the industry after nationalization I had to smooth away the suspicion of all those with a finger in their nationalization pie. The owners, perfectly aware that their days in control were numbered, were not very concerned about current output. The miners were restless and I had to make scores of speeches to them at meetings in all the mining areas to explain the need for increased production. Last, but certainly not least, domestic and industrial consumers had to be kept in as sweet a temper as possible.

One of the miners' twelve points—indeed the main one—was the immediate institution of the five-day week. It met with considerable opposition in the country, but I knew that it was a token of our good faith. With it output might not be as great as we hoped. Without it there might be no output at all. The coal strike of 1919 might well have been repeated.

The miners got their five-day week. They got better pay. I was told at meeting after meeting with the men and their representatives that I would get all the coal I wanted. The British miner is a sincere but temperamental man and I know that those promises were given in complete faith. There were unofficial strikes over pettifogging disputes. Men who still remembered years of life on the dole fought obstinately against the introduction of machinery that I told them was labour-saving, but which they regarded as job-destroying.

Dealing with the problem which arose was not made the easier because of the set-up within the Ministry. The organization was a dual one, with skilled and experienced mining men on the production side, and the administration in the hands of civil servants; many of them were apathetic or antagonistic to nationalization, but I may mention that Sir Charles Reid, whom I regard as one of the greatest authorities on coal-mining, did agree with me that nationalization would save the industry.

There were times when difficulties arose and he wished to resign, but I always talked him out of it. It was said, I believe, that he found Labour politicians impossible to get on with—except me.

The consumption of coal rapidly became the biggest problem of all. It was constantly in my thoughts during consultations and conferences with my officials preparing the Bill. Increased production throughout industry was demanding supplies of electricity and gas on a startling scale. Most factories and domestic consumers were quite unaware that a crisis was upon us. It was of little comfort to me that I had foreseen it in the war years as, for example, when as Chairman of the Labour Party Reconstruction Committee we considered the possible effect of full employment. When I was Secretary for Mines in 1924, coal was coming from 2,718 pits. The number of men on colliery books was 1,172,000 and the year's output reached 267 million tons. I now had a mining force of a little more than half that of 1924, and the number of pits had dropped to 1,634. During the war this problem of future supplies had been a constant worry to me, although I held no ministerial responsibility.

In 1940, after the occupation of Western Europe and the cessation of our coal exports there, I had visualized the steady deterioration in output. In fact production dropped from 227 million tons in 1938 to 183 millions in 1945. The roots of our coal problems were in this cessation of exports. In 1938, 36 million tons had gone abroad. In 1942 it was under 4 million tons. I had seen what this change had meant in my own constituency, in the centre of the worst affected area, the North-East. Unemployment was severe as the men were dismissed from the pits and waited to be taken up by war industry. Lives of families and villages which had revolved around mining for generations were changed without regard for the future. Huge numbers of the men went into munition factories and moved their families away from the mining villages. Among the younger men—the miners we needed in 1946 and still need to-day—many went into the forces.

I tried in vain to stop the rot in time. In 1940 I saw Lord Hyndley, then Coal Controller, and suggested that the coal should be mined just as it had been when Western Europe took it. I said that with a long war ahead the storage problem would be acute but it could be taken to the Western Highlands and stockpiled. Hyndley was sympathetic, but both of us knew that in the press of manpower problems which the war potential and the services created there was little likelihood of any such planning for peace at the time. My fears were justified. The mines which had catered largely for the export trade were allowed to slow down. The other pits were living on men of forty, fifty, and even seventy years of age.

These problems were always in my mind. When, in 1948 (no longer Minister of Fuel and Power but Secretary of State for War), I made a speech at a meeting of the Co-operative Productive Federation and suggested that we had gone into coal nationalization without sufficient examination I was referring to the absence of plans for joint consultation, not to the hectic work which began immediately after the formation of the Labour Government in July, 1945.

Some of my colleagues criticized me severely for this speech, notably the capable but sometimes impetuous Jim Callaghan, who wrote declaring that I had struck a deadly blow at nationalization. Others demanded my resignation. The complete answer to my excitable and nervous colleagues came in a letter to Attlee a few days later:

Dear Mr. Prime Minister,

I trust you will pardon my intrusion into what, according to the Press, has become not only a Parliamentary Labour Party matter, but also a subject being considered by the Cabinet. I refer to the "After-Breakfast" speech delivered by the Secretary of State for War at the Co-operative Congress Breakfast provided by the above Federation.

I have read almost every daily newspaper and most of the weekly papers on this subject, and I consider the general treatment of Mr. Shinwell's speech to be deplored. I would also add that this is the opinion of not only myself but the members of my Executive and guests present on this occasion.

Mr. Shinwell's statements concerning the nationalization plans of the Government were received by an audience representing prominent officials of the Co-operative, Labour and Trade Union Movements with understanding and appreciation and many comments were made by the guests, concerning the frank and honest way Mr. Shinwell expressed an opinion which many of them, to my own personal knowledge, had expressed previously on the basis of assumption.

In my humble opinion, and I know it is shared by many of those present, Mr. Shinwell's opinions did not in any way reflect any criticism of the Labour Party, and further, rather than do harm to the Party, they strengthened the support of these people by the realistic appreciation of the facts.

May I give one example from many I could quote. One of the guests, a man who from my own personal knowledge has given valuable service to the Labour Movement since the days of Hyndman and the S.D.F., spoke to me after the breakfast as follows: "Well, I started off with a definite prejudice against Shinwell, but his speech this morning was exceptionally good. I've always been worried about him, but after this morning, so long as we have men like him in the Party, we've nothing to worry about." Before writing this letter I have spoken to this gentleman and received his consent to include this quotation. I would also add that the company in which this statement was made warmly agreed, and the company comprised what is usually termed the " professional types."

Speaking for myself, and observing as strict an objectivity as possible, I admired the honesty and frankness of Mr. Shinwell's comments, for in my opinion he put the whole question in its correct perspective and let the audience realize quite definitely that the road to a Socialist Britain is beset with many hazardous problems and difficulties, a necessary corrective to the blissful unthinking ideas of a large number of members of the Party who imagine that with a Parliamentary majority, all problems disappear.

It would be presumption on my part to say that everyone accepts my personal opinion, but from the comments of those present, made to myself, my assistant and members of my Executive, and the considerable pleasure expressed when Mr. Shinwell concluded his speech at our breakfast, in so far as those present are concerned, his speech did more to strengthen faith in the Party than some of the speeches we have read and heard in the past from various prominent members of the Party.

As to the reading public, I cannot say, but you also, sir, have experienced what Kipling expressed as " seeing the words you've spoken twisted by knaves to make a trap for fools," and if we, and I use the plural advisedly, are to be blamed for honest expression of opinion by members of our own party and organization (and here let me say, as an Official of the Co-operative Movement and its

National Authority and a Party member, I deplore the attack made by Mr. Callaghan, merely on the basis of a Press report), if as I say, we are to be blamed for honest expression of opinion and in this case an opinion that has been expressed to me by Members of the Parliamentary Party and which is in fact printed in a book written by one of the group, then the freedom, I and many others in the Party have worked for, is of a diminishing quality in the Labour Party.

I have presumed to write in this strain because I detest injustice and I consider that in this case an injustice has been perpetrated, first by the Press, who desire to make party capital at any cost, and secondly by a person, who in my opinion, should have known better.

I must apologize for the length of this letter, but feel sure that you will appreciate the desire that prompts me to write it. I think I need hardly add that I have not met Mr. Shinwell, either before or since this occasion.

> I am,
> Sir,
> Yours faithfully,
> ARTHUR HEMSTOCK, A.I.I.A.,
> *Secretary*,
> *The Co-operative Productive Federation Ltd.*

Member National Co-operative Authority and Joint Parliamentary Committee of the Co-operative Congress.

It is sometimes forgotten that the fuel crisis came upon us before nationalization took effect: the private owners were still in control. This factor may have caused a minor decrease in output but it would not have staved off the shut-down of industry. If the years of mismanagement and strife are ignored then the coal shortage cannot be blamed on any section of the industry.

Industrial activity with full employment made the coal situation at the electricity power stations and gasworks alarming. Gas production increased from 2,020 million therms in 1945 to 2,239 millions in 1946—a record. Electricity, with 38,611 million units in 1945, went up to 42,742 millions in 1946.

The Central Electricity Board, then in control of the grid scheme, could not, of course, have forecast this phenomenal increase. There was no precedent for it. The officials gave me the best estimates of their future fuel needs which their experts could prepare, but the figures were constantly altered. By the time I gave the House of Commons an estimate the figure would be out of date, as the new reports from the power stations were being submitted. I was in the hands of the experts; they were in the hands of economic factors which they could neither foresee nor control.

CHAPTER TWENTY

THE FUEL CRISIS OF 1947

THE coal crisis, so far as the public was concerned, began with the great freeze-up which started in the latter part of January, 1947. The risks of such a crisis had been occupying our attention at the Ministry of Fuel and Power for at least seven months.

On 17 June, 1946, I drew the attention of my colleagues to declining manpower, low rate of output, and high rate of absenteeism, and asked that steps should be taken to increase the attractiveness of the industry. The number of men in the pits was falling at an average rate of 1,000 a month during that year, and clearly something was wrong with mining as compared with other forms of employment.

On 30 July, 1946, an extra ration of meat was approved: 1s. worth a week to be given solely to underground workers, and in cases where miners took main meals in the canteens the units of extra rations had to be surrendered.

The next day I suggested methods of bridging the gap: increased production of open-cast coal, substitution by industry of coke for coal, improved distribution arrangements to reduce stocks standing idle at distribution points; economies by gasworks; increased use of fuel oil. I added that even if these measures were successful a gap of 4½ million tons would have to be bridged by increased production. It was agreed that I should be given the highest priority for production of mining machinery and equipment, and for the allocation of steel supplies to the mining industry; that a coal-oil conversion programme should be prepared, and that any suitable civil engineering equipment held by the services should be taken for open-cast mining operations.

On 16 September, 1946, I became apprehensive about the number of coal wagons under repair and wanted to move as much coal for domestic and public-utility purposes as possible before the end of October. Co-operation between the Minister of Transport and myself was essential to cut out transport delays, to give coal priority on the railways, and to find labour for wagon repair.

On 17 October, 1946, I submitted a revised deficit for the end of the year of $3\frac{1}{2}$ million tons. This could be met only by increased production. My proposals for global allocations of coal and making selected cuts on industrial consumers were approved.

On 22 November, 1946, I forecast that at the present rate of rail movement there was the likelihood of 1,100,000 tons of coal being immobilized in the production areas. I proposed immediate reduction of passenger-train services, prohibition of non-essential rail movements of freight traffic, consideration of the labour being used for manufacture of rolling stock for export which could have been used to repair locomotives and wagons.

On 15 November I submitted a scheme to cut deliveries, as distinct from allocations, for non-essential consumers to the weekly average in November.

On 26 November, 1946, the scheme was approved except that the gas and electricity consumption figure was cut to $97\frac{1}{2}$ per cent of the November figure.

On 3 January, 1947, five weeks before the actual crisis occurred, I warned my colleagues of the likelihood of a breakdown of electricity supply because of decreasing coal stocks and increasing consumption. Vigorous action was taken in reply to my demands. It was agreed that movement of commodities like iron ore should be delayed, movement of surplus Government stores stopped for a month, road haulage used for coal transport over short distances; as much coal as possible to go by sea; and twenty-eight of the "austerity" locomotives built for the rehabilitation of Europe brought back to Britain.

Other moves were to examine further the possibility of diverting workers on export rolling stock to repairs, cancellation of special trains, steps to clear congestion in the railway sidings by overtime and reduction of absenteeism, revision of fuel allocation to industry with increased deliveries to the power stations at the expense of industry. But there were to be no further steps to limit consumption of electricity or installation of equipment.

A week later, on 10 January, 1947, I proposed further measures: reduction of street lighting, lower setting of thermostats, extension of existing restrictions to smaller industrial undertakings, close-down of the B.B.C. at 11 p.m., and alteration of gas and electricity tariffs to discourage consumption. I also asked that consideration be given to the reduction of consumption by hotels and places of amusement.

These proposals came shortly before the blizzard which swept the country and started the freeze-up. On 5 February I reported that the Central Electricity Board had warned me of the impending close-down of power stations all over the country unless coal was forthcoming. The Central Electricity Board suggested that all supplies to industrial consumers would have to be cut off except in the vital services of food, water, sewage, and so on. I recognized the difficulty of the situation but felt that such cuts were very severe, and I asked for a daily review of the situation before they were imposed. I then prepared an emergency scheme and also arranged for the armed services to help in transport of coal and snow clearance.

On 7 February, 1947, weather conditions worsened, and as hardly any coal could be moved electricity restrictions were imposed. I have given a complete personal diary extracted from my official notes without comment. It indicates that, whatever were the causes of the crisis—increasing industrial production, failure to produce sufficient coal, transport difficulties— unawareness was not responsible.

I have been bitterly criticized for what was called "undue optimism" in the summer and autumn of 1946. I have no intention whatever of denying that I made optimistic speeches about the coal situation.

The reason may perhaps be simply expressed by the comment made to me by the late King George VI when he asked me about the newspaper reports of a coming coal shortage. I told him the facts, of course, and he remarked: "It's sometimes difficult for a Minister to say in public what he knows and says in private."

Miners were not only my constituents. They were my friends. I had faith in them, and the statistics on my desk in the summer of 1946 gave no reason to alter that faith. The much-advertised absenteeism did not affect 85 per cent of the men who worked steadily and hard in the worst job in the country. Many a miner had a "chip on his shoulder" for he has been victimized too often in the past. I believed that in spite of fewer men the coal would be produced. I may have erred in not finding expert advice to forecast the phenomenal rise in industrial consumption of coal and power, but I could not prophesy the weather. When the freeze-up started more than a million tons of coal were at the pits, and in the railway sidings, in the early stages of transit. At the height of the North-East storm one hundred colliers were held up on Tyne- and Tees-side, unable to reach the Thames.

As the man responsible for fuelling the nation I could not help but feel many misgivings at the accent put on export trade irrespective of the needs of the coal industry. I recall at the outset of my career in the Ministry of Fuel visiting a Manchester electrical engineering works and seeing forty or fifty generators marked "export." I knew that they would have been an almost priceless investment if installed in Britain, whatever the actual revenue in foreign currency from their export sale might be. I wanted modern mining equipment for an industry which had been allowed to run down and was hopelessly old-fashioned. The United States was the only country making much of the equipment. My plea for dollars to buy this equipment was at first regarded as inimical to the country's economy. When I wished to develop open-cast coal-mining, so successful in meeting urgent war-time needs, I met with bitter opposition from landowners and from scores of M.P.s on both sides of the House. There was also a machinery problem. When I heard of a triumph of British engineering—an enormous grab—which had been made and was ready for shipping to Finland, so desperate was I to get this machine that I took possession of it. I was severely questioned by Sir Stafford Cripps, who was naturally anxious to increase exports, on this admittedly unethical move, and the machine duly went to Finland.

It was natural that the Tories and the newspapers should attack me when the misery of the freeze-up began. I expected it, and would have been disappointed in them if they had not apportioned some blame to me. It was, however, disconcerting to find that some of my colleagues sought to lay all the blame on my shoulders. Some refrained from saying anything in public but made up for it in private. Their off-the-record comments inevitably came to my ears as fast as if they had made them at a Press conference. A few of my colleagues were notable exceptions. Attlee defended me in no uncertain fashion in a speech in Lancashire a few weeks after the crisis ended. Jim Griffiths was also a constant tower of strength and encouragement in this worrying period of my career which has had its share of crises and periods of loneliness in the wilderness of politics.

Aneurin Bevan was anxious to help but could do little. Herbert Morrison, whom I saw in hospital, was quite powerless because of illness. George Isaacs gave me quiet and valued encouragement.

Cripps sent me a welcome letter at the height of the crisis:

My dear Mannie,

I want you to know how much I sympathize with all your difficulties in the present critical time. You have had to bear the brunt of a situation that has come upon us and I know how terribly anxious and worried you have been.

I am sure that all your colleagues are anxious to help in every way they can and to share both the responsibility and the kicks!

Good luck to you,

(Sgd.) STAFFORD

There were also hundreds of letters from the rank-and-file of the Party, both in the House and outside, which showed great sympathy. As I have experienced on other occasions, the more virulent the Press campaign the greater the number of messages of good will which arrived. Fleet Street is often unaccountably out of touch with national sentiment—and especially as regards the British sense of fair play. Many of these letters came from men and women who stressed that they disliked my politics but regretted my being pilloried on exaggerated charges of incompetence. The letters from workers—many unemployed because of lack of fuel and power for their factories—were simple and short. They showed that even in such a testing time the ordinary people had not lost sight of basic principles or lost their loyalty.

Of course, there were the anonymous letters—fascinating

material for a psychologist because of their venom and indecency. I often wondered why these ladies and gentlemen, with their very expensive note-paper, troubled to hide their identity. I could have respected a signed attack, however wild and personal. The anonymous attack, sinister with its prurient asides, can only arouse pity.

Spring came and with it the situation eased and the outcry died down. My personal difficulties continued unabated, however. Those in the party who were hostile were gleeful when Cripps declared that the fuel crisis had cost the nation £200 millions. How this figure was arrived at I do not know. I personally consider that it was a wild exaggeration, but I realize that any estimate is meaningless. He might have made if £2,000 millions and backed it with some superficially convincing statistics.

I did not enhance my popularity when the Press started a storm of abuse because of my "tinker's curse" reference. It was alleged that I did not value any Briton who was not among the organized workers at even this lowly price. Remarks of that kind, true or not, do not in fact affect elections one way or the other— the British public is too level-headed to vote for or against a party because of one remark by one man—but some of my Cabinet colleagues were much alarmed at the harm I had done and about the effect at the next election. It was said I had insulted the middle classes.

Fortunately, the remark was made in a speech which, though made, as is my custom, without precise written preparation was taken down verbatim by a shorthand writer. The occasion was the conference of the Electrical Trades Union at Margate in May, 1947. The relevant passage was:

> "That there should be criticism of the Labour Government does not surprise me; that there should be criticism of the Labour Goverment is quite proper in the circumstances. There is nothing like criticism for urging you on to the right things and doing them speedily and effectively. There is nobody in the Labour Government, certainly not myself, who would complain for a single moment about criticism. We know that you, the organized workers of the country, are our friends—and indeed it could not be otherwise. As for the rest, they do not matter a tinker's curse. (Acclamation)."

There was no reference to the middle classes at all, and the passage dealt only with my reaction to criticism of the Labour Party, its value and lack of value.

The coterie of the party which heartily disliked my handling of the fuel crisis became more stringent in their demands for my removal. The Prime Minister took no notice of them for some time, but eventually summoned me to his office and said that he was considering making a change. The Minister of Fuel was no longer to be in the Cabinet.

My meeting with the Prime Minister was quite brief. It was clear that the Cabinet reshuffle was only beginning. I was offered the War Office, and at once firmly refused it. I was then asked to think over three possibilities: Minister without Portfolio with a Cabinet seat, Minister of Defence, or remain as Minister of Fuel —the last very doubtful.

I was again summoned to the Prime Minister's room a day or two later, and gained the impression that there was some anxiety lest I should go to the Back Benches. Attlee told me that the Minister without Portfolio would have to go to the Lords, so that was out. There was no vacancy in Defence. As regards staying in Fuel—"there was no chance at all of my staying." In confirmation of this he had Whiteley, the Labour Whip, come in who confirmed that there was criticism of me in the Parliamentary Labour Party over the fuel crisis. I was left in no uncertainty. It was the War Office or nothing.

In all sincerity I can say that my motive in not immediately deciding to go to the Back Benches was out of Party loyalty. An old campaigner like myself had seen too much of the struggle to attain the Party's present position, and had known too much of the fatal weakness which internecine strife could bring, to make a gesture of personal satisfaction. I was then Chairman of the Labour Party. I had been dubbed the "miners' best friend." Strong elements of the trade unions were wholly on my side. I was a minister. My resignation would have caused a political sensation and serious dissension. If I wanted to cause trouble this was the time to resign from the Government; if I wished to consolidate the Party this was the time to suppress personal desires for a show-down.

My mind was finally made up after a conversation with my

late friend Harold Laski. He considered that there was plenty of scope for a reorganizing hand in the War Office, and plenty to do to make soldiering a better profession. At the end of our conversation, in which Colonel Wigg, my Parliamentary Private Secretary, took part, I lifted my telephone and spoke to Attlee. I told him that I would accept the Secretaryship of State for War, but added that I was not happy about it. Nor were my family and many of my friends; they thought I should resign.

It was with no surprise that I learned soon afterwards that Hugh Gaitskell was to be promoted from his position as Parliamentary Secretary to be Minister of Fuel and Power. With Cripps Minister for Economic Affairs and Dalton starting his brief term as Chancellor of the Exchequer it was virtually certain that Gaitskell would be their nominee. He had done good work on the committee stages of the Coal and Electricity Bills. His abilities in this regard had assiduously been made known to the Prime Minister. It is a tradition for a Parliamentary Secretary to dream of the day when he will be at the head of a Ministry, and Gaitskell, with his ability, and strong ambitions, was one who was fortunately able to achieve this goal more quickly than most.

But he seems to have had as difficult a task as I did—as, indeed have all my successors—Noel Baker and Geoffrey Lloyd. There is still a coal crisis, and as I write in the autumn of 1954 I can only trust more miners are at work, and that the winter ahead is not like that of 1946-47. Such an experience is more than enough for one century.

The announcement of my transfer from Fuel to War had considerable repercussions. I was flattered to learn that Washington was interested. The Ambassador to Great Britain, Lewis W. Douglas, in testimony to the Senate Foreign Relations Committee, was asked by Senator Connally whether the fact that I was out of the Ministry of Fuel had brought about any change of policy.

"His successor has not been in office for any period of time," Mr. Douglas replied, "but I think there will be a change in policy."

Praise comes from unexpected places. Connally commented: "I think Shinwell is a very able man. I heard him debate in the House of Commons with Mr. Eden, and I thought he made a very fine showing." Yet I wonder why the United States

Government were concerned about a moderate policy in a British Government Department. Had I been too ready to concede to the miners' demands?

Interest in the change was aroused nearer home and was much more important. The Labour Party in my own constituency of Seaham called upon the Prime Minister to give a full explanation of the reasons for my exclusion from the Cabinet and why I was not permitted to remain at the Ministry of Fuel and Power. My friends there were very angry and mystified and insisted that I should visit them. I held a meeting at Blackhall Colliery which was attended by more than a thousand men. The chairman was Councillor George Pritchard, one of the most respected of miners' lodge officials, and he made a very pugnacious speech, calling my transfer "an affront to the miners" and a "tragedy." There was mounting excitement as he concluded with a resolution condemning the Prime Minister for yielding to pressure and insisting that if I were not left at the Ministry of Fuel the men in the area would strike.

I would be an emotionless person if I had not felt gratified by the loyalty of the men for whom to the best of my ability I had worked, but I was disturbed by the applause and electric atmosphere. I had news of other mining areas where similar moves were being discussed. The Press was present in unusually large numbers, including many political correspondents from London. They also were expecting some sensationalism. I disappointed them. I wanted no strike, no demonstration. "I remain a member of the team, and I shall play ball with the rest," I said at the outset of my speech.

One or two pressmen put away their note-books. Their journey had been in vain. There was not even a sentence to be taken out of context and used for a scare headline.

There have been times when I have upset reporters by complaining about newspaper reports. I may say that there have been many more times when journalists have upset me by unfair treatment. I have many friends in Fleet Street and among the editorial staffs of the provincial newspapers. I know that the shorthand reporter does an accurate and conscientious job. He would be fired if he did not. I wish I could say as much for the sub-editors at the offices who write the headlines and re-write the reports. At the sub-editor's table objectivity ends and policy enters. The constant quest for a story angle does on occasion garble and distort stories. That is what I am told by journalists themselves. But I bear no malice: on the whole I have lost nothing through Press criticism.

I returned to London to clear away my papers—records of the stormiest period of my career. The same day I was asked to make a brief statement on my aims in my new job at the War Office. "I would like to do as much for the soldiers as I did for the miners," I replied. I do not think it was a bad ambition.

CHAPTER TWENTY-ONE

THE WAR OFFICE

M Y appointment to the War Office caused, as I expected, a certain furore in the Press, and the Tory Party tried to make political capital out of it, with little regard for any considerations of patriotism. My personal feelings, apart from the vestiges of resentment at the change, were pleasant enough. I knew the War Office and was quite unafraid of the General Staff.

The Permanent Secretary of the War Office, Sir Eric Speed, was, I knew, unfavourably disposed towards Socialism, but the tradition that the best type of civil servant is above politics is no mere convention; it is a fact. My previous experience with Sir Ernest Gowers at the Mines Department and of Sir Herbert Creedy at the War Office was convincing. Unfortunately there are some who allow their personal political views to colour their actions if the Minister fails to assert himself and keep policy securely in his own hands. Sir Eric gave me every assistance in departmental matters until he left for Australia to take up a private financial post—an unusual move for a civil servant. Most of them accept the fact that the heads frown upon anyone succumbing to the temptation of the richer rewards and better prospects which often come their way in commerce and industry. About the only serious difference of opinion that we had was on the subject of national servicemen. Sir Eric had doubts as to whether vast numbers of them could be used in key defence situations; I felt that given justice, a worthy cause, and a country worth fighting for, backed by proper administration and decent conditions of service, a citizen's army could ably promote our security.

I had not been in office more than a day or two before Montgomery came to my room. I knew there was great speculation

At the War Office: the author (then Secretary of State for War)
with Viscount Montgomery (then C.I.G.S.).

With the soldiers. Emanuel Shinwell (Minister of Defence) surrounded by
men of the 49th Armoured Division, Territorial Army, in camp at
Tidworth, Hampshire.

Washington, 1950: With the American Secretary of State,
General George C. Marshall.

Washington, 1950: With Harry S. Truman (then President of
the United States) and M. Picciardi, Italian Minister of Defence,
after a conference with Truman and his Cabinet.

(*Above*): Washington, 1950: Memorial ceremony at Arlington Cemetery. With the author (second from right) are Marshal of the R.A.F., Sir John Slessor (extreme right), Sir Anthony Eden (at author's right), General Bradley, United States Chief of Staff (second from left, middle row), and Field-Marshal Sir William Slim (at left of middle row).

(*Right*): N.A.T.O. delegation meeting at Brussels, December, 1950. With Emanuel Shinwell (Minister of Defence) are Ernest Bevin (Foreign Secretary) and Sir John Slessor (Chief of Air Staff).

(*Right*): N.A.T.O. Conference at Washington, 1950. Dean Acheson, then American Secretary of State, sits at the left of the author.

(*Below*): With General Dwight D. Eisenhower, January, 1951. Emanuel Shinwell greets General Eisenhower (then Supreme Commander of the North Atlantic Treaty Forces in Europe), on the latter's arrival at Northolt aerodrome. The General was on a tour of N.A.T.O. countries.

as to how we should get on, and some wishful thinking in some quarters that the C.I.G.S. might use his well-known forth-rightness to make matters awkward for me, thereby not only ending my connexion with the War Office but smashing my political career for good and all.

Shortly before the time for his appointment Lt.-General Browning, the Military Secretary, introduced himself. He was pleasantly outspoken and told me jocularly that the generals were going to resign. "They won't have you here," he told me.

I laughed politely, not knowing how much truth there was behind the lightly spoken statement. In fact, as later experience proved, I think there was more in it than I suspected at the time. On the day I left office two and a half years later to go to the Ministry of Defence, Sir James Steel, the Adjutant-General, repeated the resignation story and then added: "Now we really are going to resign because you're leaving us." Steel, like Monty, an Ulsterman, is one of the shrewdest men I have met. When he gave advice I knew it was the epitome of careful consideration and given only after cautious deliberation.

Then Monty came into the room. Damon Runyon would have described his greeting as "the loud hello." I gave an equally friendly response, and, although we had only met at formal gatherings in the past, by the end of our chat we were on terms of old friendship. As he left I said that I would in future call him Monty, as other titles were too formal. He agreed.

So began a friendship of which I am proud. I liked him for his genuineness and his single-mindedness. He had a gentle humour which on occasion could lighten life's minor exaspera-tions. There was one general whose grim and melancholy attitude aggravated me. I asked Monty to arrange for someone else to take his place so far as personal contact with me was concerned.

Monty pondered a moment. Then he advised me: "Take him out one night and make him tight. That will change him."

I never risked it, though I had the means. Monty had his allotment of whisky from N.A.A.F.I. now and again; he used to give it to me with a warning to use it only as a medicine. I agreed to keep his exclusively for this purpose, but any other Scotch I got hold of would be treated in the usual manner. When Monty left my supplies ended. Field-Marshal Slim, his successor, is abstemious but is not an abstainer.

Monty is, of course, a legend, and as in most legends, the details expounded about him are largely inaccurate. Those who at best know him at second-hand claim that he is intolerant and didactic. It is true that he would argue on behalf of his own viewpoint with all the vigour and obstinacy of an experienced politician, but in all my dealings with him both at the War Office and at the Ministry of Defence I can claim that he never tried to force his views on me instead of winning me over by discussion.

He was adamant about any impropriety in the service. His sense of absolute incorruptibility meant that any offender, whether general or private, would have to be punished. There was a case of a high-ranking officer about whom there were grave suspicions. He had influential friends who saw both Monty and myself on his behalf. Monty would not give way, and I supported him. This loyalty to the service could also produce implicit faith in a man who served it well. He would fight tooth and nail for such soldiers. I did not personally care for one general and refused to have him near me. Monty knew that I never allowed such personal feeling to colour my decisions—there were some men for whom I suggested advancement even though I disliked them personally as much as I admired their ability—but he was anxious that the breach between us should be healed. He was at pains to tell me one day. "You know, —— has a great admiration for you." Few soldiers who have risen high since the dark days of the war can know how quietly and steadily Montgomery has probably fought on their behalf for advancement.

The only criticism which a hypocritical world can make about Monty is that he is transparently honest. He will never mince his words and nobody, however important, is left in any doubt about his views on any subject which comes within his purview. I did not find him severe or strait-laced; on the contrary his temperament was easy, humorous and broadminded. Because, as an abstainer and non-smoker, he despises those who drink excessively and objects to the smell of tobacco in his presence, it is hardly a reason for describing him as a puritanical bigot. But when I learned that he is also very abstemious in his diet I suggested that under such conditions life must be hardly worth living. He changing. While it may be important to maintain the traditions of the various regiments I query whether so much ceremonial both in public and within the messes is wholly necessary. Britain is a Great Power and as such must keep herself fighting fit while the various foreign offices of the world are incapable of justifying their existence. In such a world antiquated uniforms which prevent a fit and healthy young man going in the wet because he would ruin £100 worth of taxpayers' supplied clothing, ancient ceremonial which has no military significance, and exhausting ritual have little place. I know my views will upset many retired officers and the public which loves a show, but a modern Army can look smart and give an impressive exhibition of itself while keeping prepared for its potential task. In particular, there is a farcical situation that first-rate N.C.O.s have to refuse commissions in such regiments because they cannot afford what is a luxury. It is difficult to believe that units still exist in the British Army where an officer must have the private income to enable him to keep a horse and others where membership of a hunt is the tacit pass to a position of responsibility of defence in atomic war.

I did my utmost to encourage officers to come to my room. Provided it was not prejudicial to discipline I wanted to hear their views. The same "open door" policy applied to the civil staff. I believe it was appreciated, for it is good but all too rare for a minister to make the personal acquaintance of the men and women who work for him.

For the War Office rank-and-file I arranged staff meetings which were attended by many hundreds. I also was responsible for arranging a social gathering at the Albert Hall where 3,000 of the War Office staff met one another socially for the first time in their careers. We had the Kneller Hall band there, not merely because it was under War Office control but because I felt it was high time more people realized the unsurpassed musical ability of Kneller Hall.

Such was the background for my work at the War Office during a particularly stormy and dangerous period of post-war history. In 1946, shortly before I took my appointment, the effects of demobilization were being felt in the services, and with the hopes of real peace dashed by the infiltration of the Soviet

Union into Eastern Europe the Government had to introduce the National Service Bill. The first proposal was for eighteen months' service, but objection was so strong that A. V. Alexander, then Minister of Defence, had to give way and the period became twelve months.

By 1947 the accentuation of the cold war meant that it was necessary to supplement the regular forces in the trouble spots with conscripts instead of keeping them as a large reserve, as had been intended. The twelve-month period of service further aggravated the situation and resources were strained to the limit. Almost immediately we had to send an additional division to Germany (where there were two at the time) and later on we further increased this force to one infantry and three armoured divisions. The Malayan situation was deteriorating and we were worried about Hong Kong. Meantime, there was no possibility of withdrawing forces for these areas from other zones. Berlin, Austria, Trieste, and Suez needed every man and woman they could get. As is well known, we inevitably had to increase the period of national service to eighteen months.

I did not care very much for the job of defence preparation. I regarded it as a necessary evil which someone had to tackle, and having accepted the post the best thing was to do it as conscientiously as possible. A service minister is never popular in a Labour Government. The party tradition is against it through the idealistic attitude that all war is evil. The staggering expenditure on defence by all the Great Powers during this century has been regarded by Socialist speakers as the greatest obstacle to social progress, as, of course, it is. Consequently, the figures in a defence budget are anathema to anyone in the Party who has not the worry of helping to govern the country and protect it from its enemies. The Minister who acts on Cabinet instructions bears the whole brunt of the onslaught.

On one occasion at a Labour Party Conference, Emrys Hughes, well known for his sincere but bigoted pacifist views and with an equally well-known reputation for personal pugnacity, attacked me by saying I was doing the dirty work in the Party. While I have never been a pacifist I recognize and respect those men and women who are genuinely and conscientiously against war. How these worthy and well-meaning folk consider that a

Labour Government can ignore its responsibilities to the nation in matters of security I do not know. In any event the people will never tolerate a Government which fails in its duty to organize adequate defence—a fact which was well known to Baldwin, who carefully disguised the true facts about our defence situation in the thirties when France wanted to curb the Hitler menace and who found an apt pupil in the arts of misleading the people in Chamberlain at the time of the Munich crisis in 1938.

In view of the strong criticism in the Labour Party over the decision to increase defence expenditure in this period the history of it needs to be recorded. At the outset, tension in Europe was not so serious as it soon was to become. Cripps as Chancellor of the Exchequer was exerting every pressure to cut expenditure to meet the rising cost of the social services. He insisted that the maximum for the three services—at a time when the Ministry of Defence cost a quite insignificant sum—should be £700 millions. My colleagues, Lord Hall (Admiralty), Arthur Henderson (Air Ministry), and myself were anxious to help him but we had to point out that because of the run-down of stores, the obsolete equipment, and the growing cost of national service, there would be grave risks in cutting the defence budget. The Chiefs of Staff at that time—Lord Fraser of North Cape, Viscount Montgomery, and Lord Tedder, with their finger on the pulse of Europe and Asia, made it known that the danger of another major conflict could not be ignored, though they realized the need for economy. Their job was to look after the security of the country, and for this they needed money.

Cripps was at first adamant, and for a time, as trouble brewed in Malaya and the European situation worsened, we service ministers simply got Cabinet orders to do this or that on existing resources. I protested strongly. None of us wanted to spend more money, but we were expected to do our job. There was no escape from responsibility. I had not wanted to go to the War Office, but on accepting the appointment I had told the Prime Minister: "If you send me there at least give me a chance to do the job well."

It soon became obvious that the annual estimate system was useless. It gave no opportunity for long-term planning. Tension meantime increased still more. Berlin was blockaded and the fantastically expensive air-lift was in progress. There were difficulties in Hong Kong and trouble in Palestine. Bevin was not meeting with any success in his negotiations with Egypt. He was in constant correspondence with me over a reduction of our forces in the Canal Zone. I helped him by running down the forces a little, but it was soon learned that compromise on this question was impossible. He was equally unfortunate in his negotiations over Palestine. He had once brashly said he would stake his reputation on getting an agreement with the Jewish commanders. He underrated their fighting qualities, and this embittered him so that some of his utterances had the flavour of anti-Semitism. One result of his defeats in these discussions was that he then felt our forces must be built up in readiness for trouble. His insistence resulted in Cripps's maximum figure being raised; the task of the service chiefs became easier.

My job with these two powerful Cabinet colleagues was not easy. On one side there was Cripps demanding financial stringency and on the other the Foreign Secretary demanding a strengthening of the forces. Occasionally I had to take a firm line and say to both that to do my job I must have a fair crack of the whip. In this I had the support of the Prime Minister who always tried to help when matters became involved.

My colleagues and myself were attacked as warmongers, despite the fact that most of us had spent our lives trying to convince others that war is wasteful and avoidable. A few men, like Fenner Brockway, Jimmy Hudson, Victor Yates, and Harry McGee, deserved the more respect for their pacifist opinions by refraining from personal and malicious aspersions.

Of course, there were the attacks from the other side. The Tories in Parliament and Fleet Street were complaining that we were not doing enough and spending too little. The most vociferous moanings came from a group who became known as the Brigadiers' Trade Union. I have no doubt whatever that some of the minor adventures which the Russian General Staff risked at this time were undertaken because of the criticism levelled at the Labour Government on the state of our defence organization by Tory M.P.s.

Churchill, of course, contributed to the verbal onslaught on us at this time, although with more probity and with more satisfying invective. He rediscovered some of the fine language he had used with telling results on the "guilty men" in the pre-war days. It gave an opportunity for some of the parry and thrust which we both secretly—and possibly not so secretly—enjoy.

He told the House that he had no confidence in the service ministers in the Labour Government. I reminded him "that the Rt. Hon. Gentleman, when he was out of office during the Baldwin and Chamberlain Governments, said he had no confidence in either: that it was well known that he had no confidence in his present associates, and that the only person in whom he had any confidence was the Rt. Hon. Gentleman himself."

CHAPTER TWENTY-TWO

OVERSEAS VISITS

THE Tory Press scraped the journalistic barrel to keep up the onslaught on the Labour Government and on me personally. Some of the incidents were so small that even the results in print of the sub-editors' talents failed to convince the most susceptible reader that Shinwell was jeopardizing the safety of the realm. A typical instance was on a visit to Edinburgh in my official capacity. I looked forward to this visit to the castle as I knew it would give me an opportunity of looking down on the prison I had occupied more than thirty years earlier, but I was dumbfounded to learn that through some hoary regulation of the dim past when the English insisted on blatant deference from the Scots it was customary to give the Secretary of State for War a salute of seventeen guns.

I could think of many holders of my office who doubtless delighted in this expensive and futile disturbance of the peace, but I had no intention of having the cannonade for myself and I used my position to forbid it. This must have pleased the nervous members of Edinburgh's population and certainly gave some justified satisfaction to the patriotic Scots who had long disliked this "English conquering hero" business, but the Scots Press decided it was as good a reason as any to make an attack on me, and with the help of some lovers of antiquated traditions they made quite a fuss. However, I had no salute, and whatever noise was made in the Scottish Command was made by myself.

There was another example of this sort of attack during a visit I made to the British forces in Germany. A review of the troops and armour was scheduled to take three hours to pass. It was raining when I mounted the dais and the rain fell in growing intensity as the troops passed. It was uncomfortable enough for the military, but at least they could keep their helmets or hats on. As a civilian I took the salute of unit after unit bareheaded, until my back and neck were so saturated that I kept my hat on as one armoured unit passed. Shoals of pictures were taken of me during that review, but needless to say Fleet Street pounced on the only one which showed me with hat in place.

A flood of letters from retired officers and others awaited me on my return, all demanding my resignation for this insult to the forces of the Crown. The *Daily Telegraph* was particularly venomous about it, as I expected. I fear that much earlier I must have upset Lord Kemsley at a dinner when I told him that I regarded his newspaper as very unfair, not to me, but to the Labour Party. He did not mind that, but he showed his annoyance when I added some cogent views as to the reason why the average, intelligent reader should never take any notice of the political leaders in his paper.

I spoke to Kemsley, himself a kindly man, without malice. The Press can have their fun; may I not have mine at their expense in return? Many times horrified friends and colleagues have advised me to sue newspapers for libel. To such statements I have always said: "I shall—but only when they stop talking about me."

This German visit was one of many overseas tours in Europe and elsewhere. I think that I was able to inspect most of the British units in the occupation forces. On one visit I was accompanied by Lt.-General Sir Kenneth McLean and my Parliamentary Private Secretary, Colonel Wigg, M.P. for Dudley. McLean was one of the most intelligent officers I met, a skilful soldier and a wideawake man, whom I admired greatly. He is an example of the errors which occur through the promotion problem. He was retired after I left the Ministry of Defence, and the termination of his job was the country's loss.

I was never able to make as many overseas visits as the commanders hoped. There was a great temptation to visit Malaya, Hong Kong, and other British outposts in the Far East, but while it is invaluable to see things for oneself I do not think it is advisable for ministers to be away too long from the office.

I was, however, able to make a tour of the Middle East, which I found especially interesting. My first stop was at Tripoli, under the command of General Murray. The visit was, I think, a success, although my prestige took a fall when the general's personal staff induced me to play a game of snooker. They were really delighted at my discomfiture when I was abysmally defeated.

I went next to Benghazi and Tobruk, where I met the head of the state and discussed with our military staff the possibility of constructing a cantonment in Cyrenaica. I was struck by the utter desolation of this historic battle area—the turning point of the war—when I visited the great military cemetery at Tobruk, and as I looked on the row after row of graves it was impossible not to be stirred by the sense of duty to our dead—to work to make the country for which they died a worth-while place and to do one's utmost to see that such sacrifices were not needed again.

Then I went on to Fayid and the H.Q. of our forces in the Canal Zone. General Sir John Crocker and his charming wife received me with great cordiality. Crocker has retired since, but he is one of the ablest officers we have had in the post-war period. When Montgomery went to the chairmanship of the Brussels Treaty Staff Committee there was considerable interest in the appointment of his successor. Crocker was second in the running to Slim, who, of course, was given the appointment of C.I.G.S.

I discussed the possibility of Templer who, I thought, would have been a good choice. Though a man of considerable ability and undoubted integrity, he is not easy to get on with, for he is brusque in manner and says things which a man more sensitive than I might have greatly resented. Eventually he went to the Far East, from where he has since returned with an enhanced reputation. Slim, retired from the Army and a member of the Transport Commission, was far from anxious to give it up. But no soldier could really pass up the opportunity of being C.I.G.S. There was some opposition in the War Office to the appointment —the forebodings were unnecessary. Slim made an excellent C.I.G.S. He was a great contrast to Monty—quiet, patient, and would, I think, start and win a battle without all the meticulous preparation which is Monty's virtue and secret.

Lady Crocker, my hostess at Suez, has family ties with Scotland and is the sister of Rosslyn Mitchell, a man long associated with the Labour Party in Scotland. He was M.P. for Paisley for some years, where he defeated Asquith.

At the time of my visit the strength of our forces in Suez was far less than at the period as I write. Even so it was in excess of the number to which we were entitled under our treaty with Egypt. The staffs were extremely worried about the Middle East situation and wanted to retain the men in case of emergency. Incidentally I never met any officer who believed that the area was defensible without Egyptian support.

I was appalled by the living conditions of the men and equally disgusted with the extortionate rents which the officers were compelled to pay. I met some of these rapacious landlords and could scarcely refrain from kicking them out when they moaned that they could get even higher rents from civilians. I made a speech referring to the need for better accommodation which aroused the suspicions of the Egyptian Government, who disliked my visit as they imagined Britain was "up to something." I could well appreciate the Egyptian Press and Government twisting my words about living conditions into a proof that the British intended to stay in the Canal Zone, but I found it wholly extraordinary that my Tory adversaries in Parliament, who might have been expected to regard such a suggestion as wholly in tune with their policy of "no scuttle from Suez," nevertheless used the incident as an opportunity to criticize. It was another example of their entire lack of interest in the national welfare if carping and malicious political criticism proved more to their liking.

During my tour in Suez I flew to the Gulf of Akaba to see our troops there. It was a detestable place with nothing but sand, flies, and heat. I climbed an observation post to see the Israeli camp about a mile away. In 1953, as I describe in the next chapter, I visited this camp.

On the return home I stayed at Cyprus as guest of the Governor. The Cypriots knew about my visit and I was told that it was feared there might be a demonstration against the British Government in favour of union with Greece. I was advised not to show myself in public too much because of the risk of trouble. I had thought at the time that much of the Cypriot propaganda was artificial and unrepresentative of the people in general and I assured the military that I had no intention of skulking in hiding in British controlled territory. In a car with a couple of soldiers, one of whom was the driver, I set out from the Governor's house at the edge of Nicosia, one of the loveliest places I have ever seen, to the shopping centre. A crowd quickly gathered, and one or two anti-British banners were waved in a desultory fashion on the edge of the crowd. However, those nearest me began clapping and they politely shuffled behind me as I went shopping. Unfortunately I could not buy anything. In every shop the owner insisted that there was no price for me; I could have what I wanted as a gift. Perhaps it is the custom of these kindly and pleasant folk, but I found it embarrassing and hope that I did not unduly upset them in refusing their gifts.

From Cyprus I went to Malta, where I stayed with the Governor, my old colleague Lord Douglas, who had once been M.P. for Battersea. Both Lady Douglas and he gave me a true Scottish welcome and I enjoyed their hospitality in this beautiful island and among its fine people. If they occasionally give the Mother Country a little trouble then that is a British custom and privilege, and it all stems from pride. The George Cross Island has a magnificent past but a future with problems worthy of its history. The population is increasing and there are no real industries. The so-called British aristocracy living there contribute little to the solution of the island's problems.

My last call was at Gibraltar, where once again the conditions in which the men lived worried me. The barracks in some cases date from the eighteenth century and were poor and hurriedly built specimens even of that period. Troops have good reason to talk about being "Rock happy" after a few months there.

Wherever I went during my tenure of office I took a special interest in the working conditions of officers and men, feeling that the old theory of the bad old days that soldiers are a sort of lower-grade organism to be kept in order by discipline was useless with an army composed largely of civilians doing their eighteen months of national service (as it then was), and with a nucleus of intelligent and skilled men who had to be persuaded that the Army is a fine life, which it can be.

Abroad and at home I made every effort to meet the N.C.O.s and men. I was often very angry when I saw how some of the men were being fed and housed. I expressed myself in no uncertain terms when a C.O. failed to pay sufficient attention to my views. Soldiers like plain speaking and I did not find that a verbal castigation went amiss. The king-pin of the Army is the C.O. If he knows his job and takes an interest in his men then the unit will be a first-class one. Occasionally I met officers who complained that my reference in public to bad living conditions would adversely affect recruiting. Once a general blustered away with this view. After I had told him and the lesser lights my precise opinions of fraudulent advertising of the Army as a career I received no more trouble of this kind.

Not only the men's conditions needed change. I recall a visit to Wellington Barracks where I thought that at least the Guards would have accommodation commensurate with their prestige. The men's quarters were poor enough, but the housing for the junior officers was appalling and I told a monocled adjutant so in no uncertain terms. This gentleman loftily disagreed and cynically added that they must be brought up the hard way. His manner and speech infuriated me and I let him know it. I gave instructions for alterations to be put in hand, to which he replied that they could not be done for some time. I informed him that he was to report within one month—or else. I imagine that the subalterns of the Guards have found things rather better as a result.

That is one thing about the Army. The notices which used to hang up in S.E.A.C. headquarters in the war—"the difficult can be done immediately, the impossible takes a little longer"— were no hyperbole. The Army can do anything when it is ordered to do so. It has an amazing capacity for speedy organization and improvisation. I am certain that no commercial concern has such an ability as the Army in this regard. Almost automatically the officers will say a job cannot be done, and having been told to do it, they achieve miracles.

As an example, I wanted a march-past through London in connexion with a Territorial Army recruiting campaign and suggested some bands and a battalion. The Army Council put a general in charge of the organization. When he came to see me he brusquely explained that the whole thing was impossible. There were no units to spare and no bands available. I listened to his summary of where the units were and what the bands were doing and then said: "I'll tell you how to do it."

"Yes, sir," he said with the typical discipline of the good soldier, general or private.

"Go and do it. That's how to get it done."

I do not suppose that such an order could be given anywhere but in the Army. He simply drew himself up, turned, and left the room. Of course, he made a first-class job of the whole thing. All he wanted was a definite instruction and the right language. He got both.

Of course, the resources of the Army are enormous. The public has no conception of its ramifications. Depots, stores, vehicles, manpower, workshops, land, and all the rest comprise a stupendous machine capable of tackling anything. Its defects are due to its inevitable complexity, and the risk that the needful co-ordination and concentration will be lacking. There are vested interests which are not easy to cope with, for officers will fight tooth and nail on behalf of their own commands, regiments, units, battalions, down to companies. I managed to do a little to bring some rationalization into this valuable pride.

The difficulty when a minister or a notable personality makes an inspection is to see through the dressing-up of which the Army is a past-master. "Putting on a show" is an Army talent which would do credit to a theatrical impresario. It is no use anyone saying that it does not happen. I know it does. I was always entertained by the methods of the conducting officer in edging me along the route he wanted and not the one I did. I remember inspecting a camp in Germany and was shown the rooms where education was being given. I stepped aside from my host, a general, and walked into a room. I saw a class of ten men with an instructor. On the blackboard was a statement about Parliament. It was stated that the Prime Minister's salary was £10,000 (correct) and that Ministers' salaries were £7,000 each (instead of £5,000). As I continued my tour with the general I remarked that I was delighted to hear that I had had a rise but that the Treasury had not informed me about it.

Politicians can often treat these visits too lightly. When visiting Trieste I had the pleasurable honour of being received by the U.S. Army H.Q. staff. I inspected the men by walking along the ranks in the customary fashion. Then I inspected the band and had a word or two with the conductor. This simple action assured success, for the bandsmen had been hurt a few weeks earlier when the U.S. Secretary of State for War had ignored them. It is strange how small are the details which make or mar these formal visits.

The Army educational system caused me some thought. I wondered whether it should tackle the job because of the expense and through the difficulty of getting the right teachers. The reflection of the country's educational system in the heavy proportion of illiterates which are conscripted into the forces places a heavy burden on the Army, which does its best for them but at a great cost in money and time. It "carries the can" for the local authorities and Ministry of Education. I discovered that many schools' attendance inspectors must be very lax, for many young men told me that they had never been to school at all. Nobody seemed to have discovered the fact. Others, who attended school, seemed to have been able to sit in a blissful coma for term after term without teachers worrying about it. By no means always is the illiteracy due to a poor mentality.

So with the election of 1950, my tenure at the War Office came to an end. In spite of all the difficulties, the criticism in the Press and the nagging attacks of the Tory brigadiers in Parliament, the constant reiteration that what the War Office needed was anybody but myself, I had been accepted, and was in fact reaching the most unusual state for my career of being almost popular. The generals were talking about me, and talking favourably. They let the Prime Minister know that they approved of me, and there was the satisfactory feeling that comes from a loyal and friendly staff which makes a job worth while. Harold Laski had been kind enough to send me a note in March, 1948, in which he said:

"I think you may like to know that I have seen a number of officers recently, both serving in Germany and here. All of them spoke with appreciation of the tone and atmosphere in the W.O. under its new management. One high-up hoped you could be persuaded to stay there ten years!"

I was glad to know that the good relations had not been altered in the light of their experience as the months sped by.

The 1950 election gave me no trouble. I was able to spend some time in other constituencies and was returned with a majority of 29,000. My new Tory opponent, however, received

9,000 votes, which I considered far too large for a mining division even if the facile solution of the swing of the electoral pendulum is taken into account. In the new Government Attlee asked me to go to the Ministry of Defence, once again with a Cabinet seat, which I had not had while at the War Office.

CHAPTER TWENTY-THREE

MINISTER OF DEFENCE

THE Ministry of Defence owes its existence in no small measure to Clem Attlee, who spoke frequently on the need for machinery to co-ordinate the three service departments before the war. He is rightly regarded as one of the principal originators of the Ministry.

When I went there after the 1950 election it was little more than an office with a small staff. There was no Parliamentary Secretary. That it has since grown should not disturb the taxpayer. It is a department of government which as long as defence measures are essential to our security should pay for itself in rationalizing and dovetailing the activities of the services, and eradicating waste.

My first task was to create the machinery for effecting co-ordination among the three service Ministries—a rather delicate task, particularly in the case of the Admiralty, where the Lords of the Board are extremely conscious that they control the senior service —the only one, they believe, which matters.

I never had any intention of amalgamating the three services. The organization would have been too unwieldy. Jealous as the service chiefs may be for their own branches of defence, matters went far more smoothly than might have been thought. It is fortunate that the British temperament puts the country first in any critical matter, and there is in this country none of the internecine strife which has tarnished—and continues to tarnish—the history of the defence organization in the U.S.A., where, by all accounts, the war between Navy and Air Force, or Army against either, has on occasion reached bitter proportions.

I brought the principal people together for frequent talks on matters of mutual concern and interest. There was a weekly meeting with an agenda, and I also saw that the junior Ministers of the departments attended occasionally to give them first-hand experience of the work in hand. Michael Stewart at the War Office, Jim Callaghan at the Admiralty, and Aidan Crawley at the Air Ministry were most useful. The emphasis of civilian control which my constant meetings indicated was not resented. On the contrary the meetings were welcomed. The men in uniform were glad to be told "where they were," even if the position might on occasion be unpleasant.

The work was never dull—nor easy. Apart from the differences among the three services on function, and on allocation of expenditure, equipment, and priorities, there were constant discussions with the Ministry of Supply and also with the Foreign Office. These activities brought me into close contact with Ernest Bevin. Throughout the many years that we had known one another, our relations had not always been too friendly. He said to me at the outset: "Well, we've got to work together, so we may as well make a job of it." We did. All the time that I was at the Ministry of Defence he did all he could to help, and the differences of the past were swept away. He was, of course, by then a dreadfully sick man. He carried on from a sense of duty and also because of an obstinate, forlorn hope that he could by himself bring peace to the world. He must have known that the goal would elude him. Once, as I walked slowly beside him down the stairs at Carlton Terrace, he said: "Well, I've been fighting for forty years; now it's coming to an end." His last ambition was unfulfilled, but Bevin could look back on a life not without its major triumphs. He could be cruel and so disguise the kindly side of his character. The quality which had stood him in good stead from his triumphs as the Dockers' K.C. at the Court of Inquiry in 1920 was his capacity for persuasion.

How far away was Bevin's hope of a world where "you could go to Victoria Station, buy a ticket, and set off for anywhere" the world realized with a shock when the Korean War broke out that summer. The service chiefs had to act as if world war was imminent, and indeed there seemed an inevitability about it, particularly in the autumn when General MacArthur began his ill-advised activities on both the military and political sides.

At meetings held under the ægis of the Ministry at this period

I renewed friendships with many of the Army chiefs, and also got to know the leading chiefs of the other services. Montgomery used to come over in his capacity as Chairman of the Brussels Treaty Military Organization. He, of course, I knew well. His contemporaries impressed me as men well fitted for their onerous tasks and for any eventuality which might occur.

There was Marshal of the R.A.F. Tedder, looking younger than his sixty years. Sometimes he spoke rather unimpressively, but this did not disguise the fact that he was most acute, agile-minded, and with a keen intelligence. His quiet tones and almost placid appearance belied the power he could wield as an antagonist in discussion.

The Air Force has produced in its short life a tradition among its top-ranking officers which is impressive and unique—quite different from the type of man who runs the Navy or Army. Among the R.A.F. officers whom I met at this period I recall Sir John Slessor, forceful, vigorous, and blessed with an obstinate determination to get what he wanted. It was for this reason sometimes difficult to get on with him, for compromise was not a word he easily accepted. I regarded him, however, as one of the most brilliant men in the R.A.F.

It was of interest to contrast these essentially modern-type officers with Lord Fraser of North Cape, First Sea Lord from 1948-51. There could be no doubt of his knowledge of modern naval warfare. He commanded the Home Fleet, Eastern Fleet, and British Pacific Fleet from 1943-46 and he can hardly be rivalled for the experience that these contrasting theatres of war provided, yet there was about him the bluff sea-dog manner which would not have been incongruous on the deck of Drake's *Golden Hind* or Nelson's *Victory*. I admired him for his unswerving loyalty to, and implicit faith in, the Royal Navy. Whatever else happened, he was determined that Britain's sea power should be ready. He was bluff, though sometimes tongue-tied. He appeared to me to have a ready regard for the joys of life—a bachelor popular with all who met him.

Earl Mountbatten was another naval officer who on occasion attended these conferences. He did not speak very often, but when he had something to say he expressed it with great cogency. A highly intelligent man, possibly of an unusual character for a service chief: he had a keen and lively interest in the political world, and I gained the impression that behind his affability were eyes and ears which saw and heard far more of the situation apart from the purely military one than his colleagues realized.

On the Army side the personality of Field-Marshal Slim interested me. No one can doubt the ability of a man who has risen as he has from the ranks. Although the Army lost a great leader when he became Governor-General of Australia in 1953 the ties of the Commonwealth thereby became closer. There have been times when Governor-Generalships have been given to highly unsuitable men in view of the strong class hatred and vigorous democratic spirit "down under." Slim, as events have proved, could combine the difficult feat of upholding the dignity of his office with a popular regard from the people of Australia.

The interests of the men and women who formed our fighting machine were not forgotten during this period of crisis. When I took the job I was determined to do something about the general conditions of the forces as I had managed to some extent while I was at the War Office. The basic problem of pay presented an irrefutable argument for me to put to the Cabinet. It was impossible to have general wage and salary increases throughout the country (despite the alleged policy of wage restraint) without doing something for the officers and men. When I first joined the Ministry Cripps was still the supreme economic power in the Government. He gave little away. He retired through ill-health in October, and Gaitskell became Chancellor. He proved unyielding until I told Attlee and Bevin that we should have real trouble with the strength of the Regular Army unless something was done.

I did not consider pay increases as the panacea for all the troubles of the services. This was the solution vociferously and interminably put forward by the Tory military spokesmen in the House. They insisted that higher pay would produce all the recruits we wanted. They have since learned how wrong they were.

But pay was certainly bad, and bore no relation to the working conditions in civilian life. A recruit at that time received 4s. a day. After six months he might get 5s. and thereafter go up to 8s. or 9s. Officers up to captain and the equivalent ranks in the Navy and Air Force were also badly off. Their rates were really still based on the long-outmoded concept that "an officer and a gentleman" had private means. I never missed an opportunity to get to know junior officers and senior N.C.O.s—to learn of their personal problems in regard to the welfare of their families and their own prospects in their service careers.

My demand for increased pay was resisted by the Treasury very strongly, but after a series of meetings they rather grudgingly agreed to make some concessions. I was not in a mood to meet them half-way, or even a quarter. I felt as strongly over this question of service pay as I had over the miners' five-day week. A number of my colleagues sided with me, and as a result I eventually got the money.

My next task was to help the three services to do their job. Not knowing the position from one year to another curbed any long-term planning of the kind which modern weapons of war made absolutely essential for a first-rate fighting arm. Somehow we had to find a compromise which retained the annual estimates so that Parliament had full control of expenditure but also gave the departments a fairly rigid three-year budget so that they could adequately plan for their commitments. I asked the Chiefs of Staff to state their requirements, taking into consideration the international situation, the potential dangers of the future, the place of new weapons in future strategy. I also stressed the need for caution in demanding weapons which, on a yearly blue-print, might be the best that could be hoped for, but would be wasteful on a three-year plan unless care about orders was shown.

They were impressed, although they were worried about the possibility of finance for the fantastically expensive equipment of modern war. All three were beset with misgivings about the manpower situation, particularly Air, where the need for air crews was urgent. I told them to let me know what they wanted to defend the country and to fulfil obligations to our allies.

On scores of occasions the Labour Party has been charged with hasty and panic-stricken moves in the rearmament programme. The facts prove otherwise. Military assistance to South Korea was endorsed by the Security Council of the United Nations on 27 June, 1950. The election of the second Labour Government was on 23 February, 1950. By March I was at work, not admittedly on a vast rearmament programme, but on our security needs for defence. Many discussions took place and plans had been tentatively made, long before even the Cabinet was formally told of the service departments' financial needs.

The North Atlantic Treaty had come into force on 24 August, 1949. We expected that through the contribution of the member countries of men and armaments Britain's expenditure on defence could be steadied or even reduced. I knew something of the War Office's requirements, but was not fully aware of the Admiralty and Air Force position. An inquiry began which was detailed and complete. It took some weeks. The result was an estimate which frightened me. The Chiefs of Staff stated that it comprised our minimum needs if we were to avoid the risk of being caught napping by a sudden deterioration in the international situation and a failure of diplomacy.

I took into account the industrial needs of the country, the lack of raw materials, and the shortage of labour—and pruned the service demands to a realistic figure, one which I felt would get the support of my colleagues when backed with cogent argument. This was the basis of the plan which resulted in the three-year £3,700 millions programme.

As a temporary measure prior to this I had obtained approval for the expenditure of an extra £200 millions on new weapons and research. This, by comparison, minor figure but a substantial one for peace-time, indicates that the main rearmament programme was no hastily conceived measure.

My colleagues in the service departments at that time gave me all the help they could. Strachey was Secretary for War. His appointment had not pleased some members of the House of Commons and there was evidence of opposition to him at the War Office. Whenever he was attacked I defended him; he never was lacking in co-operation with me on defence matters. I do not think, however, that he was altogether happy there and this possibly affected his interest in the department's affairs.

At the Admiralty was Lord Hall, better known as George Hall, with whom I had been on cordial terms from the days of the first Labour Government. He is one of the kindliest of men and would not willingly offend anybody. This does not mean, however, that he acquiesces easily to circumstance. Nobody fought harder when he considered the cause to be worth fighting for; he has for many years given great service to the Labour Party.

Arthur Henderson was Air Minister. He is a Queen's Counsel, and I have since doubted whether his qualities were used to their advantage at the Air Ministry, as they had been in a number of other posts of the Labour Government. Sincere, earnest, and transparently honest, he was often worried by the clashes he experienced with some R.A.F. officers, and he suffered inordinately far more than others might have done from the mental disturbances such arguments caused. His great interest is in foreign affairs and I felt through the intimacy of long friendship with him that although he showed no lack of enthusiasm for the Royal Air Force his heart was in the Foreign Office.

Although our defence programme met with criticism from some members on the Labour benches it was accepted as a necessary evil. A few pacifist members put forward the argument that no defence against the atom bomb was possible and that the Soviet Union had no evil designs in any case. Genuine as their pacifist motives may be, it is always difficult to follow their reasoning. The typical pacifist does not pretend to have a constructive alternative to offer. The attitude to war is like the Irishman's to sin: they're "agin it."

Their objections, born of the emotions rather than the intellect, are at least honest. The attitude of the Opposition, led by Churchill, was less understandable. I am bound to place on record that Churchill's conduct during this period was deplorable; the pages of Hansard afford conclusive proof. While we were quietly formulating our plans he and his supporters demanded more defence measures. When, rather to their chagrin, we presented a thoughtfully planned and realistic programme they suggested it was the wrong one. Like the pacifist members, they had no alternative, except possibly that if only the Tories were in power all would be well.

The Tory arguments consisted of four charges against the Government. The first was that we had no magician as Prime Minister; with Churchill at the head of affairs his superhuman influence would disentangle all problems. It is of no comfort whatever to me to see that he has so far had no more influence in Washington or Moscow than Attlee.

Secondly, they would be able to persuade more men to join the regular forces. In fact since the Tory Government came to power the position has worsened.

Thirdly, they declared that we were wasting money. Neither then in argument or since in practice have they shown where the waste was occurring.

Fourthly, they claimed that only under a Tory Government would the patriotic fervour induce men and women to join the Territorial Army, Royal Naval Volunteer Reserve, and R.A.F.V.R. Again there is no comfort in the knowledge that the numbers in the voluntary reserves have declined since 1951.

The Opposition took every opportunity to weaken their country in the international sphere by airing unfounded views of this kind, and added some more for good measure. Some of their charges they have since regretted. There was, for example, the demand for a strategic reserve. It has not been produced. On Egypt, too, they claimed that settlement was possible; it was a settlement which would leave Britain in full control of Suez. Time makes many ill-advised critics eat their words, and never more forcefully than in the Tory Government's action over Suez in July, 1954.

It is true, of course, that amid the yelpings from the other side of the House there was occasionally a word of congratulation from Churchill. In a number of debates he praised me for what I had done in the defence sphere. Sometimes these eulogies may have been genuine and untrammelled, but his long career in party politics has taught him all the tricks of his trade, and sometimes his compliments were a device to sow dissension in our ranks.

This reminds me of an incident at a Foyle's literary luncheon in the autumn of 1953 held to launch Hugh Cudlipp's book on the history of the Daily Mirror, *Publish and be Damned*. The chairman was Randolph Churchill, who took the opportunity to make his sensational attack on almost every newspaper in the country on the grounds of pornography and irresponsibility. It was a bitter performance which produced an air of embarrassment and annoyance. In his final words Randolph Churchill changed from the general damnation of his theme to words of high praise for me.

When I got up to speak I tried to restore an easy feeling among the guests by saying that I was most alarmed to hear such praise.

Churchill interrupted with: "But why?"

"The last time I was praised by a member of the Churchill family," I explained, "I lost my seat on the National Executive of the Labour Party!"

At this period the situation in Korea went from bad to worse. By early November Chinese forces from Manchuria were fighting in Korea, and the defence programme had been presented with its £4,700 millions budget, so that we could loyally support the United Nations, despite the feeling of many in the party that there were many faults on the South Korean side.

The estimates from the Chiefs of Staff on which this programme was based did not, in fact, differ materially from their earlier figures. There was therefore no question of hasty improvisation to meet an emergency by the military, naval, and air force staffs.

The Cabinet was well aware that circumstances might arise which prevented the expenditure of the whole sum, and I made this point quite clear in a White Paper. Much of the money was needed for buying weapons of a conventional nature which could be produced speedily for an imminent crisis. I myself was constantly absorbed in striking a nice balance between these needs and the desirability of not having a vast amount of obsolete material on our hands at the end of the three-year period if the crisis passed. I was also very anxious to spend as much as possible on research and the budget for this purpose was raised.

Our defence troubles were materially increased through the lack of co-operation and energy among the members of the North Atlantic Treaty Organization. The Treaty came into force in August, 1949. It began to gather some strength when Eisenhower assumed command of its forces on 19 December, 1950.

This appointment was, of course, a major step forward. Previously Ernest Bevin had gone to the U.S.A. for a conference with Dean Acheson and Schuman. The three Foreign Ministers had to deal with a situation in which defence of the West was jeopardized by the failure of France to meet her commitments. Acheson voiced his alarm, and said that the time had come to permit Germany to rearm as the only solution. Bevin at first resisted this proposal. In face of the facts he later reluctantly consented in principle, as did Schuman. Subsequently the British Cabinet, after misgivings, also accepted the proposition in principle, specifically rejecting any attempt to proceed immediately, because there had to be safeguards against any possibility of a resurgence of German militarism. France was still divided on the decision with the Socialists and De Gaullists opposed to Government acceptance even with the safeguarding words "in principle."

As a result of these abortive discussions the Defence Ministers were summoned to New York. It was there that I first met Dean Acheson, who struck me as the most able of the American statesmen of the time. Suave, diplomatic, with a polish that is more usually characteristic of an Englishman, he gave the impression of being aloof and superior, though as I got to know him better I felt this was due to shyness. Of course, as the representative of the U.S.A., he was listened to at all the conferences with great respect, particularly by some of the other ministers who always seemed to be hoping for financial aid. But he was by his own ability the driving force of the conferences I attended. His marshalling of facts was superb.

Schuman's tactics were very different from those of Acheson. He has none of the spectacular fire of Bidault or Pleven but in his subdued but quiet manner he managed to make out a splendid case for his country. On occasion his approach to a problem reminded me of Attlee: quiet but forceful, always putting the case with calmness.

The other Defence Ministers of the "Big Three" at the conference were General George Marshall and Jules Moch. Marshall is a man of great vision and determination. He is a gentleman in the real sense of that maligned word: kindly, courteous, ready to give way to anybody with a point to make. It is, of course, generally said that he fostered Eisenhower's rapid rise during the war and afterwards. After meeting Marshall I can well believe it, for he is the type of man with the ability to choose men and, having done so, to see that his faith in them is justified. Such faith may well have meant that he sacrificed his own destiny. I regard General Marshall as a statesman greatly superior to Eisenhower, and I believe that he would have made an illustrious President of the United States.

Jules Moch, a Socialist, is perfectly ready to argue for hours on end. He is a capable man—a fact about which he himself has no false modesty. His actions are coloured by the memories of the sufferings of his family at the hands of the Nazis, and at the conference held at Washington two months later he opposed a German contribution to Western defence though he accepted the situation sufficiently to propose a scheme in which Germany would supply small combat units not larger than a brigade and never exceeding in size the contribution of any other member. The delegates all argued at great length about this proposal. I wanted more details. Marshall rejected it as of no value and asked me privately to let the others argue it out. The only minister in favour of the French proposal was Colonel de Greef, of Belgium. He read his case from a brief which was doubtless the work of Van Zeeland, the Foreign Minister.

In the end, with no other country ready to give unqualified support to the Moch plan, no decision was reached. It was clear that the remainder of the delegates, if they had to accept the inevitability of a German contribution, wished it to be controlled through a Supreme Commander and N.A.T.O., with safeguards against the emergence of a German General Staff. For some reason Moch regarded me as the most powerful opponent of his scheme, and our personal relations became rather strained. He said: "You make difficulties for me." He did not like my retort that he had made difficulties for us all. It is remarkable that since that conference Moch has been the most bitter opponent of E.D.C., which was in fact partly his own creation. Moch's acerbity was the only jarring note; my relations with the other ministers were most cordial. I received much personal kindness and in official matters my views seemed to meet with respect. Whether this was a compliment to my person or to the country I represented I cannot say. I like to think it was based on both.

Not the least of the burdens of any conference in the United States is the amount of hospitality for the delegates. It is provided on a lavish scale and arranged on the assumption that one has illimitable energy, a cast-iron digestion, and strong head. I dislike cocktail receptions, public dinners, and all the rest of such functions attended by large numbers of people. They are boring and time-wasting. Small functions, where one can talk with a few interesting people, are another matter. I recall a pleasant dinner at the British Embassy in Washington. Sir Oliver Franks was the host. Before his appointment I had invited him to join the Coal Board, but he declined. I think this was a pity, for he would have been an asset. He is regarded as a philosopher and therefore suffering from such a person's alleged defect of inability to make decisions. Philosopher Sir Oliver may be, but I regard him as one of our ablest men, and I have no doubts about his administrative qualities.

His guests included President and Mrs. Truman, General and Mrs. Marshall, the Bishop of Washington and his wife, and Anthony Eden, who was in the States on a private visit. My neighbours were Mrs. Truman and the Bishop's wife. Mrs. Truman struck me as a very womanly person, concerned with domestic matters more than the problems that beset her husband. She was full of the arrangements for some church in Alabama which was about to receive a banner, and I admired her for telling me all the details rather than attempting conversation on matters which were not so interesting to her. The main conversation at the table centred around Truman and Marshall, who exchanged reminiscences in rare style. It was obvious to me that Truman greatly admired his Secretary of State.

Washington is one of the finest cities I have ever visited, with splendid buildings, beautiful parks and wide roads, with the Potomac never very far away. I took the opportunity to walk round the city to see how the ordinary people lived, taking my excellent breakfast of fruit juice, coffee, toast, and two fried eggs for half a dollar in the cafés, and some of my other meals in the drug stores where perfectly cooked food served at the counter is available at extremely reasonable prices until late at night. Hotel meals and accommodation are, by contrast, very expensive by British standards.

Several times I visited the district inhabited by the coloured population. While there is a certain amount of segregation in Washington these people seemed very prosperous and if the housing conditions sometimes contrasted unfavourably with those of white people the American negro in Washington lives at a much higher standard than many Europeans.

One day I was driven to the Arlington cemetery for the unveiling of the memorial to Sir John Dill, and I passed the house which was then being used as the presidential residence during the alterations to the White House. There was a considerable crowd in the vicinity and many police. Only later did we know that there had been an attempt on the President's life by Puerto Ricans. When Truman appeared at the cemetery and spoke he showed no sign of distress.

I made a second visit to Washington about the adoption of a standardized automatic rifle. The American experts were against the British model of which the War Office was very proud. I backed the adoption of the British weapon partly because of the impressive evidence of my experts and also because I prefer British products. There was something of a paradoxical situation over this rifle, with Churchill seemingly liking any weapon but the British one. Perhaps I was wrong, for who am I to evince more patriotism than he does? Still, I can gain some comfort from the knowledge that never have I allowed my political beliefs to affect my attitude to my country when I have been abroad.

It was obvious to me that the Pentagon was adamant against the British weapon, and seeing no reason to stay wasting time and words I made arrangements to return home. There was a beauty contest in my constituency which I had promised to judge, and it seemed to me that to stay in Washington would be no more valuable than to attend this modest little function. I jokingly told the American reporters so—and they produced the headline in the evening papers: "Shinwell prefers legs to arms." On this occasion it was correct.

General Eisenhower's emergence from semi-retirement as President of Columbia University to become Supreme Commander of the West European Defence Forces was due, of course, to President Truman. On Eisenhower's arrival in Britain on his way to his new post I had a talk with him, and found him full of assurance and confidence, despite the enormous problems that awaited him at S.H.A.P.E.

There was also a private luncheon given by Mr. and Mrs. Attlee for Ike at which the other guests were Ernest Bevin and myself. At the end of the meal, Mrs. Attlee rose and Eisenhower gallantly hurried over to open the door for her. I, of course, stood up as well, and as this informal function was in a small room at No. 10, I moved the chairs back so that she could pass.

Unfortunately Eisenhower did not notice them, and to my embarrassment he flopped to the floor. He took it very well indeed and dismissed my profuse apologies with the famous Ike grin. I hoped that he did not privately think that this was an example of British anti-Americanism by direct action instead of the verbal type we are always hearing about.

Eisenhower did not, I think, have any reason to complain about our co-operation. Alone among the nations of Europe we did everything we promised. We offered four divisions and supplied them. Pleven and Jules Moch of France made optimistic and generous promises of the number of divisions they would supply but never did so. Belgium and Holland failed in the same way. These and promises other members made both in private conferences and in the N.A.T.O. council meetings were not worth the time they took to make.

I am not backward when it comes to talking at conferences, but some of my European colleagues amazed me not only with their verbosity, but with the lavishness and optimism of their promised contributions. Some of them could have been fulfilled with a comparable sacrifice to that of Britain; others they must have known were merely empty gestures.

One of the most garrulous of the delegates was the Portuguese Foreign Minister. He spoke at length on every subject. His words helped to disguise the fact that his country's proposed contribution consisted merely of a brigade, and I doubt whether even now a properly equipped unit of even that size could be transferred to N.A.T.O.

There was no attempt at co-operation when we announced that we had decided to increase the period of national service to two years. We had a number of reasons for this: additional training was necessary for men going overseas, the time in transit left little time for actual active service. We stressed that this was only a temporary arrangement.

Other N.A.T.O. nations opposed the idea. Their conscription varied from ten months to two years, but it was not clear whether men were actually conscripted for the legally maximum period.

At one of the conferences at Fontainebleau I was one among more than two hundred high-ranking officers and three other Defence Ministers. The exercise was controlled by the late General

Shinwell with his constituents. At Easington, at the time of
the colliery disaster, May, 1951.

The author at a Durham Miners' Gala, July, 1950.

The author with two of his ten grandchildren.

de Lattre de Tassigny, in my opinion one of the ablest officers France has had in the past twenty years. Afterwards we four ministers were invited to speak.

Jules Moch of France spoke first. He is a great orator but spoke from a few notes. He was followed by conventional speeches by the Belgian and Dutch ministers.

When I rose as the fourth speaker I used no notes. I took as my theme the need to do everything possible to avoid war, but to be ready with strength and adaptability if it came. I criticized the apparent apathy of the member-Governments. I suggested that there was a need for creating a compact and well-equipped organization with smaller divisions. I stressed that in speaking on military matters I was merely using my experience at the War Office and in the Ministry of Defence.

The speech went down well, and was greeted with more applause than those of my colleagues. Later I was told that Moch had reproved his generals for applauding me; I was just a street-corner orator. He had no need to be jealous: I have no ambitions for the brief term of office as a French Minister of Defence, but his criticism illustrates how personal and difficult co-operation can be.

I had my troubles in the House of Commons while in the Ministry of Defence. Either my friends behind me or the Opposition in front were moaning and complaining. I preferred to get on with my job in the office, for despite the general view that those who are reputedly good speakers are poor administrators and take unwillingly to the chair and office desk I do not think this is true. I enjoyed my work and was interested in the problems with which I had to grapple. I found that administration consisted of taking pains with details, of hard and consistent work, and of getting on with the people around you. So far as I am able to judge, I succeeded.

Prolonged and contentious as the defence allocations debates were the major event in this Government was of course the resignation of Aneurin Bevan and Harold Wilson in April, 1951, over the financing of the health services. The sequence of events which led up to this gesture by two ministers warrants telling as it was seen by a member of the Cabinet.

During Cripps's chancellorship Bevan received as many

orders as I did that expenditure had to be limited. Cripps wanted to put a ceiling on the cost of the health services. Bevan resisted vigorously, his argument being that with the increasing prices and claims a ceiling would jeopardize the whole purpose of the service. Under Gaitskell the controversy continued, and he proved as adamant about expenditure as his mentor.

It has been said that the resignations came as a protest against the £4,700 millions defence budget. This is not so. Both Bevan and Wilson accepted the figure, though doubting, like many of us, that the country could stand the cost or whether it could be spent within the allotted time. Bevan, indeed, spoke in the House in defence of the estimate when it was attacked by Churchill.

Gaitskell's Budget of 1951 demanded a cut on the health services of about £13 millions for the current year and £30 millions in a full year. Many of my colleagues were doubtful about the wisdom of the cut. They hoped for a compromise, but Gaitskell, in a difficult financial situation, was in no mood for compromise. Bevan is not by nature a man to give way. In the event, if some patience and tolerance had been shown the matter would have resolved itself, as in a very short time delivery delays on the defence programme proved that the money would not be expendable.

There seemed to be an underlying motive for these gestures against the Chancellor. Bevan was absolutely sincere in his determination to preserve the health service, but elsewhere the animus concerned the struggle for governmental positions. An able servant of the party, Bevan with longer service may have regarded himself as more entitled to the chancellorship than Gaitskell. Apart from membership of the party's Ottawa Tariff Committee in 1937 (of which I was chairman) Gaitskell had played no prominent part in the Labour movement prior to 1945. His ministerial appointments, and in particular that to the Exchequer, caused considerable surprise, and among some members (not only Bevan's supporters) a considerable amount of misgiving at the time.

The party has a traditional dislike of nominees, preferring democratic discussion and election to high rank. Gaitskell, while possessing considerable merit, had, it was thought, been nominated by Cripps. Bevan was at fault in taking such a vigorous and impatient view of the proposed emasculation of the health service he had created. On the other hand no one can really claim that the Treasury view, that the country's financial well-being would have suffered by keeping the health service intact, can be justified. That is just like Tory propaganda.

My own view at the time was that Morrison should have become Chancellor and Bevan could have best served himself and his country by remaining at the Ministry of Labour. He is, contrary to some views, a good administrator. Morrison would, I think, have been happy and successful at the Exchequer. He did not seem to enjoy the Foreign Office, for which appointment I happen to know he had little enthusiasm when he was given it in face of some competition after Bevin's death.

In all this unfortunate affair I did my best to prevent further trouble. My severest critics will admit, I hope, that I have never been one of the desperate seekers after office, and so I was able to stand on the sidelines during the somewhat hectic period of rumour and counter-rumour which occurred. I wish to see the people of Britain, and the world at large, living in conditions of prosperity and security—that is my ambition, and of greater importance than who shall be Chancellor of the Exchequer or Foreign Secretary in a Labour Government.

There can be no doubt that the resignations did the Party much harm. They may not have been the sole cause; they were however a contribution to our defeat in October, 1951.

CHAPTER TWENTY-FOUR

A VISIT TO ISRAEL

IN the autumn of 1953 I was able to fulfil a long-standing invitation to visit Israel. I must confess that through the long years of Zionist activity which began after Allenby's victories in Palestine in 1917-18 and the ensuing agreement regarding the traditional home of the Jews, I had done little or nothing in public to help the movement. My activities were confined to conversations and assistance behind the scenes. But no economist or politician, of whatever creed or race, can to-day afford to ignore this amazing experiment of creating in the span of one generation an integrated state of the kind which elsewhere has taken hundreds and even thousands of years. The briefest perusal of the Old Testament will indicate the strategic and commercial importance of this tiny land, once a buffer state among the great nations of pre-history: Ur, Assyria, Babylon, Persia, Egypt. It has straddled the crossroads of the ancient overland trading routes from the dawn of civilization. Now Israel is an independent nation standing between East and West as well as a junction for air, sea, and land trading lines.

Israel will, to my mind, become increasingly important in global politics. As a young, virile, and idealistic country she will never allow herself to become a shuttlecock to be tossed this way and that in the game of power politics. But the Great Powers which have the acumen and vision to treat her as a valuable ally will not regret it. The accent on the more spectacular danger points of the cold war sometimes blinds us to the real issues in the political struggle, and I have long felt that the Middle East, as always, is potentially a more dangerous powder-keg than many of the places which have come into the recent news.

It may be said without fear of denial that Israel is Western

in concept and entirely democratic in attitude. She has as hearty
a suspicion of communistic regimentation as of the jungle conditions of unrestricted capitalism. In these factors lies the reason for
the antipathy of her neighbours more than any problem of
religious clashes. The Islamic states, not because of their faith,
but because of their political régimes, consist of a few people of
fabulous wealth and huge numbers existing in appalling poverty.
Israel has suddenly brought into this area a glimpse of Western
civilization with its trend towards equality and its principles of
justice, welfare, and respect for human life. There are, of course,
tragic scenes among the Arab refugees moved from Israel, though
it may be noted that the enormously wealthy "petroleum sheik-
doms" and the larger Arab Powers are content to allow Western
welfare organizations to look after them. But equally there
are many thousands of Arabs who live happily in Israel in
conditions of prosperity which none of their race know except in
such British-controlled areas as Jordan, Aden, and the Canal
Zone—and then not on anything comparable in scale. In my
travels about Israel I was frankly surprised to see so many Arab
villages where the people had the appearance of being better off
than many of the Jewish refugees who had recently arrived in the
country. Bedouins pursued their nomadic existence, moving with
their flocks of cattle, goats, and sheep as they have done from time
immemorial. They were also, of course, better off than their
neighbours in Egypt and Syria—a fact which was noted by the
latter.

My principal reason for going to Israel was to visit the military
establishments, and especially the Nahal, manned in the main by
men and women trained to use arms but pursuing normal work
while they remain ready for defence—ploughmen with a rifle
slung across the back, road builders ready to man defences within
minutes. In the three weeks I was there I was able to combine
these visits with a varied itinerary covering all facets of the nation's
life. Israel is certainly not the land which nature has caused to
flow with milk and honey as tradition suggests, though with
irrigation and patient development it might well return to this
state. Possibly few of those working for this goal to-day will live
to see it, but if the first enthusiasm continues their children will.
The optimism of many of these people is inspiring. Naturally

there are tremendous personal problems involved in the achievements, which are little short of a miracle.

The Israeli people, scattered for two thousand years, have little reason to venerate theories of race. They have in any case learned that to be a Jew by religion does not always mean that it is easy to get on with other Jews. From the Arab states have come immigrants like the Yemenites, living just as they did three thousand years ago, and happy with a tent for a home and fried vegetables for food. Alongside them may be a Polish Jew whose memories from childhood are of Hitler's concentration camps, while his comrades are a young couple from the East End of London and some idealistic young man who left a luxurious home in New York in order to contribute his services to the re-emergence of the land of his ancestors. As an example of this admixture I watched a mortar unit in training. The four men were by birth a Greek, a Turk, an Iraqui, and a Sabra (native of Israel).

For such people to co-operate and live together is not only a personal problem; it is a national one. Human nature being what it is, some of the first enthusiasm has evaporated in some cases, with the people leaving the farms, industries, and civil engineering projects to set up shops and small businesses. Enormous numbers of people are working fanatically hard, but some are working too little, and some are not working at all.

When I was in Israel the state was five years old. At the beginning many of its farmers left the country. In their place came the immigrants, the vast proportion of whom knew nothing about farming or building. The Jewish population was thereby increased from 650,000 to $1\frac{1}{2}$ millions. The farm units had then increased from 16,000 to 36,000. From a very low level agricultural production had risen so as to provide about 60 per cent of the country's food requirements. By 1957 it is hoped that the figure will reach 80 per cent.

Before this goal is reached the labour problem of farming will have to be solved. The country will have to decide whether to continue and develop the communal agricultural organization which was the pioneer method; whether to foster agricultural settlements on the private enterprise principle; or whether to introduce state farming employing hired labour. Whichever method comes to the fore there is no doubt in my mind that the

Israelis will have to find a substitute for that first fiery zeal. It is naturally evaporating a little—life at fever heat for a prolonged period is impossible.

It seemed to me that more self-discipline was needed. They will have to work in more generous co-operation one with another, abandoning excessive individualism and facing the fact that in the long-term task of building a country from nothing idealism is not enough. At the back of this tolerance there must also be a compromise between the orthodox and less orthodox sections of the community. The religious life of the country will not be weakened by recognizing that time marches on.

Success or failure depends on many things: the individual attitude already mentioned, capital investment, technical training —and also on the workers' movement. The Israeli Federation of Labour is much more than a trade union. It is engaged in industry, housing, transport, and agriculture. The Histadrut was formed in 1920 with 4,500 members. At the time of my visit its membership exceeded 472,000, or about 70 per cent of the total working population. It is not an industrial or craft organization but a personal union for the worker, who pays between 4 and 5 per cent of his wages as his subscription. More than 50 per cent comes back in the form of direct social and medical services. One interesting feature of the Labour movement in Israel is that employment exchanges are run by the movement under Government control. The country's wage set-up is tied to a cost-of-living index and although there is the usual lag between price increases and wage increases disputes are rare.

Histadrut is responsible for producing 70 per cent of the mixed farming produce of the country. A co-operative supplies these farms with everything from seeds to tractors, and another co-operative sells their products. It is the largest building construction company in the country, with its own quarries, brick factories, cement works, and iron foundry. Ninety per cent of the urban and inter-urban passenger road transport services are run by co-operatives affiliated to Histadrut.

Despite opposition from the reactionary right and the extreme left Histadrut has gone ahead with its efforts to treat Arab workers fairly, and its organization has 12,000 members in sixty Arab villages. Arab and Jewish workers are paid the rate for the job—

a standard which applies not only in industry but also in the Government and municipal services.

Histadrut will undoubtedly continue to play a vital rôle in the country's economic policy, yet its work and that of the Government, and of the country's friends outside, will come to naught if the hatred and fear of the Arab countries around Israel is not ended. I frankly doubt whether the country can prosper; its survival may even be in danger if this problem remains unsolved.

Of Israel's ability to fight there can be no doubt, as earlier clashes have shown. There are officers in the Israeli Army who served in the British and American forces, and also many ex-British N.C.O.s who have together produced a well-knit, courageous, and resourceful army. I recall the admiration of many officers of the British General Staff while I was in office, when the telling of the latest stories of Israeli prowess became a fashion.

One of our most famous generals told me that he had an intelligence report of the retirement of an Egyptian battalion in the face of a single Israeli soldier. The man had been slightly wounded in a skirmish and was lying on the outskirts of a village. As the enemy battalion moved up he thought he might as well make one defiant gesture, and he fired his automatic rifle. The enemy scattered and never returned. Such a story, apocryphal or true, merely exemplifies a lack of martial valour on one side without extolling the efficiency of the other. But my experience was that Israel, for her size, has the best defence organization in the Middle East. Its value to the West in future defence strategy must not be underrated. During my tour and conversation I began to realize the immense value of an alternative base to Suez which could be built up on Israeli territory. Naturally Israel would have to have sovereign rights, but Haifa as a naval base— a possibility which has become infinitely more important since the agreement to evacuate the Canal Zone was signed in the summer of 1954—could be a bastion of democracy in a Middle East Defence Organization closely associated with N.A.T.O. As an insurance against the severance of lifeline between occident and orient its value would be incalculable. For Israel the revenue obtainable for the construction of such a base might well be her economic salvation.

My immediate and vivid impression from the first moment of my arrival at Lydda airport when I was received by the Director-General of the Ministry of Defence and other officials was of the friendliness of everyone to Britain and myself. The keynote was set by the address of welcome from J. Sprinzak, Speaker of the Israeli Parliament: "I welcome you as a leader of a great workers' movement, as one who was the Defence Minister of a great country, and, above all, I welcome you as a brother. . . . You once wrote a book *The Britain I Want*; I hope that during your stay here, while seeing our accomplishments and our difficulties, you will understand and you will feel what the State of Israel means and what is 'The Israel We Should Like to See'."

All the officials I met had a lively knowledge of my work in association with the War Office and Defence Ministry at home, and seemed to share my pride in the fact that I had been both Secretary of State for War and Minister of Defence. I was impressed with the ministry officials, of whom I met most. Ben Gurion was still Prime Minister although he told me he wished to retire. He struck me as a great idealist who was beginning to realize that ideals could best be achieved by hard work and by the removal of internal and external political problems—a realization which might well be taken as an example by the population as a whole. Sharret (who succeeded Gurion as Prime Minister), Lavon (Defence Minister), and Mrs. Myerson (Minister of Labour) struck me as first-class ministers. In the permanent staffs of the Government departments there was an unusually high standard of personnel, but I believe that greater efficiency might be achieved by a closer copy of the British civil-service system.

I made many speeches, including one at the largest of indoor meetings ever held at Tel Aviv. Although I was sometimes critical I found that my remarks were taken in the spirit they were intended. Of course, all Israelis were anxious for my views on the recurrent border clashes, but I told them: "I prefer to wait until my return to Britain before expressing an opinion on these clashes. But it would be wiser for people outside the country not to get too excited about recent events. It may suit Foreign Ministers in certain countries who are faced by an impasse in the Far East and in Trieste (there was trouble between the Yugo-slavs and the Italians at the time) each to seek to divert attention to events in Israel. It is an old device which will not deceive those who are familiar with such political activities. Unlike some of my political adversaries in Britain I don't believe in criticizing my own country when abroad. I prefer to say what I have to say in England."

In village after village the contrast between East and West, between ancient and modern, was fascinating. Nazareth is an Arab town, inhabited by many Christian Arabs. Safid is a very ancient Jewish town where everything is strictly orthodox and the customs can have changed but little in three thousand years. Beer-Sheba, where Abraham dug a well and lived, has every appearance of a modern town, with magnificent schools, hospitals, and workers' houses. Possibly the place which has captured the spirit of modern Israel best is Holon, south-east of Tel Aviv, and not far from Jaffa. In ten years it has become one of the country's major potential industrial centres. More than 130 factories and workshops turn out a variety of products from plastics to silverware, from fruit juices to nylon hosiery.

One of the border areas I visited was Elath on the Gulf of Akaba. There was a British military camp about a mile away which I had visited during my period of office as Secretary for War. The Israeli commandant arranged for me to go out in a launch. The young officer in charge told me he had been a lawyer, but had transferred to the Navy as a more useful type of work. I agreed with him that Israel needed more men ready to sacrifice professional careers for the good of their country. I had hoped that the British C.O. would have asked me to land, but in the uneasy situation which pertained in the area he doubtless felt that the visit of an ex-British Minister in an Israeli boat might upset Egypt and cause an "incident." However that may be, there was no sign of life, although naturally my presence in the vicinity was well known.

The facilities afforded by the Israeli Government enabled me to travel as far north as Metulla and as far south as the Dead Sea at Sodom. The country in the north is of rare beauty; in particular does the description apply to the neighbourhood of Galilee, the scene of so many historic events. In the south, principally in the Negev, the long range of hills and valleys presents an appearance of grandeur, but the absence of fertile land and water is at present one of the principal obstacles to the continued progress of the state.

I had the privilege of paying a visit to the Israeli Navy at Haifa. I was piped aboard a frigate where the officers treated me with the utmost cordiality. They were in appearance as like those in the British Navy as two peas. In dress and in routine one might have been on a frigate or destroyer in Portsmouth Harbour. On one of the motor torpedo-boats, purchased from Britain, I was taken for a trip round the harbour of Haifa and had a full view of the port, one of the finest in the Mediterranean.

The town of Haifa created a most favourable impression. The fine buildings, splendid shops, the morale of its people, together with the fast-growing industrial development on its perimeter give hope of progress exceeding the expectations of those Israelis who lived there when the Arabs were in control. Indeed after what I saw there I could not help remarking how much more impressive were its potentialities than the achievements already gained.

In my time I have visited many cities. None has been more interesting than Jerusalem, a city of pilgrimage for three great religions. I hope that one day it will be an easy place to reach for anyone who wishes to visit it. Certainly its potentialities as a tourist centre are enormous. Time means little in Jerusalem. Modern blocks of flats stand near buildings two thousand years old. Young men and women in modern clothes pass whiskered Rabbis and other Orthodox natives. East meets West across a street—and barbed wire and sentries proclaim the tragedy of schism. I had hoped to visit the famous Wailing Wall, but even though it was a matter of ten minutes' walk the Israeli officials hoped that I would not pursue the idea even if the Jordan Government gave permission. A chance shot, an unintentional brush against a passer-by in the narrow street—and trouble might break out. That is the uneasy state in which Jerusalem lives, but no one seems to care very much. They carry on. Jerusalem has some similarity to Berlin in this regard, except that in the German city the zones are clearly marked and wide thoroughfares shield the danger points. In Jerusalem a labyrinth of passages and narrow streets can lead either side to disaster in a moment of time or a few yards of space.

Yet Jerusalem, symbol of independence and home to the Jews, is one of the historic cities which are the common heritage of humanity. Like the country in which it stands, it has both the immediate omen of potential tragedy through international strife and also the hint of hope for peace. In Israel, youngest of the nations of the world and being built on a framework which embodies all that is best in modern civilization, there are the ingredients of progress and peace for its inhabitants and a useful contribution to the defence and prosperity of democracy. They need more technological help, though young men and women are coming along in increasing numbers for training. They need water to make the desert bloom—the Negev has immense possibilities under irrigation—and they need oil. The prospect of advancement depends almost entirely on the eventual ability of Israeli and Arab to live in peace with one another. With that, the future is rosy indeed; without it, there are sombre signs of ultimate catastrophe. The shadow of hostility from the reactionary nations around Israel is the menace never far from the people's minds.

I shall ever be grateful for the opportunity I had of visiting this remarkable country. Her leaders have given more than a million immigrants unity; I hope to live to see the Israelis grasp their opportunity.

CHAPTER TWENTY-FIVE

SOME THOUGHTS ABOUT
THE FUTURE

O N 25 October, 1951, despite the greatest vote for one political
party in the history of the country, we were defeated. I am
a realist, and I had expected this was likely to happen. The
disputes in the Party had not helped the situation, but the main
reason was the public's mental reaction to the financial position
of the country as described by the facile-minded economists who,
whatever the state of the British economy, enjoyed a splendid
boom proving that while production and exports had increased
far beyond expenditure, the country was on the verge of
disaster.

The modern economist is in the happy position of being able
to prove almost anything, given time and verbosity. The facts
were that the country was far better off than it had been in 1945
when Labour took office. The nationalized industries, described
in one of the most outrageous campaigns of unjustified attack
and unbridled complaint on record as a disastrous experiment,
were in fact proving a success, not only in management-employee
relationship, but as trading organizations.

My personal view was that as a party we had little to be
ashamed about; in a memorandum for private circulation which
I prepared in the early part of 1951 I stated: "The Government
cannot be accused of failure to redeem the pledges given at the
general election of 1945. A substantial section of the nationalization programme has been carried through. . . . In addition there
has been a considerable expansion of social services accompanied
by strenuous efforts to promote economic recovery. So far, both
the Government and the Labour Party can claim to have delivered
the goods."

I then proceeded to analyse the reasons for our reduced majority in 1950. I cited dissatisfaction at the results of nationalization and criticism by the workers in those industries of the numbers employed in white-collar jobs; disquiet among consumers on the prices of coal, gas, and electricity and on the "remoteness" of the control when complaints or inquiries were made.

As regards future nationalization I suggested that we should not embark on any scheme unless (1) we were satisfied that privately owned industry failed to measure up to conditions laid down by the Government as regards the benefits to users and employees, and (2) unless the monopolistic character of the industry constituted a menace to the state.

My estimate of the needs of a successful appeal to the nation at the next election was to satisfy the public that nationalization was working well; to reduce the cost of living (which might be achieved by coming to grips with the distribution cost problem); to impart a greater sense of urgency to the housing programme; and to iron out the continuing variations of the standard of living among the classes.

With these questions adequately met I stated that I believed we could win a sufficient majority to carry out the mandate of the majority of the people. I still believe it would have been possible. But generally speaking the problems enumerated were not faced, and Labour lost by the narrowest of margins in constituency after constituency where precisely those questions were asked—and were unanswered.

The election results provided few sensations. The pendulum, as always, was swinging, but only a little. The movement was sufficient to bring narrow defeat for Labour in place of slight victory. In the area of special interest to me, the North-East, we retained most of our seats, but our solidarity was damaged because of the loss of seats at Darlington and Middlesbrough.

The elation of the Tories in Parliament was second only to the joyous acclaim of the Tory Press. It seemed that Fleet Street's ominous reports of the nation's state had been, after all, exaggerated. They were, whatever they were, of such a temporary and artificial character that all would now be well. As an old political campaigner I must confess that I found the Tory staging superb. In the arts of legerdemain the actors and managers could hardly be improved.

The Tories soon put into operation their schemes for the de-nationalization of the transport and steel industries, and legislation designed to destroy rather than create became a feature of Government policy, taking up most of the time of the House. The Tories did not, of course, dare to tamper to any extent with the social services. The Welfare State would not have come into being without the Socialist Government, but it was now an accepted condition of life which neither the 1951 Government materially changed nor any other Tory régime will dare to alter.

In the realm of foreign affairs the situation began almost immediately to deteriorate. Unfortunately Churchill's claim that he would by both instinct and experience do better than Labour has been falsified by events, nor could his ministers transform the defence situation.

Shortly after the new Government was in action I made my Party's and my own views on the international question quite clear. "We of the Labour Party accept the need for defence preparations because at present there appears to be no satisfactory alternative. But, simultaneously, we must direct attention to the need for promoting peace in the diplomatic sphere."

Incidentally, in this debate, Churchill upset some of his colleagues by paying my speech the compliment of intervention before the War Secretary replied.

"I should not like," he said, "the speech of the late Minister of Defence to go without its due and proper acknowledgment from this side of the House. We have our party battles and bitterness, and the great balance of the nation is maintained to some extent by our quarrels, but I have always felt and testified, even in moments of party strife, to the Rt. Hon. Gentleman's sterling patriotism and to the fact that his heart is in the right place where the life and strength of our country were concerned. . . . I am so glad to be able to say tonight in these very few moments, that the spirit which has animated the Rt. Hon. Gentleman in the main discharge of his great duties was one which has, in peace as well as in war, added to the strength and security of our country."

We have in our time paid one another compliments and hurled our invective. When the Churchillian periods were honeyed I have on occasion suspected the political motive behind them. But I accepted the fact that in the security of a new Parliament the Prime Minister was extending his hand across the barrier of party. How high this man can rise above the midget stature of his colleagues! It was not unamusing to watch their faces as Churchill intervened in this way. Hansard's pages record no approval from the benches behind him for his remarks.

A series of internal disputes has since 1951 minimized the Labour Party's prestige in Parliament, and if permitted to continue could jeopardize its immediate future in an election.

The dissension is traditional. Throughout the history of the Socialist movement there have always been disputes about policy and tactics. This is a healthy and democratic feature. The secondary motive, born of ambition for leadership, is more insidious. The former feature of the movement is not merely a national characteristic. It can be found in all countries. In Russia the Bolsheviks and Mensheviks were an example of the lengths to which disputes among the disciples of Karl Marx could go. In Germany and Europe generally there have been similar instances of quarrels between those who wanted to follow Marx and those who preferred to believe that a more moderate policy would suffice. In the United States, where no Labour Party in the political sense exists, there is the dissension between the trade unions who operate on a craft basis and those who have adopted a more revolutionary policy with organizations comprising all sections of workers.

The British record is replete with examples of personal troubles among those at the head of the Socialist movement. At the turn of the century Hardie was at loggerheads with Blatchford. Later MacDonald was bitterly opposed by others who disliked his conception of Socialism; this situation was complicated by personal animosity between MacDonald and such men as Snowden and Henderson. Before the last war the thread of dispute continued with incidents such as Ernest Bevin's attacks on Lansbury.

One thing both our supporters and adversaries must not be mistaken about. These disputes will not in the long run hamper the Party's progress. The public will tolerate, and even be stimulated by, the news of divergence of views among the leaders, but they will not put up with apathy and inactivity.

On the whole "Turn Left" has led to the best road. This is natural enough, for the world will not stand still, and history of progress is impatient about timid and moderate leaders. The series of "crises" since 1951 have revolved around the dispute on future policy. On the one side are those who prefer moderation and on the other those who are forced to adopt a more vigorous and extreme line, partly because it is the traditional one but also, in some cases, because they are personally ambitious and have eyes on future leadership in the Party.

An almost exact parallel exists in the trade-union movement. The divergence of attitude between the Electrical Trades Union and the Transport and General Workers' Union, for example, is greater than that in the hierarchy of the parliamentary party. Here, as in the political sphere, there can be no doubt that any dampening-down process is destined to fail in the end. An ardent and vigorous character is bound to come to the top sooner or later.

The future will bring more of these internal duels. They are unimportant compared with the outcome of the battle against Toryism—a struggle which will become far more intense than in the past. Moves for purely political ends have been indicated in the denationalization of transport and steel; the inquiry into the electricity supply which is in hand as I write is a pointer to the fact that some sections of this profitable service are in danger of being brought into the ambit of private enterprise, not through alleged inefficiency, but simply because there are prospects of private profit from them.

Such matters are merely items in the general picture. The main campaign must be to eradicate the divisions among the classes. The improved conditions of the workers and the slight restriction of fortune among some sections of the capital classes have done but little to remove the class divisions. There has, in fact, been a retrograde movement in this regard. The democratic spirit which rose under the pressure and common danger of war has largely disappeared. Despite Labour's legislative measures the National Theatre is again divided strictly into stalls, gallery, and pit, and the segregation of one section from another is as stringent as ever. Indeed in parts of the so-called social world the distinctions to-day are more reminiscent of the Edwardian period than of that between the wars, except that the vulgarity and ostentation are now greater, and the good manners fewer.

It will not be easy to break down these distinctions, unjustified in themselves and fraught with danger to the country. One of the first tasks of any future Labour Government must be to institute free education for all, with no privileges except those attained by ability and work. Britain's educational system, with its potentialities second to none in the world, is, I find, an enigma to overseas people. Even in the United States the segregation of children by caste is not understood, while in an enlightened country like Switzerland I have been told that my hosts have disbelieved me when I have described our private and public school systems running alongside what is theoretically—and often in practice—the finest state educational system in the world.

There is, I must admit, some need for the Party to remove the proverbial mote from its own eye before dealing with the beam in the nation's. There are indications for any Socialist of my generation that the ideals of the past pioneers are in danger of being forgotten. I often ask myself whether those members of the Party who are well-to-do would be ready to accept the conditions which would apply in the Socialist state for which they are fighting.

It is easy to speak glibly of equality, but harder to accept it. But there is no justification for cynicism about it by repeating the allegations that the caste system emerges whatever happens. We hear much about the social situation in the Soviet Union, with members of the Communist Party, Government officials, and officers in the armed forces living luxuriously under a caste system as rigid as that which existed during the Czarist régime. I am chary of accepting any story without evidence, and therefore I hasten to add that no one has ever given me direct evidence of the truth of this statement.

In any event, we must accept that one of the most powerful elements of appeal to vast numbers of people in the world is the concept of a classless society. However much we may deprecate the imperialist flavour of the modern Soviet Union it is futile to adopt an ostrich-like attitude to the irrefutable fact that to large numbers of the less fortunate peoples of the globe this offer of an abolition of the anomalies caused by accident of birth or inheritance of wealth is far more attractive than anything the capitalist countries can offer.

Acceptance of this fact is a condition of Western survival. We must face the truth that the great struggle in the world is not so much between freedom and the slave state, but between the competitive system as to-day typified by the United States of America on the one hand and the gradual, albeit blundering at times, approach to a different way of life in Russia, China, and other Communist countries. The world must move forward; never backward. Not being possessed of divine knowledge, but merely of human idealism and hope, man can only march blindly and courageously into the future; he goes backward at his certain peril and to inevitable doom. Civilization after civilization has collapsed because of this inability or refusal to face the future.

This is the precipice on which reactionary countries are to-day blissfully existing. Two world wars have created an artificial and temporary prosperity; between the boom periods emergency sops have alleviated the misery of the masses. On this insecure foundation the capitalist countries have managed to maintain their particular systems to a greater or lesser degree. The balance between the masses' complacency and revolt is far more delicate than ordinary people realize, and in the increasing tempo of economic life to-day the dangers of revolt when the machine of capitalistic competitive industry breaks down through slump must not be ignored.

I have no desire to see Britain brought to her knees and possible doom by such a situation. That is why the Labour Party must patriotically press on with its Socialist proposals without regard for Tory protests or, for that matter, the anxiety of some Labour leaders to hasten slowly.

We need to entrench ourselves for the future. Far too much of our policy is based on a day-to-day attitude. Far more must be done to educate those who intend to take up a political career. The trade unions' and party's educational schemes are excellent but need extending. Many of our best young people are hamstrung by the lack of education; few of those who have had university training have the knowledge of working-class conditions which they need. I make no claim to be the doyen of political knowledge. My experiences of failure and success have helped me, but in

241

retrospect I realize that my lack of education has been a serious personal handicap.

Service in the political sphere demands many and varied qualities. The "gift of the gab" may be of value, although I know of many men who have rendered great service who are tongue-tied. Debating ability looks well in the pages of Hansard and can stimulate interest in public halls or over the air, but to turn and twist an opponent's argument is not in itself a service to democracy.

Far more important than these is the simple virtue of honesty of purpose. It is vital to believe in one's actions, to be forthright even if it contravenes party policy and banishes one into the political wilderness. There must be such a faith in one's views that they are worthy of the unpopularity which may result. There should be no cowardice about making mistakes, so long as there is a readiness to admit error.

We need to ensure that the Party has good leaders for to-morrow—and the day after. In their hands lie possibilities of greater achievements than any at present attained. This is for the distant, not the immediate future. The repeated cry for young men alone has no validity. They need experience if they are going to handle the reins of future government. The experience is of greater value when obtained before ministerial rank is reached. I have known men between thirty and forty who have contributed little or nothing to the success of the Party's progress during their membership of the House and, in some cases, in governmental office. On the other hand, some of the veterans have been active in their contributions.

It is my belief that new M.P.s will have to come in greater numbers from the trade unions, and they must be men with sound and practical knowledge of political affairs. In advocating this type of recruit to the Labour ranks I am not belittling the value of the so-called intellectuals who have by their record shown that they are often capable of doing more for Socialism than many of the workers. A judicious mixture of both types would be admirable.

In the past and to-day—and this applies to all parties—there can be some justification for the view that we suffer from a ple-thora of lawyers. Brilliant advocates seem often (though I readily admit the exception) to lack political judgment and sensitivity; witness Simon, Cripps, Hastings, all of whom appeared to have this Achilles' heel in their otherwise powerful intellectual armour.

There will, I hope, be young men who may read this book because they are stirred with the ambition to take up a political career and hope that the words of someone who, through events and a certain streak of obstinacy mixed with idealism, has survived the buffetings of political life, will provide some clues to the sign-posts on this difficult, wearisome, exasperating, but satisfying road. To them I say that it is wiser for their own comfort and better for the country if they temper personal ambition with a more selfless attitude to the real aims of the Party. Like so many of our younger men at present in Parliament, there is no reason why time and circumstance will not reward them with high office, but they will be beset with disappointment if they impatiently seek out those posts. All of us cannot share the responsibilities and prestige of the offices of Prime Minister, Chancellor of the Exchequer, and Foreign Secretary. They may even find that duty demands that they be ready to become a Minister of Defence—a certain method of ensuring their unpopularity if they are members of the Labour Party, as I have reason to know.

Let there be no cynical belief that "politics are a dirty business." Britain has a code in these matters, and I say categorically that patriotism, idealism, and honour are the impellent forces which activate the majority of members. Such men and women are of greater value to the people they represent than those who appear to believe they have a right to rule and in fact have no qualifications for office at all.

Such men may be dangerous. Their severe disappointment in being left out of the Cabinet or without ministerial rank does harm to the party and touches those whose jobs they think they ought to have. Occasionally—very occasionally—I believe that this lobbying of the Prime Minister and those reputedly in his confidence for jobs achieves selection for a minor post. I have at times been amused and amazed at the names bandied about in this regard. I recall travelling by sleeper on an overnight train journey to the North. The walls of these compartments are thin, and apart from hearing criticism of myself I heard how so-and-so ought to have a job. The talkers were both of Cabinet rank. The

M.P. whose welfare was being so assiduously nurtured was hardly known to me and quite unknown to the public outside his constituency. I might add that he did not get the job.

Within the parties on both sides of the House are many young and not-so-young members who imagine themselves at the helm. Consuming ambition of this kind blinds them to their real usefulness. In the Labour Party, where we can afford to tolerate this reasonably harmless vice, we refer to the Amalgamated Society of Potential Foreign Secretaries and the Society of Theoretical Chancellors of the Exchequer.

Time alters all things. When I was younger and fired by the Socialist ideal I envisaged a future where Britain was a land of pleasant cities with well-built houses, fine parks, wide streets; of smokeless factories providing full employment at good wages; of free and excellent education; of opportunity to broaden the outlook by travel. These things were, of course, the mental contrast to the scenes around me: of waste heaps and ugly buildings; of beggars and unemployed; of men and women drinking to excess as an anodyne for their misery. In the zest and impatience of youth I believed that all good could replace the evil within a few years once Labour came to power. Experience has not eradicated this vision of the future, though I am less optimistic about the time it will take to achieve. The Party is no longer a young one and it too accepts the dimensions of its task more realistically than it did fifty years ago. But it must never lose sight of the ideal. Considerations of practicability are no excuse for cynicism or acquiescence.

I do not believe that in order to banish our material problems we need to wait until the whole of industry is nationalized. Those industries and services which are indispensable to society and which are in danger of becoming private monopolies run for profit must come under public ownership, and any Labour programme which evades this issue is failing its past founders, its present supporters, and its future adherents.

Equally there are many industries and services which, with state direction and guidance to ensure that the public and the employees are well served, can remain in private hands.

I used to believe that with the satisfaction of material needs all problems would be automatically solved. Deeper thought has convinced me that while the material requirements must come first, because an empty stomach becomes more important to its owner than a filled brain or satisfied soul, afterwards we must tackle the problems of the mind and spirit; the relations of one caste, creed, and race with another; culture, leisure, tolerance, honesty, and citizenship.

The history of civilization is a record of the Martyrdom of Man. The world is still young, the future illimitable. I believe that now, and only now, are the technical, material, and intellectual resources available to eradicate the evils which have beset the mass of men and women from the dawn of time. Britain, by her example, can truly save the world. We must look forward rather than backward. I dislike the nostalgic trend towards the Elizabethan Age of the sixteenth century, the accentuation of the past in traditional rigmarole and ceremony. They smell of senility and the smug satisfaction that Britannia can well afford to rest on her past laurels. I believe that with the recruitment of everyone who can give service to our ideals the greatest renaissance in history is possible.

It will bring with it the first real democracy; democratic in fact and not merely in name. Society will not suffer if we weed out some of the meaningless symbols of the past; lavish spending habits, obeisance to a few elements on the grounds of hereditary position, the pomp contrived by medieval costume, the award of titles.

The people get the government they deserve. Electors have a greater responsibility than they sometimes realize. The franchise, which is society's gift to every young man and woman at twenty-one (unless he be a peer or a lunatic), is not one to be accepted lightly. Too often the elector is ready to be misled by glamour and wealth, and even more often by self-interest. The elector who votes for the Party which promises to reduce income tax, to increase subsidies, and similar examples of self-centred advantage to the individual concerned, is no more honest than the politician who seeks after his own interests.

I have never believed that the Golden Age was in the past. It lies in the future. If this country can show the way to it the rest of the world will surely follow. Then the labours of the social reformers and agitators, of whom I would like to count myself one of the most humble, will have been worth while.

INDEX

ACHESON, Dean, 217
Adamson, William, 59
Aircraft Production, Ministry of, 157
Alexander of Hillsborough, Viscount, 90, 118, 133, 154
Amery, Leopold, 137
Anderson, Sir John (Lord Waverley), 164, 166, 172
Anderson, W. C., 127
Attlee, Clement, as new M.P., 90
    in General Strike, 100
    in 1931 Parliament, 121
    and Parliamentary Labour Party, 133
    intrigues against, 134
    requested to join 1940 Coalition, 145
    wartime policy, 152
    criticism of author, 158
    electors' opinion of, 170
    letter to, regarding nationalization, 176
    his 1947 Cabinet reshuffle, 186
    support of author, 198
    luncheon to Eisenhower, 221

BAKER, Noel, 187
Baldwin, Stanley (Earl Baldwin of Bewdley), 78, 87, 88, 99, 101, 132
Barnes, Alfred, 134
Barnes, George, 53
Beaverbrook, Lord, 156
Bell, Tom, 36
Bellenger, Fred, 161
Bevan, Aneurin, in Opposition to National Government, 133
    expelled from Labour Party, 134

visit to Spain, 141
    debating prowess, 149, 162
    and 1945 Election prospects, 169
    and fuel crisis, 184
    1951 resignation, 223
Beveridge Report, 159, 161
Bevin, Ernest, on origins of Labour Party, 40
    in 1931 crisis, 110
    anger at MacDonald, 129
    approached to lead Labour Party, 134
    organizing ability, 150
    difficulties as Foreign Minister, 198
    author's relations with, 210
    in U.S.A., 217
Blatchford, Robert, 36, 37, 41, 47
Blum, Leon, 140
Board of Trade, 91
Boer War, 23, 24
Boothby, Sir Robert, 161
Bower, Commander, 137
Brace, William, 92
Bracken, Brendan, 155
Brains Trust, 163
Britain I Want, The, 163
Browning, Lt. Gen., 191
Buchanan, George, 79, 137
Buckmaster, Lord, 93
Burns, John, 16, 37, 47

CALLAGHAN, Jim, 176, 210
Campbell Case, The, 95
Carson, George, 37, 41
Cazalet, Thelma, 137
Central Electricity Board, 178, 182
Chamberlain, Neville, 137, 144

Chiang Kai-Shek, 155
Churchill, Randolph, 216
Churchill, Sir Winston, his speeches,
    47
  as Minister of Munitions, 80
  prospects of Premiership before
    1940, 87
  and General Strike, 100
  as Chancellor of the Exchequer,
    104
  forms 1940 Government, 145 *et seq.*
  author's criticism of, 153
  "Gestapo" Election broadcast, 171
  criticism of Labour's defence policy,
    198, 215
  compliments author's patriotism,
    237
Citrine, Lord, 110
Clarion, 36, 41
Climie, Robert, 42
Clyde Workers' Committee, 54
Clynes, J. R., 59, 83, 90
Communist Party, 27, 36, 128, 173
Cook, A. J., 99
Co-operative Production Federation,
    176-8
Crawley, Aidan, 210
Creedy, Sir Herbert, 190
Cripps, Sir Stafford, in 1931 Parlia-
    ment, 121
  and sanctions on Italy, 132
  forms Socialist League, 134
  attitude in fuel crisis, 183 *et seq.*
  as Chancellor of the Exchequer,
    197
  retirement, 212
  attitude to Health Service costs,
    223
Crocker, General Sir John, 202
Cudlipp, Hugh, 216
Cunninghame Graham, R. B., 34, 47

Daily Mail, 100
Daily Mirror, 216
Daily Telegraph, 201
Dallas, George, 42

Dalton, Hugh, 132, 150, 187
Darwin, Charles, 23
Davies, Clement, 161
Davies, Rhys, 139
Defence, Ministry of, 186, 209 *et seq.*
Defence of the Realm Act, 54, 56
Dollan, Sir Patrick, 44, 63, 102, 127
Douglas, Lewis W., 187
Douglas, Lord, 204
Duncan, Joe, 37, 41

Eden, Sir Anthony, 187, 220
Eisenhower, General, 221
Elections, 1923, 90
    1928, 101
    1931, 121
    Seaham, 127 *et seq.*
    1935, 132
    1945, 168 *et seq.*
    1950, 207
    1951, 225, 235
Electrical Trades Union, 185, 239

Fabian Society, 13, 17, 35
Fairchild, E., 127
Fisher, Victor, 37
Food, Ministry of, 146, 156
Forward, 80, 114
Fraser of the North Cape, Lord, 197,
    211
Fraser, Sir William, 89
Fuel and Power, Ministry of, 158, 168
    et seq., 180 *et seq.*
Fuel Crisis, 180 *et seq.*

Gaitskell, Hugh, 187, 212, 224
Gallagher, William, 35, 64, 65, 67
Gee, Bill, 127
George VI, King, 182
Gilmour, Sir John, 147
Glasgow, 18, 21 *et seq.*
Glasgow Trades Council, 36, 39, 40,
    43, 48, 61, 78, 115
Glasier, Bruce, 37, 127
Gowers, Sir Ernest, 91, 190

Grayson, Victor, 47
Greenwood, Arthur, 90, 133, 146, 150
Griffiths, James, 149, 184
Gurion, Ben, 231

HADDOW, Martin, 37
Haldane, Lord, 91, 93
Hall, Viscount, 118, 197, 214
Hardie, George, 82
Hardie, James Keir, 17, 34, 37, 40, 41, 43, 47, 113
Hastings, Sir Patrick, 91, 95
Havelock Wilson, 48 *et seq.*
Henderson, Arthur, 55, 84, 110, 122, 132, 197, 215
Hinchingbrooke, Lord, 161
Hogg, Quintin (Lord Hailsham), 161
Horner, Arthur, 173
Hughes, Emrys, 196
Hyndman, H. M., 17, 35, 47, 177

INDEPENDENT Labour Party, 17, 34, 43, 83, 102, 115
International Labour Office, 106
Isaacs, George, 184
Israel, 226 *et seq.*

JENKINS, Arthur, 146
Johnston, Tom, 80
Jowitt, Earl, 161

Kemsley, Lord, 201
Kerr, George, 41, 60
Keynes, Lord, 165, 166
Kidd, James, 88, 101
Kirkwood, David, 55, 62, 64, 67, 80, 85
Kneeshaw, J. W., 127
Korean War, 210 *et seq.*

Labour Magazine, The, 125
Labour, Ministry of, 150, 153
Lamond, James, 89
Lansbury, George, 127, 132
Laski, Harold, 187, 207
Law, Bonar, 62, 78, 87
Lawson, Lord, 118, 141

Leon, Daniel de, 36
Livingstone, Angus, 89
Lloyd, Geoffrey, 187
Lloyd George of Dwyfor, Earl, 54, 59, 78, 84, 87, 94, 101, 165
Lloyd George, Major Gwilym, 155

MACARTHUR, General, 210
MacDonald, Ramsay, his peace campaign, 1916-17, 53
election as party leader, 83 *et seq.*
forms first Labour Government, 90 *et seq.*
and Zinoviev letter, 97 *et seq.*
intrigues of, 102
and 1931 crisis, 106 *et seq.*
his character, 112 *et seq.*
as author's opponent at Seaham, 127 *et seq.*
Mann, Tom, 37, 67, 75, 127
Marchbanks, John, 41
Marshall, General George, 218, 220
Marx, Karl, 27, 35, 46
Maxton, James, 79, 83, 102, 127
May Committee, 109
McGovern, John, 138
McKerrel, Tom, 42
McLean, John, 35
McLean, Lt. Gen. Sir Kenneth, 201
McLean, Neil, 27, 36, 62, 127, 137
McManus, Arthur, 36, 56, 97
McNeill, Ronald, 137
Miaja, General, 142
Milne, Lord, 104
Miners' Federation, 94
Mines Eight Hours Act, 101
Mitchell, Rosslyn, 202
Moch, Jules, 218
Montagu, Fred, 127
Montgomery, Field Marshal Viscount, 190, 192 *et seq.*, 197, 211
Morris, William, 17, 35
Morrison, Herbert, 47, 133, 141, 159, 169, 184, 225
Mosley, Sir Oswald, 135

Mountbatten of Burma, Admiral Earl, 211
Murray, General, 202

NATIONAL Service Bill (1946), 196
New Party, 136
North Atlantic Treaty Organization, 214, 217, 219 et seq., 230

PARMOOR, Lord, 91
Paul, William, 36
Pethick-Lawrence, 90, 149
Poland, 13

QUELCH, Harry, 37

REID, Sir Charles, 174
Roosevelt, Franklin, 155

SAVE Russia Fund, 155
Scottish Union of Dock Labourers, 48
Seafarers' Union, 47, 56
Seaham by-election, 127 et seq.
Seamen's trade unions, 48, 52, 117
Second Front, 154 et seq., 163
Shale industry, 88
Shaw, Tom, 103
Shinwell, Emanuel, birth, 13
  ancestry, 14-6
  childhood, 17
  in Shields, 18
  school at Glasgow, 18
  first job, 21
  self-education, 23
  tries to join Navy, 24
  return to Shields, 24
  first interest in Socialism, 25-7
  marriage, 25
  unemployment, 38
  work at clothing factory, 39
  membership of Glasgow Trades Council, 39
  campaigning for Scottish I.L.P., 41
  children's education, 43
  union work on Clydeside, 48 et seq.
  and Military Tribunal, 53

  his prospective constituency of West Lothian, 58
  and 40-hour strike, 60
  involved in Glasgow riots, 62
  charge and trial, 64 et seq.
  prison experiences, 67 et seq.
  first elected M.P., 76
  at I.L.P. meeting regarding MacDonald's election, 83
  maiden speech, 85
  re-elected M.P. in 1923, 88
  joins Mines Dept., 91
  defeated in 1924 Election, 97
  wins 1928 by-election, 101
  at War Office, 102
  goes to I.L.O. Conference at Geneva, 106
  views on Ramsay MacDonald, 112 et seq.
  defeated in 1931 Election, 121
  work as Socialist speaker, 122 et seq.
  wins Seaham by-election, 128 et seq.
  House of Commons incident with Commander Bower, 138
  visit to Spain during civil war, 140 et seq.
  Churchill's offer in 1940, 145
  criticism of war-time shipping programme, 147 et seq.
  clash with Ernest Bevin, 150
  views on Second Front, 154
  renewed invitation to join the Government, 155
  meeting with Lord Beaverbrook, 156
  views on Beveridge Report, 159
  campaign for post-war planning, 159 et seq.
  views on 1945 Election prospects, 167 et seq.
  views on Clement Attlee as party leader, 170
  becomes Minister of Fuel and Power, 171 et seq.
  work on mines nationalization, 172

Shinwell—*continued*
  criticized for speech on nationalization, 176
  and 1947 fuel crisis, 180 *et seq.*
  colleagues' attitude to, 183
  criticized for " tinker's curse " speech, 185
  offered War Office, 186
  impressions of Montgomery and other Army personalities, 190 *et seq.*
  cold war problems, 195 *et seq.*
  visits to overseas commands, 200 *et seq.*
  wins in 1950 Election, 207
  becomes Minister of Defence, 209
  friendships with Service chiefs, 211
  plans for rearmament programme, 213
  attitude of Churchill to, 215
  work on behalf of N.A.T.O., 217 *et seq.*
  visit to Israel, 226 *et seq.*
  views on 1951 Election defeat of Labour Party, 235
  on future policy, 236 *et seq.*
  Churchill's compliment to, 237
  on Labour's internal disputes, 238
  on Britain tomorrow, 241 *et seq.*
Shipping Federation, 50, 56
Shipping, Ministry of, 147
Silverman, Sidney, 141, 162
Slessor, Sir John, 211
Slim, Field Marshal, 192, 202, 212
Smillie, Robert, 41
Smith, Sir Ben, 158, 172
Smith, Ellis, 162
Snowden, Philip (Lord), 44, 84, 90, 99, 101, 104, 109, 115
Social Democratic Federation, 13, 17, 35, 37, 43
Socialist Labour Party, 27
Socialist League, 17, 134
Spanish Civil War, 140 *et seq.*
Spearman, Alexander, 161
Speed, Sir Eric, 190

Spoor, Ben, 96
Sprinzak, J., 231
Stalin, 155
Steel, Sir James, 191
Stephen, Rev. Campbell, 80
Stewart, Michael, 210
Stockholm Peace Conference, 117
Stokes, Richard, 162
Strachey, John, 214
Strauss, George, 134, 141
Strikes, seamen's, 1911, 49
  miners', 1915, 54
  40-hour, 60
  General, 57, 100
Supply, Ministry of, 210
Swaffer, Hannen, 94, 141, 143, 157, 169

Tedder, Marshal of the R.A.F., 197, 211
Templer, General, 202
Thomas, Albert, 107
Thomas, J. H., 84, 90
Tillett, Ben, 127
" Tinker's curse " speech, 185
Trades Union Congress, 40, 56, 99, 100, 101, 108, 110
Transport and General Workers' Union, 56, 130, 239
Transport, Ministry of, 181
Truman, Harry, 220
Turner, Ben, 106

Unemployment Insurance Act, 104
United Front, 135

Walker, James, 41, 48
Wallhead, Dick, 127
War Office, 102 *et seq.*, 190 *et seq.*
Watt, Harvie, 153
Waverley, Lord (*see* Sir John Anderson)
Webb, Maurice, 122
Webb, Sidney, 90, 93, 119
Wells, H. G., 26, 46, 163
Welsh, James, 37, 91

Wheatley, John, 75, 83, 85, 94
When the Men Come Home, 167
Whiteley, Will, 170, 186
Wigg, George, 187, 201
Wilde, Oscar, 36
Wilkinson, Ellen, 133, 141
Willey, O. G., 127
Wilson, Harold, 223

Winterton, Earl, 47, 137, 161, 162
Woodburn, Arthur, 149
Woolton, Lord, 146, 161, 162
Workers' Weekly, 95

YOUNG, Douglas, 101

ZINOVIEV letter, 36, 97